JOSH
A RE-TELLING

AN ALTERNATIVE JESUS STORY

Ian Smith

JOSH: A RE-TELLING

Copyright © 2010 by Ian Smith

ISBN 978–1–4467–0820–0

The Scripture quotations contained herein are from the New revised Standard Version Bible, copyright © 1989 by the Division of Christian Education of the National Council of the Churches of Christ in the U.S.A. Used by permission. All rights reserved.

*For Mum and Dad,
who gave me what I needed
to set me on the way.*

Contents.

Acknowledgements 7

"It's Jesus, Jim, but not as we know him." 8

The Setting. 14

1: A Nice Young Man 17

2: Starting Out 35

3: The Lines Are Drawn 52

4: The Officer And The Showgirl 72

5: Battle Joined 93

6: Give Me To God 112

7: Life And Death 131

8: Close Relatives 151

9: A New Take On It 172

10: King Of The World 192

11: Into The Dark 214

12: Never Look Back 235

13: Remember The Wine 255

Notes 277

Acknowledgements.

This is where I get to say a big, richly deserved thank you to everybody who's helped.

First come the encouragers. The world needs more of you. As the kind of person whose default position is 'It probably won't work' but who'll try, and do, almost anything appropriate if only somebody encourages me, I can say that you got the project this far. You know who you are, my wonderful friends. You've coaxed Josh into the light of day and inspired much that he says and does. Thanks, thanks and ever thanks. For many things.

Also, I have to give a mention to the intrepid Bill Stirling, who gave the boost that got the whole thing off the ground; to proof-reader *extraordinaire* Jim Gatherall, who went meticulously through the whole thing, possibly even utilising that hallowed briefcase, and has loyally refused to report me to denominational HQ; and last but not least, to the management of the world's best bistro, Gusto And Relish, who let me sit there hour upon hour so I could write a lot of the best bits: I still have the bottle of Creative Ambience.

Ian Smith
December 2010.

"It's Jesus, Jim, but not as we know him."

So might Dr. McCoy have said had he tried to explain *JOSH* over a nutrient synthesis in the Enterprise canteen. The good doctor may well have elicited an 'illogical' from Mr. Spock in the process. And not surprisingly, because the first thing you notice about these scripts that flaunt themselves as a 're-telling' of the Gospel's accounts is that there isn't a character called Jesus. The main man is somebody called Josh Davidson, who works in an office, hangs out at his local, likes to keep up with the footie and has a favourite comedian called Wally Trotter. All right, he does go along to his parish church, but even then he upsets the vicar.

This probably won't remind anybody of Jesus, whatever their picture of him may be; and in a way that's the point, because I'm trying to tell the story in an 'alternative' way that's unfamiliar and fresh. That's why there isn't a sandal in sight.

JOSH is a series of scripts for radio that tell the story of Josh Davidson. These plays, currently in process of being recorded, are my attempt to provide an alternative telling of the Jesus story. Why am I trying to do this? Well, there's this person, you see, who's quite startlingly, inexhaustibly beautiful and fascinating. He's turned out to be far better than everything people have tried to say about him (including me) and far, far better, even, than a lot of his followers have let on. He's even better than Aslan. To me, he makes sense of life and is the best guide to how it should be lived because he speaks as somebody who's found what really matters. I also find he's the best clue to what God's really like (despite what they've told you) and therefore the best clue to what the world ought to be and what one day it will be. I want to be involved with him, not because of a Book, an institution, a Glorious Truth, a Timeless Message or a supreme morality, but just because of...him. Call it a personal loyalty, a developing friendship or something like that; but do realise it's a person thing.

Actually, to be quite honest, I often feel like dropping the term 'Christian' because of all the depressing baggage that's got attached to it. You can probably think of examples without much trouble. A new name probably wouldn't catch on though, so just let me say it's all about this excellent individual as real and specific as whoever's sitting next to you while you read this; and I'd like the excellent person I'm talking about to get noticed.

So, these scripts are an attempt to tell his story and bring him to the attention of whoever might read or listen to them. But aren't there enough versions of the Jesus Story already without this one? Certainly, Jesus has taken his place as a leading character in the sword-and-sandal genre, for better or worse, and some results have been, shall we say, inappropriate. Take, for example, the 1961 *King of Kings*, where nobody, not even Jesus himself, seems to get particularly excited about his being raised from the dead. His resurrection becomes a ho-hum few minutes tacked on after the crucifixion to get you to the credits. Well, that's that: anyone for an ice cream? Admittedly this does take in the call of several individuals who, at the sight of somebody off-camera, suddenly abandon the fishing industry by dropping their nets and wandering slowly out of shot to strangely stirring music. Odd that the Biblywood response to history's most starting event should be to flip into a trance-like catatonic state, stare intently at who knows what and wander away. Fortunately there's now excellent medication for this sort of thing, but you can't help feeling the filmmakers have missed something. I mean, is that it? Why did they bother? Oh yes: it was a good excuse to have lots of scenes of Romans hammering Zealots. Deep stuff indeed.

Even the Christian media doesn't always seem to know quite what to do with Jesus. He's ethereal, detached, a good ol' American boy or an ecstatic charismatic, cheesy, gushy, bland, harmless, permanently cheerful, infinitely above the nuts and bolts of life, rarely like somebody you'd meet in the street and *take to*. I think he was *so* real you might not notice him.

By the way, for a good antidote to the above, try Pasolini's gutsy work *The Gospel According To St. Matthew*. He actually used real people instead of actors (including his own mum as Mary) and the terrific results touch many a nerve.

There have been endless attempts to re-create Jesus' life in its historical setting 'as it really was', but the sword-and-sandals approach, however excellent the production, has a distancing effect that makes it hard for moderns to connect with what they see and hear. Mel Gibson's *The Passion of the Christ* has his Jewish characters speaking only Aramaic, the Judean language of the time, with the intention of taking the viewers back, pulling them into the story, so that they feel they're eavesdropping on what is taking place. This certainly brought an immediacy to the film, but generally the historical approach can easily leave you feeling it was all back then and over there and not much to do with you and me.

We see Jesus and his followers talking about ideas like Messiah, the Kingdom of God, sacrifice, Passover, the temple and other things a million miles away from the daily lives of most of us. Romans talk about 'the gods', 'divine Caesar', 'upstart messiahs' and how they can't understand Jews, or get philosophical. They also model violence and oppression and become all too understandable. Still, it all happens in a culture remote in time and alien in its thought. Possibly that bunch of people who do the goat sacrifice behind the gasworks on Tuesdays and venerate the Exalted Arthur of Bogthorpe Road would get the point (it was only Exalted Arthur's influence that got them the Health and Safety certificate) but really it's a bit lost on the rest of us.

So: is there anything for us in all this (the Gospels, I mean, not Exalted Arthur)? Well, I'd say yes, because the significance of Jesus and what he had to say isn't tied to any one time or place, so that only one specific people-group could ever appreciate it. He was a member of one specific culture and explained himself in terms familiar to that culture, but his importance isn't built into it in a way that becomes meaningless when we step outside it. The Jesus story has had loads of differing cultural expressions. We can build bridges across time, space and people-groups. Why? Because people are people, with human needs and longings, wherever they are in history, or in your town, and Jesus addresses them as human individuals. For example, the 'poor in spirit' are with us in every age – we *are* the poor in spirit (well, I am anyway; don't know about you). Another example: if you wonder how to decide how to deal properly with people (or the be theological, what does God want?), Jesus would say that the principle that decides all that is love for God and (practically the same thing) love for people. That's what he said to his contemporaries. If he told them that it meant following some rule that was part and parcel of Judean culture – and *only* Judean culture – that wouldn't have worked for any other culture in any other time; but loving people and seeking to apply that is a principle that relates to anybody, anywhere. And so we can include this in what Josh Davidson says in our contemporised, alternative version, even though it sounds different coming from Josh.

Another difficulty of the familiar story is that it *is* familiar. *JOSH* attempts to bypass the 'heard it all before' reflex. Hopefully, nobody will listen to *JOSH* and slip into 'been there, done that' mode. For those that haven't yet worn the T-shirt, send your size and a large donation. The series offers a 'parallel' account: the same, but different. So far as possible, it avoids *everything* that's familiar or able to numb people by over-acquaintance. There isn't even a character called Jesus. In other words, if you didn't know much about the Gospel accounts, you might not realise that that was what you were listening to, since there would be hardly any obvious connection to the original; and you would, hopefully, still enjoy the plays as a ripping yarn. Then somebody might say, 'Well, have you ever read…?' and you could cross the Josh Bridge to the original story of Jesus.

Of course, our characters will re-state and re-enact the Gospels' stories as different people in different circumstances. We can compare this with the way Bible translators deal with the text in the original languages. They look for words that may not be literally 'the same', but are a 'dynamic equivalent', something that's alive in the minds of the people who'll read their work. *JOSH* adopts the same approach, which is why it will, at times, seem very unfamiliar indeed. Here's an example (and it's true, so don't laugh): translators were preparing a version of the Bible for the use of people using an Eskimo dialect. It turned out that straight translations of phrases like 'lamb of God' and 'the lost sheep' were useless, for the simple fact was that their potential readers had never seen sheep in their lives and had no idea what they were, sheep being conspicuously absent within the Arctic Circle. The result was that their Bibles contained phrases like 'the lost seal' and so on. 'Sheep' would have been pointless, but 'seal' meant something, no matter what English-speaking readers were used to. Unfamiliar to us, but alive, correct and meaningful. No doubt dwellers in the Galapagos Islands can ponder passages like 'All we like iguanas have gone astray', while the parable of the lost yak will warm their hearts in the Himalayas (*can* you lose a yak?). Josh Davidson's story is a 'translation', a 'dynamic equivalent' that's different from the original while hopefully the essence of the original comes through.

Of course, if *JOSH's* story were *completely* different, it would be telling a different tale, saying different things. So there are certain necessary points of contact with the original. Probably most of the uninitiated – and maybe some of the initiated – won't spot them, but they're there. For example, you could hardly give an account of Jesus without mentioning God, who was the centre of his life, or 'the kingdom of God', which was the core concept of what he had to say. Oops, theology alert! Don't worry, theology (decent theology) is better than you think: when it's done right it's actually about living. In fact the God-element in our re-telling has to be essentially the same as that of Jesus' own thinking, or we'll end up with a version of the story that's just a restatement of our own preferences and misunderstandings. While frankly recognising that Jesus-followers do in fact sincerely differ on the interpretation of some passages (you noticed, hey?), we need to make the effort. Being deep for a moment, getting the story's God-dimension right is a way of working out loyalty to Christ in literary and dramatic terms.

Not always easy of course. It's not about regurgitating time-hallowed phrases, or necessarily giving audiences what they like to hear and see. That approach just confirms people's comfortable habits of thinking and keeps them safe within their current understanding. They might even be threatened or restricted by their current understanding and need your work to open the door to freedom. Perhaps they will remain with their familiar perceptions, protected by them from significant realities of life and their relation to the real Christ. A lot of artistic work has very extreme features not because the people who produce it are out to shock people for the sake of it (well, some of them maybe) but are trying, sometimes desperately, to jolt their audiences into realising something important.

Is *JOSH* preaching, then? Aargh! No! Not if you mean moralising and throwing abstract concepts-to-be-obeyed at people from a safe distance. The sad fact is that writing or painting often fails when it begins to preach. What the artist wants to say becomes the only thing that matters and the actual work of art itself doesn't really go for much. Thus, we end up with what Nigel Forde brilliantly called 'a pot of message'. The play, painting or novel has to succeed *as* a play, painting or novel, quite apart from what it may be trying to show you. If not, it fails as art, and it's banality and unimaginativeness will obscure and spoil even the most marvellous thoughts, which can really alienate lots of sensitive and thoughtful people. Is this Jesus-event as stereotyped and remote as the works that try to point to it, they wonder.

More could be said about this; and I'm not saying it's impossible for somebody's life to be revolutionised by the local parish youth group's Easter play. Forge ahead, youth groups everywhere! Keep on in the strength of your conviction and ability and who knows what you'll achieve! I'm just saying that I've tried to make these plays work as plays, while trying to get them to say what the Gospels say, but to do so by showing real people getting involved with the central character, Josh Davidson (alias Jesus). Jesus spent a lot of time spelling out in no uncertain terms what he had to say about God, life and himself. He must have repeated his convictions often; and his followers have certainly done that since. But, rather like *Blade Runner* I think, Jesus doesn't date. His words are fresh and life-giving, having sprung from the heart of a real person who could not keep quiet about what he knew. One reason why they helped, and continue to help, so many people; and one reason they upset, and still upset, many people who feel they know, or wish to know, something different. With Josh Davidson, I've tried to show a real individual living out of his own vivid experience, as Jesus did: somebody who knows what Jesus knew. Have I succeeded in what I've been explaining? Hope so. You tell me.

The setting.

JOSH tries to be a version of events that took place almost 2000 years ago. How does it provide a dynamic equivalent of the historical setting? Let's look at the essentials of that situation.

Rome took advantage of Judea's internal instability to invade the country in 68 BC, thus making it a province of the empire. At first Rome appointed local kings to manage things on its behalf, the most famous and notorious being Herod the Great, who appears briefly in Matthew's Gospel. However, by the time of Jesus' public activity, the country had been divided up between Herod's three sons. Antipas, ruler of Galilee, was responsible for the liquidation of John the Baptist and encountered Jesus briefly after his arrest. Rome had decided to abandon its policy of puppet kings for the southern territory and administered it directly through resident procurators, the brutal Pontius Pilate going down in history as the procurator who signed Jesus' death warrant. Although life went on more or less normally, the Roman occupation was deeply resented. Not only was Roman rule oppressive, the very presence of the idolaters in the land whose very soil was sacred to God was a terrible affront.

The Romans knew better than to interfere with Jewish religion – most of the time, at least. Judaism was a 'permitted religion' of the empire and the observances of synagogue, Sabbath and temple continued freely. There was even exemption from the otherwise compulsory sacrifice to the emperor, the authorities being content with daily prayer *for* the emperor. However, there were limits. Jewish religious leaders, based at the temple in Jerusalem, were still the leaders of the nation and were permitted a great deal of civil authority. This elite were mostly of the group known as Sadducees and had a 'collaborationist' policy of peaceful co-existence with the Romans, knowing very well what Rome's reaction would be should the nation step out of line. Leader of this ruling group was the high priest Joseph Caiaphas, who, alarmed by Jesus' large and vocal following, concluded that his forcible removal would be justified in order to avoid Roman reprisals for the revolt that seemed to be looming.

The policy of co-operation, however practical, was certainly not shared by everyone. That heathens should dominate the land given by God to his people was a detestable thing to most of the population. The severity Rome often showed didn't help. A result of all this was the Zealot movement, composed of intense nationalists for whom patriotism and zeal for God were almost the same thing. Zealots were prepared to initiate an armed revolt, confident that God would be behind their actions. Most people, indeed, longed for the 'Kingdom' of God, his breaking into history to rule. In the popular mind, this was translated into political terms, namely the re-establishment of an independent Jewish state with the Messiah, God's appointed king, at its head. A careful reading of the Gospels shows that Jesus came up against these ideals constantly and that even his closest circle of the twelve disciples saw him and his mission at least partly in these terms.

Jesus put 'the Kingdom of God' at the very centre of what he had to say. However, he took great care to explain exactly what he meant, frequently beginning with 'the kingdom of God is like...' He re-interpreted the idea, saying that it wasn't a political state of affairs, but the exercise of God's rule in a person's life. He stated that the 'kingdom' – God's loving, powerful rule - had already arrived and was showing up in him and his actions. He also reshaped the idea of the Messiah, by joining it to another Scriptural figure, the compassionate Servant of the Lord, who is appointed by God to channel God's mercy and healing.

His understanding of how God likes to do things brought Jesus into conflict with political currents – he had to confront and refuse those groups who saw him as the new king – and with religious groups who had interpreted the legacy of the Mosaic law in terms of rule-keeping. Contemporary rabbis referred to the six levels that they saw existing within the Pharisees, from men who truly loved God down to time-serving, hard-hearted legalists at level six. It seems to have been the members of group six who came into sharp conflict with Jesus. They drew his sharpest words against their religious practice, which had become an arrogant posturing devoid of any compassion or understanding of God. These were the people, said Jesus, who placed terrible burdens on people and gave no help to carry them.

This, broadly, is the historical life-setting of the Jesus story. Distilling it to basics, we have:

- A country run by an oppressive and dangerously intolerant military government.
- A politically-minded religious establishment kept on a short leash by the state.
- A resentful population seeking a new order.
- A serious misunderstanding among religious leaders about life with God.

Transpose these essentials into a modern context and we find Joshua Davidson born in a period of upheaval and civil war. After the various military and Government factions have fought it out between themselves, the victor is the brilliant general known as The Eagle, who establishes a totalitarian military dictatorship. Although life goes on more or less as normal, people must live under a watchful, oppressive, 'Big Brother' regime. The Eagle becomes known simply as The Leader and sits for thirty years at the centre of a web of political and military power.

And that's it for starters: no more spoilers. Just a few explanations: being the kind of story it is, *JOSH* needs a few explanations to help fill out what's behind it so, out of the goodness of my heart, I've provided some notes at the end that give you historical and biblical information and comments. You don't have to read them but they might be helpful. Words or phrases that have a note are indicated by a tasteful 'bullet' like this •

Last of all, a disclaimer. Among Josh's opponents is 'The Church', an unlovely institution with vicars, prayer books, cathedrals and an Archbishop. Please bear in mind that this 'church' is an entirely fictitious creation and is not intended to represent, or say anything about, any existing religious group, of whatever faith. For the purposes of the story, which is set in an imagined alternative Britain, I needed a religious establishment that could not only affect the whole nation but go hand in glove with the State to exercise a political influence. The most culturally fitting, familiar and readily accessible features of such a body were those of the dear old C of E and I found they worked well; but this 'church' is an invention of my own, as are its clergy. Note that it never says anything specifically Christian: the alternative world it inhabits is meant to represent a world where Jesus has only just appeared. The same goes for the northern 'Presbyteries'. Likewise, the Eagle's regime isn't intended to specifically represent any current Government or political group.

Well, that's it: enjoy.

1: A NICE YOUNG MAN.

1.1 A report just in...

RADIO ANNOUNCER: It's Friday night and time to relax; and to help you do that here's the big band sound of the Joe Dempsey Orchestra.

We're interrupting our programme• for a few moments, as we have a report just in about developments in the opposition to the recent economic reforms. Prominent politicians and military leaders are calling the reforms oppressive and unconstitutional....

...saying that military action may be justified for the sake of order should current unrest continue...

...reports of polarizing opinion within the armed forces ...

...seems that anti-government forces are gathering under an unidentified general referred to simply as the Eagle...

...confirmed that the Eagle is now the leader of a full-scale military coup. The nation's political future will be decided by an internal conflict...

(Montage of battle sounds: planes, explosion, gunfire, shouting.)

...following the cease-fire, the Eagle received the surrender of the Government forces. The formation of a new government...

...a temporary state of martial law...

AUTHORITARIAN VOICE: This is the Broadcasting Executive of the People's Republic•. The commander of the victorious reactionary forces, our general formerly known as the Eagle, is the obvious focus of the hopes of our new nation. Conscious of this, he prefers to be called simply the Leader.
The Leader has decided that martial law must remain in force for the foreseeable future. He is compelled to enforce rationing and nightly curfews and promises that looting and anti-social activity will be dealt with in the severest manner...

1.2 Almost time.

MUM: Not long now, not long now. Oh, hang on, hang on, wee Josh. I'll find you somewhere safe. You'll not be born just anywhere, not you. Never mind the bad men, son, we'll get somewhere nice, so don't come just yet, hang on, hang on.

Where are we? It's just a big, cold street, son. Oh, look at the soldiers. They better not arrest your mammy. Not tonight. Oh, angel, look after him. God, look after him. Oh! Josh, you kicked me!

I think you're ready. Oh, if that Leader man knew who you were he'd give us his personal bedroom.

SOLDIER: 'Ere! Who're you?

MUM: Genghis Khan, who'd you think?

SOLDIER: Now don't you be cheeky, miss. There's a curfew on, y' know. What you doin' out at this time?

MUM: Hostel threw me out. And it's Mrs.

SOLDIER: Where's your husband then?

MUM: Under the grass in the big grave at the airport. We got caught between two sides.

SOLDIER: Well, sorry, but I'll still have to see your papers.

MUM: Listen, you look like a nice boy; can't you just leave me alone? Promise I won't murder the Leader in his bed. *(The baby kicks)* Oh! Josh!

SOLDIER: You all right, miss?

MUM: Well, yes and no. I'm pregnant and I'm going to pop any minute.

SOLDIER: Right, guardroom.

MUM: Oh, but - no! Let go! Oh, what's that?

SOLDIER: What? *(She kicks him)* Ow! Ow, me leg! You come back here! Get after her! Down there! Down that alley!

(Later:)

MUM: Right, Josh, let's try this. Looks like a shed or something – we'll be all right here.
Oh, quiet now, here's the bad men. *(Running feet outside.)*
Well, there you are, Josh. It's just our two selves. I'll settle down here in the warm and we'll find the hospital when you're ready. If it's not bombed out.
There now, that's cosy. We can have a wee sleep. Oh, I wish Ben was here. Josh? Are you coming? Oh Josh, not now! Not here! Are you ready? Oh! Oh, you're ready! Oh, Josh! Oh!

1.3 A bedroom.

EDIE: Arthur! Arthur, wake up! There's a girl in the potting shed!

ARTHUR: Eh, wot? Oh Edie! You know wot time it is?

ARTHUR: Yes, it's three twenty-four in the morning and there's a young woman in our potting shed.

ARTHUR: Eh? Wot for?

EDIE: She's having a baby, Arthur. Now, come on, go and heat some water.

ARTHUR: Don't she know there's a curfew on? She'll get us arrested!

EDIE: Never mind that. Now you take these blankets out.

ARTHUR: Why ain't she in a nursing home like decent people?

EDIE: She got caught short, Arthur. Now hurry up, will you.

ARTHUR: I don't want that sort in my potting shed, Edie –

EDIE: You know nothing at all about that young woman, Arthur Figgins, so I think you should remember that before you start making judgements.

ARTHUR: Well, bring her in here then.

EDIE: Babies come when babies come, Arthur: we can't move her. Now will you get your backside out of that bed and down the potting shed!

1.4 The Potting Shed.

EDIE: Now then, here's a blanket, my love. Good job I heard you, I thought it was the cat.

MUM: Oh, he's nearly there!

EDIE: Good. Keep breathing, love. Think it's a little boy, do you?

MUM: Oh yes. His name's Joshua. Do you believe in angels, missus?

EDIE: Yes, I do. Angel saved us in the fighting. Incendiary bounced off our roof and landed in the garden, should've gone off but not a whisper. That was an angel, that was.

MUM: An angel told me about Josh.

EDIE: Did it, dear?

MUM: Said he'd be special, said he'd be a great man one day.

EDIE: 'Course it did, dear. Is his daddy not here, then?

MUM: Er – my husband's dead. They shot him. They shot him. Oh!

EDIE: Oh, well, you'll meet another nice boy some day, help you look after the little one. Shove now, dear. Push, that's it.

MUM: Oh! Here he is! He's what I was spared for!• Oh, come on, my special boy! Oh! *(Baby cries.)*

EDIE: Oh! You were right! It's a boy!

MUM: Oh, Josh. Oh, come here, my special.

EDIE: I'll just clean him up, love.

MUM: No, I want to hold him now. Hello Josh, I'm your mum. I'm going to look after you. You're so special.

1.5 Memories in the vestry.

MUM: So – that was it. My Josh started life in Albert's potting shed with the marrows and tomatoes. I can't believe it was thirty years ago. And here I sit in your vestry Vicar, telling you all about it now he's going away.

VICAR: It's only for a short time, Mrs. Davidson.

MUM: Something's going to happen to him.

VICAR: Now what could possibly happen?

MUM: Vicar: men think, women feel. I know his life's going tochange.

VICAR: I daresay. More tea?

MUM: Oh, thank you.   **(Cups clink, tea pouring.)**

VICAR: So Joshua's going off to think through his faith.

MUM: Well...he'll think about God.

VICAR: Isn't that the same thing?

MUM: He wouldn't say so.   **(Knock. Door opens.)**

Mrs. PEMBERTON: Hello, Vicar. Sorry to interrupt, but the organist wants to know what the Introit is for this evening.

VICAR: Come in, Mrs. Pemberton. I've chosen 'Lead Kindly Light'.

Mrs. PEMBERTON: Oh, that's such a nice one. So comforting. Hello, Mrs. Davidson. Is your Joshua all packed?

MUM: Just about.

Mrs. PEMBERTON: Such a nice young man, so harmless: time he had a break. Well, I won't keep you.   **(Door close)**

VICAR: A fine woman. Organised the flowers for forty years. And thinks the world of Joshua. We all do.

MUM: I know. But I don't think people understand him.

VICAR: Well, he's not the run of the mill. But you don't usually speak like this.

MUM: Josh is special; I know he's special.

VICAR: Oh, every mother –

MUM: It's not that. Oh, I just wanted to say it. I need to sometimes.

VICAR: To Joshua?

MUM: Yes. Then he looks at me and smiles but I don't know what he means.

VICAR: Of course. Joshua will be here for Evensong, won't he? I've asked him to say something about his going away to…meditate. **(Knock, door open)**

Mrs. PEMBERTON: Sorry Vicar, only the organist says he's lost the music for
'Lead, Kindly Light.' He says will 'Panis Angelicus' do instead as they won't know the difference?

VICAR: That will be excellent, Mrs. Pemberton. Tell the organist to practice that.

Mrs. PEMBERTON: Oh, he's not going to practice, he's going to listen to the Leader on the wireless.

VICAR: The Thirtieth Anniversary speech. I remember his first, after the coup. I was in my first parish. They brought the wounded into the church hall. We tended them.

Mrs. PEMBERTON: Well, I wouldn't listen to that Leader for a pension. I'd be happy to arrange the flowers on his grave.

VICAR: Mrs. Pemberton –

Mrs. PEMBERTON: It's shocking that you have that man's picture in this vestry.

VICAR: I have to. Now do take care.

Mrs. PEMBERTON: I know – walls have ears. But I'll say what I like in my own church. This country needs a monarchy and a proper Prime Minister. I'm tired of living in a glorified barracks where you can't blow your nose without asking the Leader. Oh, don't get me started. I'll see you at Evensong. Don't want to miss Joshua. Bye, bye. *(Door)*

VICAR: Where is Joshua going?

MUM: Up north to see cousin Callum. The last time Josh saw him he was a stockbroker. Now he's a preacher. That really amuses Josh.

(Knock, door open.)

VICAR: Ah, Joshua. Just talking about you.

JOSH: Hope it was nice. Hello, mum.

MUM: Hello, son.

JOSH: Just to say, going to be a bit late, so stick my tea in the oven, will you?

MUM: Josh, again? Gallivanting somewhere?

JOSH: No. If you must know, I'll be listening to the Leader's speech.

MUM: There's a wireless• at home.

JOSH: Yes, but I'm going down the King's Head to listen there. I'm meeting Joe Silver and his dad.

VICAR: The, er, Arms of the Republic.

MUM: It was the King's Head before the coup.

JOSH: Don't worry, Vicar, I don't think they'll shoot you for knowing that.

VICAR: You will be at Evensong to say your few words, Joshua?

JOSH: I'll be there. Right. Well, Joe and his dad's waiting so I'll be off. Don't want to miss the Leader. Bye, mum.

1.6 The Pub.

DAD: 'Allo there, Josh.

JOSH: Hello, Mr. Silver. All right then are we?

DAD: Oh, can't complain. Well, I can, thanks to our glorious soddin' Leader, but what's the point, eh? What you drinking, Joe?

JOE: Another scrumpy, Dad. And one for Josh. If you can't buy a jar for your best mate, what's it all about, eh?

JOSH: Yeh, all right, you forced me.

JOE: That's the way. Here you are, dad. Is that a tenner?

DAD: No, it's a fiver.

JOE: Oh, right. What about that then?

DAD: Yeh, that's a tenner.

JOE: Here, you haven't been makin' a fortune pinching my change, have you?

DAD: You're not too old to get a clip round the ear, y'know.

JOSH: I wish you could see, Joe.

JOE: Well, I do all right. Dad looks out for me – literally – and I can remember seeing. I remember you, Josh, this little kid laughing and smiling. You had that little stuffed rabbit, remember? Red and yellow it was. When was it again? When was it when I…?

JOSH: Five, Joe. We were about five.

JOE: Yeh. You brought the rabbit round after that, so I could touch it and hold it.

JOSH: You don't usually talk like this, Joe.

JOE: No. I mean, I get by, but I've been sort of – well, sick of it. I want to see people's faces. I want to see you again, Josh; I want to see me Dad…

DAD: Here we go then, lads. Pint o' scrumpy, usual for you, Josh, and my dearly beloved pint o' bitter. Warms yer 'eart.

JOE: What about my change then?

DAD: There you are, you tight-fisted blighter. All coins, so count it if you want.

JOE: Ta very much, father, I shall trust you.

DAD: Cheeky little bleeder, i'nt 'e, Josh?

JOSH: Listening to the Leader's speech then, Mr. Silver?

DAD: 'Ere, it's nearly time. Carol! Carol!

CAROL: What?

DAD: Bung the wireless on, there's a good girl.

CAROL: Oh, right.

DAD: Thirty years of the People's Demercratic Wotsit. For what? Oughter bleedin' well apologise. Oh, here we go.

JOE: Atten-*shun!*

DAD: Now then, now then, some respect. Let's hear what the old sod's got to say.

RADIO ANNOUNCER: This is the Broadcasting Executive of the People's Republic. To celebrate the thirtieth anniversary of the Great Victory, we take you directly to the central office. Citizens of our nation, your Leader.

LEADER'S VOICE ON RADIO: It is a tremendous privilege to address you, the people of our beloved nation, on this, the thirtieth anniversary of the day when I was first called your Leader.

PATRON: Give us a song, then.

LEADER: This is a day for remembering, for gratitude; a day for weighing the lessons that three decades of responsibility and steady work have taught…

PATRON: Like keep your back to the wall!

LEADER: One of these lessons has been the importance of cohesion and unity. That is why I have decided to share responsibility with appropriate groups within the social family of the Republic.

DAD: I wish he'd speak English.

JOE: It means drinks and cigs are going up, Dad.

DAD: Does it?

JOE: S'pose so: it usually does.

LEADER: A foremost member of that family is the Church, the revered institution that has guided the hearts and minds of our nation for centuries. And so, after consultation with our Archbishop and his synod...

JOE: *Our* Archbishop!

LEADER: ...a concordat has been signed which allows the Church and it's servants to work organically with the state at the local and national level of our national life, of which it is so much a part...

JOE: Blimey, a secret police with dog-collars.

JOSH: I don't like this. I don't like it at all.

JOE: You're right, Josh. We'll never trust the vicar again.

1.7 Evensong.

VICAR: You all know the young man beside me in the chancel this evening. He is of course Joshua Davidson. Joshua won't be with us for a few weeks and I've asked him to tell us why. Joshua...

JOSH: Hello. Well, I'd better be quick, because I'm getting the sleeper up north just after this. People often say, You don't sound like your mum, and that's why. She come down south here to get married, but really she's from this wee glen• with lots of little haggises running about. A braw, bricht, moonlicht...wotsit. Sorry, mum. I'm going to get it after this.

So, I'm going because, well, I need a break, but I want a bit of time when it's just me and Dad – you know I call God my Dad• – and I'm, er – well, I'm in a bit of a rut at work and dad might head me in a different direction. Don't worry, I don't want to be vicar or anything. I'd look a right twit in a cassock and surplice – I mean, er – sorry, Vicar, I – oh, shut up, Josh.

Well, that's it basically, so if you could all spare a prayer, light a candle, that sort of thing... Right. Thanks very much. Thanks.

VICAR: Thank you, Joshua. Shall we pray. Page twenty-five, no responses. Fulfil now, O Lord, the desires and petitions of thy servant

Joshua, as may be most expedient for him; granting him in this world knowledge of thy truth, and in the world to come life everlasting. Amen.

MUM'S VOICE: Oh, God, look after him. He's so special. Send the angel. Send the angel and look after him.

JOSH: Er…right. Amen.

1.8 With Callum.

CALLUM: Come on, Josh, come on. I'm sitting waiting on you.

JOSH: Not gonna beat me, Callum•. Gonna make it.

CALLUM: Och, you'd think you'd never climbed a hill before! Look at the state of you.

JOSH: Last few yards…made it! The summit at last! Now I plant the flag and have my picture taken. Oh. What you doing up here?

CALLUM: You're an awful man, Josh – that city has ruined your lungs.

JOSH: Well, what d'you have such big hills here for anyway? What about them sarnies then, eh? Cause I am famished; I could eat – well, I dunno what I could eat.

CALLUM: I think 'scabby horse' is the phrase you're looking for.

JOSH: Whatever that is, I don't want it. What's that stuff? Looks like cardboard.

CALLUM: Oatcakes, Josh. Did your mother never give you oatcakes?

JOSH: Oh yeh. She did once, with cheese. Sends her love by the way. Always talking about you lot in Haggisland.

CALLUM: Is she still on about her angel?

JOSH: She is. I've heard about that angel since I was a little sprog. Been like a family member.

CALLUM: Not many people foretold by divine messenger.

JOSH: Yeh, maybe I should start a club. Certainly made it hard in Sunday School.

CALLUM: You never told the Sunday School!

JOSH: 'Course I did. Went down like a lead balloon.

CALLUM: Did the kids not believe you?

JOSH: Oh, the kids did. The teachers told me to shut up and stop telling lies. Kept it to ourselves after that. Our family secret.

CALLUM: You really believe it then?

JOSH: Yeh, I do, Callum. But I don't know what it means. That's one reason I'm up here, to find out. Don't wanna spend my days in some office.

CALLUM: Maybe you're going to start that revolution everybody talks about.

JOSH: Oh, no. Not the type. They want a new Leader they'll have to look somewhere else. Don't think I'd fit the job spec.

CALLUM: You would not. Is it true the Church is joining with the Government down there though?

JOSH: Yeh, 'fraid so. The New Relationship they call it. Bad enough with military all over the place without your vicar watching you as well. Be hidden microphones in confessionals next. Easier up here, though.

CALLUM: Aye, a bit. There's still the soldiers, and the Presbyteries are infiltrated, but we're still pretty free.

JOSH: You and your old reverend dad won't be stopped preaching?

CALLUM: Oh no. I'm preaching quite a bit just now, in fact. You might try it yourself, Josh.

JOSH: Crumbs, dunno. I'm not wearing no white nightie, though.

CALLUM: Have you no idea what you'll do?

JOSH: Well, there's this thing out the Bible won't go away. Can't get it out of my head. You know the bit about the feller that's just called Servant•?

CALLUM: Aye, I do.

JOSH: Well, Servant says – really strange bit – he says God's Spirit•, his own living breath, gets breathed out on him, poured out on him like oil. And that living breath, that Spirit's sort of Servant's friend, his power, sort of thing, and he makes him able to fix people and give 'em hope, makes him able to change the world.

CALLUM: Och, Josh, it seems such an easy thing for you – angels and vision and all. God's so real to you.

JOSH: Yeh, why shouldn't he be?

CALLUM: Aye, Josh. Ah, but if you were Servant –

JOSH: I want to be, Callum. Oh Dad, Dad God, I want to be like that for people. I want – I want – oh, Callum, he is so chuffed with me right now. He is so pleased with what I want. Oh, Callum, I think…I think it's beginning.

CALLUM: What, Josh? What is it?

JOSH: Can't you see him? Look at the mountains, look out where it all goes blue and misty. He's rushing down, he's breathing, he's pouring out; he's over the hills, he's in the wind.

CALLUM: Yes, I feel it, Josh. The beautiful presence, the weight of glory.

JOSH: He's the breath of my dad; he's the breath of my breath, my friend. Hello, friend, hello.

CALLUM: He broods over the world with bright wings, he has come through into our place. What is starting, Josh?

JOSH: I think I'm Servant. Gotta be on my own, Callum. Just me and my Dad; and this friend.

CALLUM: Away higher up, Josh; away up to the moors. Come back to the house when you're ready.

JOSH: Yeh, right. I'll be ready for anything after this.

1.9 The Moors 1. *(Wind moaning steadily.*
Occasional sheep.)

JOSH: These moors• are just the place, dad. Just you and me. And the sheep, but you don't mind that, eh? Oh, but dad, what's it all about? Speak up, dad, got to hear you.

WIFIE: Talking to ourselves, are we?

JOSH: Oh. Morning, darlin'. Nice day for it.

WIFIE•: This is the day the Lord hath made, young Joshua.

JOSH: Yeh. Have we, er...?

WIFIE: You are carrying the holy power of God. Your dad, as you call him. You are too familiar with the great and mighty king, but he has told me he will overlook it.

JOSH: Well, no. I love him –

WIFIE: God is stirring in this land. Oh, I have prayed for this. My sister and I have striven mightily in our back kitchen each Sabbath for twenty-five years and I'll not miss it now.

JOSH: Well, if God – I mean, er – sorry, but if *my dad* did something really big, all these people out there would...

WIFIE: The saints will be exalted. There will be great demonstrations of power. How will they know it is God if they do not see power?

JOSH: Oh, yes. Dad can do such beautiful things. All these people, all broken up and sick and miserable.

WIFIE: You make it sound like a…rescue mission.

JOSH: Yeh, I do, don't I? D'you know, I used to read things in my Bible when I was a little boy and I thought, I want to do that. If I could just touch somebody and make 'em well, or give 'em hope –

WIFIE: Well, it may start there….cures, and such like.

JOSH: I don't…

WIFIE: Young man, God will shake this nation, as my father shook me when I neglected my prayers.

JOSH: Well, you had a horrible dad then. Dad God never shook me.

WIFIE: If God is your father, you will make the Leader's tanks and his guns rise into the air and crash down on his head. You will fill the sky with fire, you will summon beasts from under the sea.

JOSH: Here! People have been getting smashed down for thirty years – I'm not going to tell them God's like that as well. Where's the hope in that?

WIFIE: You can *make* people do what is right. That's hope. Dazzle them, sweep their own thoughts aside!

JOSH: No, I won't. I can't. You can't make people love you. That's stupid –

WIFIE: I'm not speaking of love, I'm speaking of righteousness.

JOSH: You musn't do this. You musn't pull God into stupid situations just to get what you want. That's what it says. If you were such a saint you'd know that's what it says. Flying tanks!

WIFIE: Hear me, now: God is speaking to me.

JOSH: You're hearing you own voice, darling. No offence, but there's something in this for you, isn't there?

WIFIE: God has said to me –

JOSH: No! I'm not going to do anything that way, so don't try and twist me round for your empire-building.

WIFIE: Sentiment! You have missed God's moment. Good day, Joshua Davidson.

JOSH: Good day. Blimey!

1.10 Meanwhile...

VICAR: We remember in our prayers this beautiful morning Joshua Davidson as he seeks to know more of the will of God. But first, please turn to page five in the new Ministry of Religious Affairs booklet *Orders Of Prescribed Prayers*. There are no responses. Let us pray. Almighty God, who hast given us grace at this time to make our common supplications unto thee; Most heartily we beseech thee to regard with thy favour our most gracious Leader. Strengthen him and grant him in health and wealth long to live that by his governance of Church and State we may aspire to live quiet and peaceable lives, to the glory of thy most holy name. Amen.

1.11 The Moors 2.

JOSH: Crumbs, dad, what was that woman about? I'm glad you're not like her. Hello, who's this old bloke?

LEADER: Hello. Hello there.

JOSH: So much for time by myself. It's like a circus up here. Morning, sir. Look, sorry, but it looks like everybody knows me and I don't know anybody.

LEADER: You know me.

JOSH: No, I don't think – oh! You! I seen you in the newsreels. Our vicar's got your picture in his vestry. You're him, the Leader! What you doing up here?

LEADER: I'll speak plainly; you don't need a dad, you need a master•.

JOSH: But my dad's –

LEADER: You and I join perfectly. You have spiritual power, I have the power of the State. You will of course have your moral crusade, but I can make it prosper.

JOSH: Oh, no – now, look –

LEADER: I don't know what you think you have and I don't care, but whatever you preach, my forces will carry it forward. Time to expand.

LEADER: The cosy deity in carpet-slippers. When I stand astride this narrow world, I will hand you its kingdoms. Be ruled by me and they're yours.

JOSH: No, no...

LEADER: Serve me and I'll give you your dream. You'll have the world to show your dear old dad to. Just worship me...

JOSH: No, get away from me, get away from me...

LEADER: WORSHIP ME, WORSHIP ME, ME, ME, MEEEEE...
(Fades into demonic roar.)

2: STARTING OUT

2.1 The Moors.

LEADER: Serve me and I'll give you your dream. Just worship me.

JOSH: No! Get away from me, get away from me –

LEADER: WORSHIP ME, WORSHIP ME, ME, ME, MEEEE *(fades into demonic roar.)*

JOSH: No! My dad's my master! Both at once! God's the Leader! You know what it says: Worship Leader God! Don't give yourself to anybody else! Get away, get away, I'm not yours! I'm not yours! *(Scream and roar, then silence.)*
Dad, you really stepped in there. I know who that was. Dad, what are you getting me into? Somebody doesn't like it. But now I know what it is. Well, I need a rest after that. Back to the house: Callum'll have the bridies on. Nice hot bath, cup o' tea…

2.2 Afternoon Tea 1.   *(Tea cups clink.)*

MUM: Tea, Mrs. Pemberton?

Mrs. PEMBERTON: If it's Earl Grey. Thank you, dear. Fancy the Leader taking the Church under his wing. Personally, I wouldn't trust the Leader as far as I could throw him. An iron hand in an iron glove for thirty years and suddenly he's best of friends with the Archbishop. Very fishy. Mm!…is that real butter shortbread?

(Letter box.)
MUM: Excuse me, Mrs. Pemberton, that's the postman.

Mrs. PEMBERTON: My cousin used to send it down during the rationing. She was in the islands, of course. Anything interesting?

MUM: Don't believe it: postcard from Josh! It only took him two weeks.

Mrs. PEMBERTON: How nice. Are those real chrysanthemums? So tasteful. I made a chrysant arrangement for a funeral once. A little too perky, thought the vicar…

MUM: 'Weather fine, everybody here fine, I'm fine…' Mine of information.

Mrs. PEMBERTON: 'Vicar,' I said, 'in the midst of death, we are in life…'

MUM: 'Look after yourself. Don't get talked to death by Mrs. Pemb - .'

Mrs. PEMBERTON: What's that, dear?

MUM: Nothing. Just… *(Doorbell)* Oh. Oh *dear*. Who could that be? Do excuse me. *(Door.)*

VICAR: Ah, Mrs. Davidson. I'd like you to meet someone.

2.3 At Callum's.

CALLUM: Josh! Josh? Are you not out of that bath yet?

JOSH: Sorry Callum, fell asleep. Be out in a minute. *(Sloshing.)*

CALLUM: Well, come on. You should be relaxed enough by now. The bridies are nearly ready.

JOSH: Right, right. Hold your horses. *(Door)* There you go. All that Leader muck washed away.

CALLUM: You said it wasn't really the Leader.

JOSH: Oh yeh. But it's gone. Till the next time prob'ly.

CALLUM: Aye. Well, dry your hair. I'll put the tea out.

(Later.)

CALLUM: There you are, Josh. Genuine bridies, authentic bannocks.

JOSH: Just what I need, Callum. Pour the tea, will you?

CALLUM: Here you go. So, you know what it's all about.

JOSH: That I do. Mum's gonna be very interested.

CALLUM: I'll bet she is.

JOSH: What I mean is, she'll say what happened to me up that hill's got something to do with her angel.

CALLUM: Her angel?

JOSH: Yeh. Well, it told her I'd be born…

CALLUM: I knew that.

JOSH: Yeh, but it said I'd be a one-off: the pride of the whole world. She thinks everybody'll stand or fall because of me. Blimey, eh?

CALLUM: Josh! I never heard that.

JOSH: Well, we kept that bit quiet. We didn't know what it meant.

CALLUM: And is that it?

JOSH: Dunno. Wait and see.

CALLUM: And now?

JOSH: When I get back I'm putting my notice in. I've gotta tell people and it'll take all my time.

CALLUM: Tell people?

JOSH: Yeh. I think…well, people…they don't want the Leader, they want a monarchy again, or a revolution, or – something, something different. Somebody else in charge. Now, if my dad was in charge…but they don't even know what that would mean. It would be far bigger than politics.

CALLUM: They don't know what he's like. Even the Church doesn't know•. A lot of it anyway.

JOSH: Think I've gotta tell them. I've gotta show them.

CALLUM: How, Josh?

JOSH: I dunno, really. I'll start at our church and do what I can round our parish and then – we'll see. Oh, but that's really bad.

CALLUM: What, Josh?

JOSH: My tea's gone cold.

2.4 Afternoon Tea 2.

VICAR: Now, Mrs. Davidson. This fine, uniformed young man is a newly appointed Lieutenant to our Provincial Governor.

LIEUTENANT: Pleased to meet you, Mrs. Davidson.

MUM: Hello.

VICAR: The Lieutenant is here because of the new co-operation between Church and State.
He's –

LIEUTENANT: I'm here to help things work at local level. May we pop in?

MUM: Oh. Yes. Just in here, please.

VICAR: Ah, hello, Mrs. Pemberton. One of our oldest members, Lieutenant.

Mrs. PEMBERTON: Hello, Vicar. Oh, I say! I've always had a weakness for men in uniform. You do suit black with that fair hair. Is that a real firearm?

LIEUTENANT: Oh yes; but only for emergencies. You have a delightful home, Mrs. Davidson. Where is your picture of the Leader?

MUM: I don't have one.

LIEUTENANT: Then we'll give you one. Your vicar will see to that.

VICAR: Yes. Parish funds, under the new rel –

LIEUTENANT: We're compiling a kind of informal register of outstanding people in each parish. People who are capable. So, if you'll bear with me…

Mrs. PEMBERTON: Don't mind me, dear, I'll just nibble my shortbread.

MUM: Capable people, Lieutenant?

LIEUTENANT: Yes, people who are gifted in some way – insightful or intuitive, for example, or those with leadership abilities.

Mrs. PEMBERTON: Is flower arranging any good to you?

LIEUTENANT: Not at this time, but thank you.

VICAR: I thought of Joshua at once.

MUM: Josh?

LIEUTENANT: Your son's well regarded in this parish. Your vicar tells me he's resourceful, good with people…

MUM: What do you want him for?

LIEUTENANT: Well, if there were a local crisis, say a flood, or if revolutionaries attacked –

Mrs. PEMBERTON: Oh!

LIEUTENANT: Highly unlikely. Now, people like Joshua are invaluable in such emergencies. The Register would enable us to mobilise them quickly and easily.

VICAR: That's what it's about, you see, nothing sinister.

LIEUTENANT: Nothing sinister at all. Could I meet Joshua?

MUM: He's not here.

LIEUTENANT: Perhaps I could wait?

VICAR: What am I thinking of? Joshua's on holiday! Lieutenant, I'm so terribly –

LIEUTENANT: Where is he?

MUM: Er...

VICAR: Wasn't he going North, to his cousin's little town?

MUM: He...he cancelled it. A bad time: his cousin's quite ill.

LIEUTENANT: He's gone elsewhere, then?

MUM: Oh, yes. Some friend or other on the west coast. He was very vague about it.

VICAR: Really? Not like him.

MUM: Last-minute arrangement, then dashed out the door.

Mrs. PEMBERTON: There's always the postcard.

MUM: I don't think that's –

LIEUTENANT: May I see?

Mrs. PEMBERTON: Oh, that's no good – it doesn't even have a picture on it. Joshua's an old cheapskate.

LIEUTENANT: And the provincial postal service is slacking. This has somehow been delivered without a postmark.

MUM: How strange.

LIEUTENANT: Very. Well, Mrs. Davidson, at least now we know where you are.

MUM: Yes. Maybe you'll see Josh another time.

LIEUTENANT: I hope so. I do hope so.

2.5 Leaving Callum.

CALLUM: Train's in half an hour, Josh. Are you not packed yet?

JOSH: Nearly, Callum. Where's me rugby shirt?

CALLUM: Here. And here's the white trousers.

JOSH: How'd they get green stains on?

CALLUM: That's what you get for kneeling in wet grass. You can't start a mission with green knees, you know.

JOSH: Don't see why not. Anyway, what you gonna do now, Callum?

CALLUM: Just carry on. There's a lot of issues to preach about here. I think God wants to be involved with people, society.

JOSH: Never mind society, how am I going to explain it all to Mum?

CALLUM: Now that *is* the big one.

JOSH: You're right. If I can do that, the rest's a dawdle.

2.6 In the park.

JOSH: So that's it, mum. That's what happened.

MUM: Oh, Josh.

JOSH: Any more tea in that flask? So, what d'you think?

MUM: This is it, Josh. This is what the angel meant.

JOSH: And here I sit, on a park bench, feeding the ducks. Great, innit? What's this we're giving them anyway?

MUM: Some of Mrs. Pemberton's buns I didn't need.

JOSH: Blimey, don't give 'em that: they'll sink.

MUM: Well, everything's different now, Josh. This'll completely change our lives. What's the first step?

JOSH: Dunno. I asked dad to show me, but I suppose I could phone the vicar…hang on! 'Change our lives?' What d'you mean *our* lives?

MUM: It's got to affect me, I'm your mother.

JOSH: Yes, but – but I'm going to be doing all the stuff.

MUM: I can make the sandwiches.

JOSH: The sandwiches?

MUM: There's a lot of people going to come and hear you, son. Somebody's got to feed them.

JOSH: Oh. S'pose so.

MUM: I'll organise the catering, get the posters up, get the leaflets printed; and I'll hire the halls, book the hotels –

JOSH: What hotels?

MUM: You'll be travelling around. The whole country's not going to come down here to listen to you.

JOSH: Oh yeh. Never thought of that.

MUM: Of course you didn't. You've got the big things to think about. You concentrate on dad, son. I'll just…help it along.

JOSH: You're brilliant, mum. D'you know that.

MUM: Yes I do, actually. So that's two of us.

JOSH: I do love you, mum. Give us a hug.

MUM: How's this one? Mm…

JOSH: Better let go, mum. The ducks are feeling excluded.

MUM: Well, first steps?

JOSH: Well, first thing is, I'll tell 'em all about it at Evensong tonight. You coming?

MUM: No, I've heard it from the horse's mouth. And I think it might go down like a lead balloon.

JOSH: Really, mum?

MUM: They don't understand what you have, Josh, not even the vicar. You live your life on a higher and a deeper level than he's ever thought about.

JOSH: That was deep, mum.

MUM: And what you have is going to – to – burst out. It'll be so clear and bright nobody can miss it. My boy'll shine so brightly they'll either love him or hate him. There'll be nobody that just doesn't care.

JOSH: That a prophecy, mum?

MUM: Don't know. Part of me hopes not.

JOSH: We'll wait and see then.

MUM: We will. Well, see you for tea after evensong?

JOSH: No, I'm going down the King's Head afterwards. I want to tell Joe and his dad what happened to me.

MUM: Dried-out shepherd's pie for you, then. Oh…the vicar was round looking for you. He – oh, tell you later.

JOSH: See him at the church. Gotta run, mum, bye. By-bye, ducks.

MUM: Bye, Josh, bye. So this is it, God, at last. Oh, he's just starting out. I don't know where it'll end. Please send the angel again. And get it to keep an eye on the vicar.

2.7 Evensong.

VICAR: The Lord be with you.

CONGREGATION: And with thy spirit.

VICAR: You will remember that Joshua Davidson took some time away, specifically in order to pray and meditate on the course of his life – something not overly characteristic of the young people of today, so we're rather proud that Joshua is ours. He's back among us now, and he's going to tell us something of his time away. I'm sure our Lord would have no objection to a brief ripple of applause. Joshua.

JOSH: Thanks, Vicar. Ta, everybody. Well, where do I start? I just don't feel I'm the same man. No, really. And I know what Dad God wants me to do. In fact, I've put my notice in at work.

VICAR: We didn't know this had been quite so radical, Joshua.

JOSH: You've no idea, Vicar.

CONGREGATION: Bless 'im; God bless yer, son *etc.*

JOSH: Well: best thing I can do is tell you about a thing in the Bible, all right? It's a bit of what that feller Isaiah said way back when, er…

VICAR: Isaiah was a contemporary of Nebuchadnezzar.

JOSH: Oh: well, there you go then. So it's pretty old. But my Dad God said to me, I want everybody at Evensong to know it's come true. It really has come true. **(Murmurs.)** Thought that'd be a surprise. Anyhow, remember Isaiah did some poems about this special feller? Vicar, you preached about him last year.

VICAR: Er…oh, the – the Servant of the Lord.

JOSH: That's it, Servant of the Lord. Now, pin your ears back; here we go: remember the bit where Servant says God's got an agenda for the whole world? He's gonna make things the way they're meant to be. For everybody: everybody on this earth; but he's not gonna do it with armies and politicians. He'll show us what his world's supposed to be like, says Servant, and he'll do that with me. He's quite a feller, isn't he? Wonder who he is. D'you want to know? D'you want to know who it is? It's me.

2.8 In the park 2.

MUM: "To my darling great-granddaughter on the occasion of my hundredth birthday. May this Book of Psalms speak to you as it has to me. With love from your Granny Hopkins." God love you, Granny Hopkins. That wee books been in my handbag ever since. It's got some lipstick and eye-liner on it now. Sorry about that, but I look at it every day.
Well, ducks? Fancy the Psalm for the day? Never mind the bread, this'll do you good. Lift up your tails unto the Lord. Today's Psalm is number two.
"Why do the nations so furiously rage together, and who do the peoples imagine a vain thing. The kings of the earth rise up and the rulers take counsel together against the Lord and against his anointed." Hm. Granny, you used to say if you were anointed you were chosen for something. *Well...*God's chosen Josh for something all right. Hope the kings of the earth lay off him.
What's the evening Psalm? Something more cheerful, maybe. C'mon, ducks, make a joyful quack unto the Lord, here's Psalm fifty-five. "It was not an enemy who reproached me; then I could have borne it: But it was

thou, a man my equal, my guide and mine acquaintance. We took sweet counsel together, and walked unto the house of God in company." That's tough; somebody from the house of God putting the knife in. *(She gasps)* God, I really, really hope you're not trying to tell me something.

2.9 Evensong 2.

VICAR: Joshua, I am not following you. How can the Servant of the Lord be you?

JOSH: Well, it was about somebody back then, I know that, but it's me as well.

VICAR: You're making no sense, Joshua.

JOSH: Well, my dad God said, you're my boy, so I want people to see what I'm like when they see you.

VICAR: Joshua! Do you realise what - ?

JOSH: Hang on, though. He said, 'I'm the true Leader, the prototype, sort of thing: what a Leader's meant to be.' People want something political, but Dad God's 'Leader-ship' is starting to show up: as of now. I mean, nobody can do it but him, but he wants me to get it going: front man sort of thing. And when I do, I've gotta be like that Servant feller, 'cause God's like him as well. He's gonna do this his way. *(Some applause.)* He's not like that old feller down at Government HQ.

VICAR: Do you mean revolution?

JOSH: Didn't say that. You're not listening, it's not political.

VICAR: Joshua, please return to your seat.

JOSH: Let me just –

VICAR: I fear you're misguided. Sit down.

VOICE: Doesn't sound too bad to me.

VICAR: It's – unscriptural. Misguided. Think of our place in the community under the New Relation –

VOICE: We're the community; we like it.

VICAR: No. I can't allow it. Joshua, it's best if you return home.

JOSH: Nothing against you, vicar –

VICAR: Please leave us!

JOSH: Right, right. Don't get your cassock in a twist. See myself out then. *(Feet up the aisle)* G'night, everybody. *(Door closing.)*

VICAR: I'm sure we…regret what we have heard. Remember Joshua in your prayers. Let us return to our evening worship. Lift up your hearts. *(No response.)* Lift up your hearts!

CONGREGATION: We lift them up unto the Lord.

VICAR: It is meet, right and our bounden duty, at all times and in all places, to give thee thanks, most merciful Lord…

2.10 In the vestry.

(Telephone dialling.)

VICAR: Hello? Central barracks? Hello, I am the vicar of St. Genevieve's parish. One of your lieutenants paid us a call recently. Regarding the new Parish Resource Register…yes, that's him. Yes, I would appreciate that. Yes, If he's free. Yes, I'll hold. Thank you so much.

Ah, Lieutenant, I hope I'm not disturbing your evening. Oh, good. You may recall we visited a Mrs. Davidson. Her son, Joshua – he is home again, yes. Now, I mention this only because of the new state-church relationship and your parochial reg - yes, well, the point is that Joshua spoke tonight at our evensong gathering and I am concerned - he appears to consider himself more than eligible for your register of the resourceful. Ah – I'm not sure *what* it means, Lieutenant – a catalyst, I think, a social force with divine sanction, that sort of thing. Now, I wouldn't wish the

New Relationship to be threatened in our corner of the vineyard, so – well, I'd say he thinks rather too highly of – ah. Yes, yes. It may amuse you, but he thinks he has a mention in the Scripture. Thinks of God as the one true Leader. Metaphorically, I expect – yes, certainly. Yes, I can meet you there, but I do have a committee – fifteen minutes? Yes, certainly. I will telephone Mrs. Davidson – oh. Perhaps not. Yes, of course, I'll look forward to it. You know, strange as this is, Joshua has great – oh. Goodbye.

2.11 The street.

MUM: Well, never sat on that park bench so long before. Josh's shepherd's pie won't even be made, never mind dried out. Hope he gets a bite at the King's Head. Yes God, I'm well aware I'm talking to distract myself, thank you. All right, that Psalm *is* bothering me; why should it be buzzing round my head? Oh, sorry, mister! Didn't see you!

STRANGER: Preoccupied are you?

MUM: Oh, just dashing home –

STRANGER: You musn't go home, Mrs. Davidson.

MUM: What? Do I know you?

STRANGER: Yes, but never mind that. You can never go home again: not for a good while anyway. Neither can Josh. Be very careful, both of you, and read that little book. Good night.

MUM: What? What d'you - ? Where is he? Well, what a nerve! Funny man! I'll be glad to get in. Good job my street's well-lit, never know who you'll meet. From ghoulies and ghosties and funny men on street corners Good Lord deliver us. And God, why are there two soldiers outside my house? And why is the vicar standing there talking to that Lieutenant? *(Gasps)* The kings of the earth; my guide from the house of God. Oh, no! No! Oh, Josh, don't go home! Stay in the King's Head till I get there!

2.12 The Pub.

DAD: I dunno, Josh. I never thought you was in the Bible.

JOE: So, you think you've got to sort of explain God.

JOSH: Something like that, Joe. After that beautiful thing up North, I knew. I knew I'd be able to do it.

JOE: Right. You got the power then, have you?

JOSH: Yeh. I mean, not power like them people on the moors was on about. I don't want to be like that.

DAD: You wouldn't have me signing up if you were.

JOSH: I knew that a long time ago, Mr. Silver. I gotta to be like that Servant feller. It's the only way I can do it: give people a clue what dad God's all about.

JOE: Well, it's a marvellous idea what you're saying, Josh, beautiful words and all, and I can hear you're thrilled, hear it in your voice. I'm so happy this has happened to you, I really am, but life's hard and people need something they can hold on to. Something that's – sort of tangible. You understand me, don't you?

JOSH: Yeh, I do, Joe.

JOE: I mean, I go tapping around with me white stick and sometimes I think, what's it all about, y'know? I don't understand what it means that you've got a power, this light thing. What's it mean, Josh?

JOSH: I hate seeing you like this, Joe. I'm so sorry.

JOE: Not your fault. Few glasses o' scrumpy and it's not so bad. I'm just…in the dark.

JOSH: I want to be a light for you, Joe.

DAD: What d'you mean, Josh?

JOSH: I mean – I just – look, suppose I dip my fingers in your scrumpy and rub it on your eyes.

JOE: What you doing?

JOSH: Said it yourself; it's not so bad with scrumpy. Here's a jug of water. Give us your hanky. Now, you clean your face. You wipe that scrumpy off.

JOE: Well all right; but I don't know what you're about, Josh, I really don't –

DAD: Joe? Joe, what is it?

JOE: Is that you, Josh?

JOSH: It's me, Joe.

JOE: Where's that little boy? Where's that little kid with the rabbit?

DAD: Joe? What's happening, Joe?

JOE: Dad? Oh dad, you're all wrinkles and sags. Your hair's all white.

DAD: You're looking at me, son. You're looking right at me.

JOE: I see you dad. I see you.

DAD: Oh, son. Come here.

JOE: How'd you do it, Josh?

JOSH: My dad did it, I did it with him. Group hug, group hug!

MUM: Josh! Josh!

JOSH: Hello, mum. What's up?

MUM: Josh, don't go home, there's soldiers outside the house. I think the vicar brought them!

JOSH: The vicar!

JOE: What's happening, Mrs. Davidson? I think you're Mrs. Davidson.

MUM: 'Course I am, Joe – Joe! Joe, you're looking at me!

DAD: Your lad's been up to a few things, love. Here! Take a look out that window!

JOSH: Soldiers! The vicar's with 'em!

JOE: Right, out the back, sharpish! Go to my uncle Alfred.

JOSH: Joe, I'm not leaving you. I can handle the vicar.

MUM: Josh, come on!

JOE: What did I tell you, dad? Bleedin' vicars' secret police! *(Door. Silence falls.)*

LIEUTENANT: Attention! Your attention please, routine investigation.

VICAR: There's absolutely no need to be alarmed –

LIEUTENANT: I need to speak with a Joshua Davidson. Urgently. Can anyone help me?

VICAR: Ah, Mr. Silver.

LIEUTENANT: Who's that?

VICAR: Mr. Joseph Silver, Lieutenant. A very good friend of Joshua's, I believe.

LIEUTENANT: Really? Then help me, Mr. Silver. It's very urgent. Have you seen him? What can you tell me? *What can you tell me?*

3: THE LINES ARE DRAWN.

3.1 The pub.

LIEUTENANT: Help me, Mr. Silver, it's very urgent. Have you seen him? What can you tell me? *What can you tell me?*

JOE: I can't tell you nothing, sir.

LIEUTENANT: I advise you not to hinder this investigation.

DAD: He don't know nothin', he's just havin' a drink.

LIEUTENANT: I can encourage you. Rewards are substantial.

VICAR: Come, come, Mr. Silver. Joshua introduced you to me as a good friend. I've only met you once, but you do know me.

JOE: Can't say I've ever seen you before, sir.

VICAR: Well, of course you have. I met you – . Oh dear. Lieutenant, I have misled you once more. The person Joshua introduced to me was blind, whereas this gentleman –

LIEUTENANT: Is not. Well, I'm sorry to have disturbed your drink, Mr....

JOE: Johnston, sir. Frank Johnston.

LIEUTENANT: Of course. Well, Mr. Johnston, you will let us know if you learn anything, won't you?

JOE: I certainly will, sir.

LIEUTENANT: Then goodnight. Outside, men. Vicar, you will accompany me.

VICAR: I'm most terribly sorry –   *(They leave.)*

JOE: That was a close one, dad.

DAD: Yeh. Joe, I think I need some more bitter...

3.2 Running.

MUM: Better stay off the main streets, Josh. Keep running, it's not far to Alfred's.

JOSH: These Ladies' Guild fitness evenings are paying off, mum.

MUM: And I grudged that shilling• a week.

JOSH: Wait, wait, stop a minute. You saw soldiers at our house. With the vicar.

MUM: Yes, and he came round with an officer when you were away.

JOSH: An officer!

MUM: They were drawing up a list. People to use in emergencies. He said. He really wanted to meet you.

JOSH: Emergencies?

MUM: They just want to know who to keep an eye on, and you've got a reputation. The vicar's lapping it up.

JOSH: That's it! The vicar! I said dad God was the real Leader and he's run off and reported it. Didn't understand me.

MUM: Oh good grief. My son, enemy of the state! Come on, run.

3.3 The street.

VICAR: I'm so terribly sorry, Lieutenant. Perhaps that was not Mr. Silver's usual hostelry after all.

LIEUTENANT: Then redeem yourself, vicar. Investigate Silver and 'Frank Johnston' for me.

VICAR: Investigate?

LIEUTENANT: I want to know who I spoke to in that pub.

VICAR: Ah well, this area is outwith my parish, you see –

LIEUTENANT: What?

VICAR: Mr. Silver is not a communicant at St. Genevieve's. It's very improper to examine another parish's records –

LIEUTENANT: You think this is a game?

VICAR: A game? I assure you, Lieutenant, I am extremely serious –

LIEUTENANT: Your archbishop bought your church some breathing space and himself a little money. Do you think the Leader wanted to attend Sunday School? He's serious. You don't help us, you serve us.

VICAR: Lieutenant, your interpretation of the concordat is most harsh -

LIEUTENANT: Find Silver for me. Parish Registers, Cradle Rolls, Sunday school picnics. Dig up your churchyard if you have to.

VICAR: But –

LIEUTENANT: Davidson's too capable. He's a visionary, he's a leader; he *thinks*. The rest of your pew fodder isn't worth our attention, but Davidson can provide an alternative. Religion in such hands we will not have. I need to find anybody who can lead me to him.

VICAR: I think if I instructed Joshua, took him through the catechism –

LIEUTENANT: If you want to remain vicar of St. Genevieve's you will do this for me. If you want to walk the streets at all, you'll do it. Am I clear, vicar?

VICAR: Well…my moral vocation as a churchman in society is to…serve the state.

LIEUTENANT: I'd never thought of it that way. Well, on behalf of the people the state thanks you.

VICAR: My simple duty.

LIEUTENANT: Yes. And both of us live under the responsibility that servanthood• brings.

VICAR: I don't quite…

LIEUTENANT: Church and state must protect our citizens from reactionaries, from…deviants. That's why I must have Davidson. I am compelled to be ready to…punish. Am I still clear?

VICAR: Yes, yes. Don't worry, please don't worry. I'll do my duty, I'll find him. I'll find him.

3.4 At Alfred's.

JOSH: That's it, mum, just over there.

MUM: Stay away from the street light, Josh.

JOSH: Don't worry mum. They didn't know who Joe was, so they won't know where his friends live. Right, this is Alfred's gate. Nice little front garden, isn't it?

MUM: Josh, this isn't the time!

JOSH: Does his garden all by himself and he can hardly walk. Got blown up in the coup.

(Knocks.)
ALFRED *(Inside)***:** Who's that? Is that a patrol?

JOSH: It's Josh Davidson, Alfred, Joe Silver's friend. Me and my mum.

ALFRED: Josh! Wait a minute. *(Locks, chains, bolts.)*

MUM: Does he work in the Tower of London? We'll be safe here all right.

JOSH: Alf doesn't take any chances. *(Door.)*

ALFRED: What's going on, Josh? What ye dragging your mother out at this time of night for?

JOSH: Joe sent us, Alfred.

MUM: There's a bunch of soldiers after Josh. Me as well, probably.

ALFRED: What? Get in, get in. Wait, I'll put the light off. *(Feet.)* There. Careful; watch the crutches. *(Door.)* Come through here. There now, sit down. Now what have you done, Josh?

JOSH: Nothing. They think I'm starting a revolution or something.

ALFRED: So you should. Bastards, I'd give them a revolution. What's Joe got to do with it?

JOSH: I was in the pub with him when the soldiers came. He got us out and told us to come here.

ALFRED: Ahh, good laddie. Well, you did the right thing. You stay here as long as you need. If they want you, they'll need to get past me.

MUM: Oh Alfred, thank you.

ALFRED: Don't you worry yourself. Least I could do. Now: we'll fortify ourselves. You get the tea on. The whisky's in that cupboard over the wireless.

3.5 Joe's front door.

(Knocking. Door opens.)

DAD: Oh. Hello, Reverend.

Fr. JEREMIAS: How do you do? I am Father Anthony Jeremias, Archdeacon• to this diocese.

DAD: Oh, right. Here, is that your car? That big black 'un?

Fr. JEREMIAS: Yes, it is.

DAD: There's a soldier with it. Bleedin' 'ell, he's got a gun! What's he got a gun for?

JOE: What's going on, dad?

DAD: There's a bloke with a gun out here!

Fr. JEREMIAS: Am I addressing Mr. Joseph Silver?

JOE: That's me, yeh.

Fr. JEREMIAS: I'm Archdeacon Jeremias. The gentleman holding the rifle is my formal escort under the terms of the State-Church Relationship. Perfectly routine.

JOE: Bleedin' 'ell.

Fr. JEREMIAS: I am…authorised to request you to accompany me to an interview that may be important for the quiet of the community.

JOE: Well, I dunno.

Fr. JEREMIAS: It concerns Joshua Davidson.

JOE: Where is it then?

Fr. JEREMIAS: I'm not authorised to reveal the location. I'm sorry.

JOE: What if I don't go?

Fr. JEREMIAS: That would be…out of my hands. Please come, Mr. Silver, for your own sake. I will…look after you.

JOE: And you didn't say that.

Fr. JEREMIAS: That is correct. Your father is also invited.

DAD: Blimey.

JOE: Oh well. Right, dad, get your demob suit• out. We're going out for tea.

3.6 The Cathedral.

DAD: What's happenin', Joe? What've they brung us here for?

JOE: It's a cathedral, dad. What could happen in a cathedral?

DAD: It's all big and dark. I don't like it.   *(Door. Feet.)*

Fr. JEREMIAS: I'm sorry to have left you waiting, Gentlemen. May I introduce His Grace the Archbishop?•

DAD: Archbishop?

ARCHBISHOP: Mr. Silver. So pleased. And this is your father?

JOE: Yeh. If I can ask a –

Fr. JEREMIAS: Excuse me. Your Grace, Mr. Silver. We address the Archbishop as Your Grace.

JOE: Well, Y'grace –

Fr. JEREMIAS: And we stand to speak to the Archbishop.

ARCHBISHOP: Thank you, Archdeacon, you may leave us now.

Fr. JEREMIAS: Your Grace.   *(Feet. Door.)*

ARCHBISHOP: You were about to speak, Mr. Silver?

JOE: Well, sir – Y'grace – It's all a bit sudden, this. An' a bit of a shock, I have to say. When the Reverend turned up at our door, an' a soldier with him –

DAD: He 'ad a rifle.

ARCHBISHOP: Startling, yes. The fact is, Mr. Silver, that in these difficult times even clergy on an errand of importance require a degree of protection. In easier days there would have been the telephone call, the written invitation; but you understand...

JOE: Er...

ARCHBISHOP: You know of course that the Church now works in partnership with our military leaders. For the good of all.

JOE: Yeh. So they say.

ARCHBISHOP: Now, that good may be threatened. Someone says there is another Leader and that he is his representative.

JOE: I don't know about that.

ARCHBISHOP: Yes, you do, Mr. Silver. And there is a gentleman here who can confirm that. If you please, Lieutenant.

(Door. Feet.)

LIEUTENANT: Good to see you, Mr. Johnson.

DAD: Oh, 'ell.

LIEUTENANT: So you're the spontaneous remission.

JOE: Now look, I got nothing to do with no trouble –

LIEUTENANT: Of course not. You weren't yourself at the pub the other night. You were confused, you forgot your name.

ARCHBISHOP: Mr. Silver, your friend appears to harbour thoughts that would place him in opposition to both Church and State, and therefore against society as a whole. He wishes to lead a movement as representative of the 'real' Leader; he bases this upon a violently delusional interpretation of Scripture. You see how that must concern us.

JOE: Well, he never –

ARCHBISHOP: We need to speak with him. We need clarification.

JOE: Are you – are you talkin' about Josh?

ARCHBISHOP: That dangerous man.

JOE: But what am I here for?

ARCHBISHOP: You are someone he has tried to use. Let me explain. According to our findings, you were, until fairly recently, blind.

JOE: Well, I –

LIEUTENANT: Let's hear from the father. Who better qualified to confirm the wonderful cure?

DAD: It wasn't me.

LIEUTENANT: But he *was* blind, wasn't he? You watched him walk into doors when he was five. Where's the mother? Is s*he* blind? Is it hereditary?

DAD: If you please sir, Edna's been dead these ten years.

LIEUTENANT: But not blind.

ARCHBISHOP: The fact is, Mr. Silver, there is no room in our province for any third force. But your Josh, as you call him, threatens to become that force.

JOE: Josh don't want to be no force. He never said –

ARCHBISHOP: Whatever he *says*, the danger is there; and his ploy in using you is perfectly clear.

JOE: His what?

ARCHBISHOP: Isn't it obvious? Take a widely-known and, I'm sure, well-liked individual, engineer a radical change in his circumstances and *voila* – a magnificent piece of propaganda for his movement.

LIEUTENANT: How did he do it?

JOE: Eh?

LIEUTENANT: Look, Silver, you're small fry. Davidson's far away by now. We can forget about the pub incident, but we need to know how he did it. Was it surgery? Has he got doctors working for him? Herbs? Oils? What was it? I suppose you *were* blind?

ARCHBISHOP: Yes, Mr. Silver. Tell us, please, exactly what happened.

JOE: Well, not much to say, really. He dipped his fingers in me scrumpy and he –

ARCHBISHOP: Scrumpy? Scrumpy, Mr. Silver?

JOE: Yeh, me drink, and he rubs it on me eyes and says, wipe that off. So I did and me eyes was good as new. That's all I can tell y'.

LIEUTENANT: Don't insult me. You're telling me these theatricals cured you?

ARCHBISHOP: Yes, we are intelligent men, Mr. Silver. You are not addressing the man in the street.

JOE: I don't know about that, sir. All I know is I can look at you an' see you as well as anybody else, an' I think you might be glad for me 'stead of draggin' us here an' going on about propergander an' I don't know what –

LIEUTENANT: I think, Archbishop, there is a fundamental disloyalty here. In your flock.

ARCHBISHOP: Yes. Yes, of course. Mr. Silver, you leave me no choice. The olive branch that bears no fruit must be pruned. You are no longer part of the church. I declare you excommunicate•. The churches are closed to you, the sacraments are denied you, worship excludes you. This is my solemn judgement.

LIEUTENANT: Well done, Archbishop. The church is pure again. All right Silver, you can go home. You'd never try to fool me with therapeutic cider, so we'll call it a mystery, or a trick you couldn't…see through. Now, off you go and – behave.

JOE: Yes I will, sir. Thank you, sir.

DAD: Thank y', sir.

LIEUTENANT: Now, Archbishop, shall we retire to your rooms? You can pour me a sherry.

JOE: Y' Grace, can -

ARCHBISHOP: There is no more to be said. Good day, Mr. Silver. *(Leaves with Lieutenant.)*

JOE: Right, dad. We got to warn Josh: get word to Alfred's.

DAD: Oh Joe, I'm scared.

JOE: Don't worry, dad. We're not gonna hear any more from this lot.

DAD: Ain't we?

JOE: Nah, 'course not. So, tell you what - how about a nice cup of tea at Lil's caff? You can have one of them buns with cherries on.

DAD: Oh let's, Joe. I feel better already.

JOE: That's the way.

DAD: What are you going to have, then?

JOE: Dunno. I never could read the menu before. Come on then, let's get going.

DAD: Oh Joe, you always cheer me up. Even when you was a little boy…

(They leave. Feet, door closing. Another door creaks open.)

ARCHBISHOP: You truly feel this is the best approach, Lieutenant?

LIEUTENANT: Easiest, quickest, kindest. Mr. Silver will retrieve his coat from your cloakroom and never notice the tracking device. He'll lead us to Davidson in no time.

ARCHBISHOP: Well, when weighed in the moral balances…

LIEUTENANT: Yes. No coercion, complete secrecy. No misunderstandings in the common mind about the church's motives.

ARCHBISHOP: Our witness maintained•. Of course.

LIEUTENANT: Of course. You know, this really is an excellent sherry. Where did you find it?

ARCHBISHOP: Ah. You hold before you an *Oloroso*, as the Spanish call it, meaning 'scented'. This variety is a little obscure, an indulgence of a certain Andalucian vine-grower.

LIEUTENANT: Really? Well, we'll soon have a properly conducted inquiry regarding Davidson. I'm glad you feel uncompromised.

ARCHBISHOP: Quite so. You'll notice this is a darker, richer wine, Lieutenant.

LIEUTENANT: I'll keep you informed, of course.

ARCHBISHOP: Thank you. The *Oloroso*, you see, is aged oxidatively for some time – a little more?

LIEUTENANT: Thank you.

ARCHBISHOP: Much longer than, say, a Fino or Amontillado…

3.7 At Alfred's.

JOE: I tell you, Alfred, they're absolutely terrified of Josh. That Archbishop feller's wettin' himself.

ALFRED: And he's chucked you out of his Gothic social club.

JOE: He knew what he'd get otherwise, didn't he?

DAD: He said Joe's just propergander.

JOSH: No, Joe. You're not propaganda to me.

ALFRED: It will help your cause, though, Josh.

JOSH: Alfred, it's not a cause. I'm not a registered charity. It's something I have to tell people about and let people see. I've gotta be a sign, a pointer to my dad.

ALFRED: Your dad?

JOSH: God, Alfred.

JOE: I think that's what it means, me being able to see. It's like saying what sort of God there is. Is that it, Josh?

JOSH: As well as fixing your eyes. You've got it though, Joe.

DAD: God bless yer, Josh. God bless yer.

MUM: Here's the tea, boys. *(Tray, cups.)* No biscuits left, I wish you'd let me out to the shops. What harm could –

JOE: You and Josh don't show your noses out of here. I brung enough food for a few days, so you behave yourself.

ALFRED: I don't understand, Josh. You're not the type to start a revolution.

JOSH: Not the kind they're scared of.

ALFRED: They wouldn't worry about an independent health service.

JOSH: No, but it's not about that, Alfred. It's about who calls the shots.

ALFRED: Ahh, power.

JOSH: That's it. Everybody want to be a little god, Alfred. But the Leader thinks he can actually manage it.

MUM: I don't know how intelligent people obey that man.

JOSH: They're buying into being god, mum. They get a share of it.

MUM: Josh, you're just a bit too deep at times.

ALFRED: So what do you want, Josh? What do you get out of it?

JOSH: I love my dad, Alfred. I love my God: I love people. I want him to be to the whole world what he is to me. That's it, basically.

DAD: I wish your vicar wanted that.

ALFRED: I don't have the religious viewpoint, Josh. But obviously you're completely happy.

JOSH: That's right. Well, maybe not completely.

ALFRED: Meaning what?

JOSH: Well, just…I mean, you want the world to know this brilliant God and the first thing you have to do is fight the church. I get really upset about that. Really, really upset.

3.8 The cathedral.
(Knocking.)
ARCHBISHOP: Enter.

Fr. JEREMIAS: Archbishop, good evening.

ARCHBISHOP: Ah, Archdeacon Jeremias•. Please take a chair. The evening liturgy was excellent, was it not?

Fr. JEREMIAS: Yes. The Mozart *Kyrie* was particularly fine.

ARCHBISHOP: Of course. But Mozart elaborates, I feel. A touch of confection. To me, Palestrina is more rarefied, more genuinely spiritual.

Fr. JEREMIAS: Yes, of course. Archbishop, I wished to approach you regarding Joshua Davidson.

ARCHBISHOP: The matter is well in hand, Archdeacon.

Fr. JEREMIAS: Yes, I am aware. Your Grace, it struck me that we may have misunderstood him. The report from St. Genevieve's seems to have very little objectivity.

ARCHBISHOP: The lower clergy should be trusted. They are sons of the church. Our brothers.

Fr. JEREMIAS: Indeed, Your Grace. Nonetheless, I wondered if we might adopt a more conciliatory approach, possibly some form of dialogue –

ARCHBISHOP: I see no advantage.

Fr. JEREMIAS: The issues at stake are essentially religious, it seems to me, and this fact makes the state's involvement rather inappropriate. Could we not discuss with the young man within the church, in fellowship?

ARCHBISHOP: Oh, no. The lines are drawn, Father. The lines are drawn.

Fr. JEREMIAS: But I –

ARCHBISHOP: Was there anything else, Archdeacon?

Fr. JEREMIAS: No, Your Grace.

ARCHBISHOP: Then trust in God. Good night, Archdeacon.

Fr. JEREMIAS: Good night, Archbishop.

3.9 At Alfred's 2.

ALFRED: I fought these bastards. Thirty years ago, during the coup. They smashed my legs with a mortar shell.

MUM: I was carrying Josh back then. I'm so sorry about your legs.

ALFRED: Haven't worked since. Been swinging along on the two crutches for thirty years. Bastards. I'm sorry Josh, but sometimes I wonder what your dad feels about me.

JOSH: That a real question? You serious?

ALFRED: Don't tell me I must have done some terrible thing. I've had that from plenty of clergymen with two good legs that just won't admit they can't answer me. Eh? Is it a punishment? Am I just rotten? Eh?

JOSH: Nothing to do with it, Alfred.

ALFRED: What did you do to Joe anyway?

JOE: Yeh. What'd you put the scrumpy on me eyes for Josh?

JOSH: I dunno, seemed like a good idea. You're always saying things are better with a bit of scrumpy.

DAD: Very good, Josh. I like that.

ALFRED: But what put that in your head? 'Oh, I think I'll just cure a blind man.' Why?

JOSH: Well, Joe was saying how he'd really like to see and I was feeling cut up about it, and I suddenly realised my Dad God felt the same and he was doing something about it.

ALFRED: Very good. And?

JOSH: I thought, I'll join in; do what dad's doing. Help it along.

ALFRED: I see. Well. Oh, I'm none the wiser, Josh. And frankly not a little resentful. You get a clue about what God has up his sleeve and then you make it happen. You're not winning me over. No offence, Joe.

JOE: 'S all right, Alf.

MUM: I don't think it's like that. I can understand –

ALFRED: No you can't. Not with two good legs. All right then, Josh: it's a real question.
What's God got up his sleeve for me?

JOSH: All right, Alfred. Hang on.

ALFRED: What're you doing?

JOSH: Asking.

ALFRED: Josh, you know I'm not religious –

JOSH: Neither's God. Don't worry.

DAD: Stay with it, Alf.

JOSH: All right, Alfred. Ready?

ALFRED: Ready for what?

JOSH: You'll see. Drop the crutches, will you? No, go on. *(Clatter.)* Right. Now, up you get.

ALFRED: Eh?

JOSH: Stand up. Just stand up.

ALFRED: I can't. I've no crutches.

JOSH: Do it for me, Alfred. Humour me.

ALFRED: I'll make a complete fool of myself, you know that? After I've made a complete fool of you. Well, here goes nothing. Hands on the chair arms and…*hup*.
No. Aw, no.

JOSH: Try a step, Alfred.

ALFRED: A step? Well… Right foot…okay. Left foot… I'm balancing. Why am I balancing?

JOSH: You're doing fine. Come on.

ALFRED: Oh Josh, sorry. I was a wee bit rude there.

JOSH: That's all right, keep going.

ALFRED: But I didn't believe it. Why did it happen?

JOSH: Well, I think deep down you really wanted God to do something for you, only you couldn't say it. But he heard you though. He heard you.

ALFRED: I don't know what to say.

JOE: What about that bubbly in the kitchen? Say something to that.

DAD: Yeh. You been saving it since your birthday.

MUM: I'll fetch it.

ALFRED: No, you won't! I'll do it myself!

JOSH: Brilliant, Alfred!

MUM: We'll toast your legs!

ALFRED: Toast my legs? I'm not a frog!

(Laughter and clapping. Then pounding on the front door.)

JOE: What the 'ell's that?

LIEUTENANT *(Off, through loudhailer)*: This is the Regional Division of the Republican Military Police.

ALFRED: The bastards! They've found us!

JOE: Stay away from the window, dad!

DAD: There's dozens of 'em out there. They got guns an' dogs an' vans an' things!

JOE: They followed me! How'd they do that?

LIEUTENANT: Citizen Joshua Davidson is required for questioning. You must give us access.

JOSH: I'm going out. It's me they want.

MUM: No! Don't go!

LIEUTENANT: I repeat, you must give us access. We are authorised to use force. *(Gunfire.)* That was a warning salvo only. We are authorised to use reasonable force.

JOSH: I've gotta go.

MUM: Josh, no! Remember the angel!

JOSH: Get out of the doorway, mum.

ALFRED: They're out the back too.

LIEUTENANT: Bring us Joshua Davidson. You have seven seconds before forcible entry.

DAD: They'll shoot us all!

JOE: They're not having you, Josh. Hold him, Alf.

JOSH: Lemme go, they'll kill you.

ALFRED: They will anyway.

LIEUTENANT: Force entry! *(Blows on the door. Gunfire. Windows smash.)*

MUM: They're in the front room!

ALFRED: Jam this door! Through the back!

LIEUTENANT: Come out, Joshua Davidson!

MUM: What are we going to do? They're all around!

LIEUTENANT: Come out, Joshua Davidson! Come out, come out…

MUM: What can we do? Josh, Josh, what are we going to do?

4: THE OFFICER AND THE SHOWGIRL

4.1 At Alfred's.

LIEUTENANT: Come out, Joshua Davidson.

JOE: They're not having you, Josh. Hold him, Alf.

JOSH: Lemme go, they'll kill you.

ALFRED: They will anyway.

LIEUTENANT: Force entry! *(Blows on the door. Gunfire. Windows smash.)*

MUM: They're in the front room!

ALFRED: Jam this door! Through the back!

LIEUTENANT: Come out, Joshua Davidson!

MUM: What are we going to do? They're all around!

LIEUTENANT: Come out, Joshua Davidson! Come out, come out…

MUM: What can we do? Josh, Josh, what are we going to do?

ALFRED: Everybody through the back! Into the kitchen!

JOE: That's no good, they're behind the house in the lane!

ALFRED: Just do it! You cured me just in time, Josh.

JOSH: What d'you mean, Alfred?

ALFRED: You'll see. In here, in here.

DAD: I'm too old for this, Joe.

JOE: Keep going, dad. Mum would have.

DAD: She'll be telling me so in a minute.

ALFRED: Now, open this cupboard –

MUM: Under the sink?

ALFRED: Observe: my cleaning stuff swings out on a false floor, revealing –

DAD: A tunnel!

JOSH: Brilliant!

JOE: What you got a tunnel for?

ALFRED: Catching rabbits! Get in! Down there - there's a ladder. You first.

MUM: Good job I put my sensible shoes on.

ALFRED: Glad you left the ball gown at home as well.

JOE: You next, dad.

DAD: Hold me arms. You down there, Mrs. Davidson?

MUM: Yes, I've got your feet, you're fine. *(Blows on the door. Shouting.)*

JOE: They're nearly through. Get in, Josh.

JOSH: No, you go –

JOE: Get in! Right, now me. Alfred, come in and close it up.

ALFRED: Right behind you. Down the ladder on my new legs, pull this handle and - click!

DAD: Ohh, it's pitch black.

MUM: Take my hand. Hold on.

ALFRED: That's it. If they look under the sink, they'll just see cloths and bleach and a tin basin on a solid floor.

JOSH: What do we do now?

ALFRED: Kid on we're dead rats. Now button it. *(Above: soldiers break in.)* They're in the kitchen. Checking the pantry…back door…window…here they come, they're going to look under the sink.

MUM: Oh God, send that angel.

JOSH: It's not my time, dad; not my time.

ALFRED: Door's shut. Right, they're leaving. Here's the torch I had in a wee plank.

DAD: That's better, I can see now.

ALFRED: Don't wait to admire the décor, get moving: along here.

JOE: Why have you got a tunnel?

ALFRED: Well, after the coup I decided to cause the victorious pigs as much trouble as I could. Of course that meant I'd maybe have to get off my mark in a hurry from time to time – strategic disappearances, you know – and I discovered this connected with a passage in the foundations of the old terrace•. Been useful, I can tell you. It comes out at the main road; we'll be a long way from our visitors.

MUM: Are there spiders?

ALFRED: If there are they're on our side. Come on.

4.2 The road.

ALFRED: Well, nice night for a walk.

DAD: I can't walk all night, Alf.

JOE: Don't worry, Dad, we'll be all right.

DAD: How d'you know, eh?

JOE: Dunno, really. I s'pose cos we're with Josh. That's not embarrassing, Josh, is it?

JOSH: Not even a little bit, Joe.

MUM: None of us can go home, though; they know where we live.

JOSH: You're right there, mum; so I think dad God would like us to get that bus.

JOE: That's the long-distance bus.

ALFRED: We'll be halfway up the country by dawn if we get that.

JOSH: Sounds good to me. Stick your hand out. Oi! Over here!
(They all hail the bus.)

4.3 The bus station.

JOE: Blimey, this is a one-horse town all right. Tatty bus station anyway.

DAD: I brought your mother here when we was courting.

JOE: Get away.

DAD: Yeh. Before the coup of course. It was nice then, it had a funfair and all sorts.

MUM: Did it have boarding houses?

JOSH: Boarding houses, mum?

MUM: I'm not sleeping in this bus station, Josh.

DAD: They had B an' B places over there, I think.

MUM: Were they cheap?

ALFRED: Don't you worry about that. So happens I've a considerable sum in my inside pocket.

JOSH: That's lucky.

ALFRED: Not lucky at all, quite deliberate. Mind I said I had to beat it in a hurry sometimes? I always kept a big wad of cash on me in case there wasn't time to place a booking in a des. res.

JOSH: Brilliant, your own walking bank. How much you got?

ALFRED: Enough to stand you all breakfast at that coffee stall.

JOSH: Ohh, yes! I can smell the bacon butties.

DAD: I wouldn't mind a fry-up.

JOSH: Yeh. I wonder why we're here.

MUM: We're saving our lives, Josh.

JOSH: Yeh, I know, but apart from that. What's dad God up to, eh? Maybe it'll all get going in this town. Maybe it'll start with that girl there having a cup of tea. Maybe she's *so* thirsty•... Morning, darling. Nobody using that stool are they?

RUBY: No, help yourself.

JOSH: My name's Josh Davidson. Nice morning, isn't it?

RUBY: S'pose so.

MUM: Josh, we're on the run. Be quiet.

JOSH: This is my mum; friends of mine there. We've just got off that bus.

MUM: Hello.

RUBY: Oh. Hello.

JOSH: So…they got good bacon butties here then?

RUBY: Have a fried egg bap, myself.

ALFRED: Here's your butty, Mrs. D. And yours, Josh.

JOSH: Oh, ta. You starting work early, then?

RUBY: Finishing.

JOSH: Oh right, night shift. Ohh, that bacon's fantastic. What d'you do then?

RUBY: I'm an entertainer.

JOSH: Oh yeh: terrible hours. Not too good for hubby.

RUBY: Not married, actually.

JOSH: Yeh, I know. Not for want of trying, though, 'cause you've been married four times, haven't you? Four speedy disasters, just like you set yourself up.

RUBY: How'd you - ?

JOSH: You just choose the wrong blokes every time. It's like you want it to fail. You just can't commit, you can't trust –

RUBY: You a detective or something?

JOSH: Now you're living with Terry and that's not working either. No, no, I'm not a detective. I just know.

RUBY: You've been stalking me, you must have –

JOSH: Well, how's this? When I came up to you, you were standing there wondering whether to sell your record collection and that really expensive blue satin dress your sister gave you so you could have a deposit for the bedsit in Armitage Road. In case Terry chucks you out.

RUBY: The bedsit - ?

JOSH: Yeh. The one above the chip shop.

RUBY: Nobody knows about that! How'd you know about that?

JOSH: True though, isn't it? You're a really unhappy girl.

RUBY: Well…well, I…I suppose I am. Oh yeh, I am. *(Cries.)*

MUM: Ohh, darling. Here's my hanky. C'mon, gimme a hug. There you go.

JOSH: That's the stuff, mum.

RUBY: Thanks missus. How'd you know all that about me, Mr. Davidson?

JOSH: What, the bedsit and that?

RUBY: Well yeh, but you knew how I feel and why I mess things up, and – and –

MUM: There, love, there. Hold on, hold on.

RUBY: I'm really scared sometimes. I don't know what to do.

JOSH: I think I could help there. Me and somebody I know.

RUBY: I'm not going to no psychiatrist or anything.

JOSH: Well, no. I'm actually talking about God.

RUBY: What, you a vicar?

JOSH: No. I've actually been having a bit of a problem with vicars. But look, God's not the big Vicar in the sky, y' know.

RUBY: What d'y' mean?

JOSH: I mean he's not in the sky at all, he's down here with you. He told me about you so you'd know he was interested.

RUBY: You're nice. I'd better get home, though. There's your hanky, Missus.

MUM: You going to be all right, love?

RUBY: Yes, I think so.

JOSH: Be nice to have another chat. Where d'you work? I could visit you.

RUBY: No, I don't think you'd fancy that.

JOSH: You never know.

RUBY: Well, please yourself. I work over there.

JOSH: That little theatre?

RUBY: Yeh. Well, I start at ten on Friday night. Ask for Ruby.

JOSH: I will then.

RUBY: Right. Well, I'm off then. Bye-bye, Mr. Davidson and thanks very much.

JOSH: Bye-bye, Ruby.

MUM: Bye, love. *(Ruby walks off.)* Josh, will you explain to me - ?

JOSH: Tell you later, mum. Maybe it'll start here, eh? Maybe it'll start with Ruby.

MUM: In a wee theatre? Josh, I don't know – oh!

JOSH: What?

MUM: Josh, no. Not in there, there's no way you could go in there.

JOSH: Why not?

MUM: Josh, do you – do you see what that theatre is?

JOSH: Yes mum, I do. It's a strip club•.

4.4 The Governor's office.

SECRETARY: I'm extremely sorry, Lieutenant, I have my orders: no-one may see the Governor•.

LIEUTENANT: Secretary, I must make a report and deliver this package.

SECRETARY: Lieutenant, if the Provincial Governor gives an order there's nothing I can do. If you'll leave the package with me –

LIEUTENANT: It must be delivered personally.

SECRETARY: And what is the nature of the item?

LIEUTENANT: I'm afraid it's classified; but kindly inform the Governor this is a Code Amber delivery. I wouldn't want to see you disciplined.

SECRETARY: I'll buzz him. *(Intercom beep.)* Sir, your Lieutenant is here with a Code Amber delivery – *(Indistinct reply buzz.)* Very good, sir. The Governor will see you.

LIEUTENANT: Thank you. Oh, don't look so chagrined; you were only doing your duty. *(Knocks, opens and closes door.)* Sir.

GOVERNOR: Stand easy. Glad you realise there's a price for walking in on me.

LIEUTENANT: Worth paying, sir. Here is the Code Amber. *(Unwrapping package.)*

GOVERNOR: Let me see. That must have cost you. Will you join me?

LIEUTENANT: Thank you, sir. *(Glasses clink, whisky pours.)* Sir, I must inform you I'll be away for some time. Regarding the suspected revolutionary.

GOVERNOR: Your pursuit of the visionary. To date, there's been highly visible and expensive deployment, public disturbance, destruction of property and all you found was an empty house. What are you doing about it?

LIEUTENANT: The signal from the tracking device we hid on suspect Joseph Silver has been picked up in a town approximately two hundred miles from here.

GOVERNOR: You think the visionary's with him?

LIEUTENANT: I'm certain, sir. I'll be commanding a special force from the town's local garrison. We'll have him in a few days.

GOVERNOR: Well, the fates smile on you – almost said the gods; wouldn't do for a man in my position.

LIEUTENANT: Ironic, sir.

GOVERNOR: Very. I'm going to make that damned church work for me, not join it. You'll have more Code Amber?

LIEUTENANT: No thank you, sir. I have to be at sick bay.

GOVERNOR: Ah yes. How's your adjutant fellow?

LIEUTENANT: Worse, sir, I'm afraid. I want to visit before I leave.

GOVERNOR: Of course. You're very close, I believe.

LIEUTENANT: Came through the Academy together. He just didn't get the promotions. Sheer bad luck, really.

GOVERNOR: Well; trust you don't lose him.

LIEUTENANT: Thank you, sir. Thank you.

4.5 Sick Bay.

LIEUTENANT: Tim? You awake, Tim? How's things today?

TIM: The pain came back. They had to give me more morphine.

LIEUTENANT: Well, that'll help you rest. That's always good.

TIM: Hope so.

LIEUTENANT: Um – I'm going north in an hour. Just wanted to say goodbye.

TIM: Don't give up, do you? Does that fellow really want to be the Leader?

LIEUTENANT: I don't know. We'll find out when I catch him.

TIM: Bring him in here when you do.

LIEUTENANT: What do you mean?

TIM: Oh, the stories. People say they saw him cure a blind man.

LIEUTENANT: Yes, I've…heard that. Well, I'll be going. Behave yourself, don't chase the nurses.

TIM: Chance would be a fine thing.

LIEUTENANT: You all right?

TIM: Yes. I won't say goodbye, that would be tempting fate.

LIEUTENANT: Tim, don't say that.

TIM: All right then. I'll just say...well, thank you feels right.

LIEUTENANT: Thank you?

TIM: Yes. You know, people talk about your mean streak, but I've never been on the receiving end. You're a marvellous friend.

LIEUTENANT: Well – you too, Tim. I'll see you when I get back, then.

TIM: 'Course you will. 'Course you will.

4.6 The boarding house.

DAD: Cup o' tea, everybody?

ALFRED: Good idea, sir.

DAD: Nice couple of rooms we got. Good job there's a little kitchen. Even got a phone.

MUM: Josh? Come here a minute.

JOSH: What is it mum?

MUM: I need an explanation. How did you know all about Ruby?

JOSH: How?

MUM: Yes, how. I never brought you up to be a mind-reader.

JOSH: Oh, mum. Dad tells me.

MUM: God tells you about people.

JOSH: Yeh, he shows me what he's doing. Thought you knew that.

MUM: I never saw you do that before.

DAD: Where's them sticky buns you got, Mrs. D.?

MUM: The table – behind you.

DAD: Oh, ta.

MUM: And how long's this been happening?

JOSH: Quite a long time.

MUM: You never mentioned it.

JOSH: What for?

MUM: But why? What would God do that for?

JOSH: Well, I think if I just went up to somebody and said, 'God's very near you, God knows about you,' they'd probably say, 'That's very nice; now clear off.' But if I say, 'God knows about you and this is what he knows,' that's like a demonstration. So Dad gets their attention. Makes it very personal.

MUM: Well, I don't know. Josh, I always knew God had great things in store for you, but – I mean, don't you think he cares about how things look? Why would he tell you about a stripper?

DAD: Eh? What's that?

MUM: Yes, just milk, same for Josh.

DAD: Oh. Right.

JOSH: Mum, dad tells me all sorts of things. Things about people, things about himself. I understand a lot you've never heard me say.

MUM: I soon will, won't I?

JOSH: I think you will, mum. I think you will.

4.7 Arrival at the garrison.

COMMANDER: Welcome to our little garrison, Lieutenant. It's not like Governor's HQ, but we've got all you need.

LIEUTENANT: Thank you, Commander. I'll be commencing operations as soon as possible: first briefing at 0800 hours tomorrow.

COMMANDER: Right ho, sir.

LIEUTENANT: I'll examine the records of the tracking signal tonight, so if you –

COMMANDER: It's all waiting for you, sir. We run a tight ship here in the sticks•.

LIEUTENANT: Glad you're prepared. Are there…any messages for me?

COMMANDER: Oh, your friend? Yeh, they called; he's just the same. He was asking for you – bit wandered, they said.

LIEUTENANT: I see. Well, if you –

COMMANDER: We'll let you know. Think you'll catch that nutter up here, sir?

LIEUTENANT: I'm supremely confident, Commander.

COMMANDER: That's the stuff, sir. I'll let you see your quarters now.

4.8 The boarding house.

JOSH: Well, ten o'clock. I'll be off then.

MUM: You'll be off? Where to?

JOSH: It's Thursday night, mum.

MUM: Thursday - ? Oh. Josh, you're not going to that place!

JOSH: Yes, I am. Said I would. What about Ruby?

MUM: She won't be expecting you; she wasn't serious when she said –

JOSH: I don't think that girl's ever been taken seriously in her life. I'm not letting her down.

MUM: Josh, she can go to church if she's serious.

JOSH: Oh yes, very likely. I was serious, look what happened to me.

MUM: Yes, but we need to think about our reputations• now…

JOSH: Absolutely mum. Depends what kind of reputation you want, though. So I'm going.

MUM: I hate to think of you in a place like that.

JOSH: Well, Dad God's there ahead of me, so I'll be in good company. Ruby's probably in her dressing room, wondering if I'm coming.

MUM: *Dressing's* hardly the word.

JOSH: See you later, mum.

4.9 Ruby's dressing-room. *(Door opens.)*

MORRIS: Come on, my lovely girls! Showtime, showtime!

DORIS: Morris! Don't you ever knock?

MORRIS: Ahh, what you worried about, you'll be flashin' it all on stage in ten minutes anyway.

RUBY: It's about respect, Morris.

MORRIS: Ruby, Ruby! I pay you enough to cover respect, don't you think?

DORIS: Hardly covers the rent, never mind respect.

MORRIS: No offence, girls, but that's an unusual concept for ladies of your calling. Now, hurry up, my lovely girls, the gentlemen are waiting. Respectfully, of course.

(Door.)
DORIS: Well! What put that into your head, Ruby?

RUBY: I dunno, Doris. Well, I do: I met this feller at the bus station and he treated me like I mattered.

DORIS: Terry does that, doesn't he?

RUBY: No, Doris. You don't know the half of it.

DORIS: Oh, well. If it wasn't for men being swine we wouldn't have a job, would we?

RUBY: True; but not helpful.

DORIS: Yeh. Come on then, girl, let's get on with it. Got all your clips loosened? Right. Now let's see, is it Swan Lake or the Nutcracker tonight?

RUBY: Doris, you keep me going, you really do.

4.10 At the garrison.

COMMANDER: Right then, Lieutenant, look at this: we've narrowed the source of the tracker signal down to a couple of streets.

LIEUTENANT: Good work, commander.

COMMANDER: Signal's been moving a bit; he's probably gone out for a jar.

LIEUTENANT: I've allowed for that.

COMMANDER: If you take the portable tracker unit into the area, the signal should lead you to the house no trouble. Your unit's on standby.

LIEUTENANT: Very good.

COMMANDER: Will you move in tonight, sir?

LIEUTENANT: I...may.

COMMANDER: You all right, sir?

LIEUTENANT: Yes, of course. The net tightens. Commander, give me the portable unit; I'm going to make a solitary reconnaissance.

COMMANDER: You can't go on your own, sir. Might be dangerous.

LIEUTENANT: I find the house, then I radio the unit to move in: minimum risk.

COMMANDER: You've got what it takes, all right. Tracker unit's over there, sir; mind how you go.

LIEUTENANT: Thank you, commander.

COMMANDER: All happens tonight, eh?

LIEUTENANT: I do hope so, commander. I do hope so.

4.11 On stage. *(Piano music, rowdy atmosphere.)*

MORRIS: Gentlemen! My lovely audience! Welcome once again to The Well, where you get the best bucket in town. Yes, we're pub by day, club by night, with entertainment second to none – the ladies you love to love. So...let's not waste any time! Let's begin the evening with the loveliest of my lovely girls. I give you...Ruby LaRue!
(Entrance music: piano, drum roll.)

RUBY: Hello, everybody! All right, are you? *(Sings:)*
Gentlemen, let me entertain you.

Gentlemen, I won't disdain you –
You'll be astonished, You'll cry Heavens above!
When I begin the entertainment and
Re-move my glove.
Gentlemen, you know I love you, my dear gen –

VOICE: Come on, darlin'.

RUBY: I can't.

MORRIS: Dear oh dear, I think Miss LaRue's got a frog in her throat.

VOICE: Let's hear the frog then!

MORRIS: Drum roll for the gentleman! *(Drum roll.)* I like that; the old rapier wit. *(Whispers.)* Get on with it, you stupid tart; what's the matter with you?

RUBY: I can't do it. I can't do it any more! I don't want you to do this to me!

VOICES: Ohhh! Wot yer mean? I paid for this. Why not? Why not, eh?

RUBY: 'Cause I matter! 'Cause – 'cause of him: that bloke at the back. 'Cause of him!

JOSH: Hello, Ruby. Said I'd come for a chat.

RUBY: Help me, Mr. Davidson.

VOICE: Who the 'ell are you, mate?

JOSH: You wouldn't believe it if I told you.

RUBY: Is he here, Mr. Davidson? Is he down here with me, like you said.

JOSH: He's anywhere you are, Ruby: anywhere you need him to be. Now, I'm going to come up on your stage and I'll help you down –

90

PATRON: Gerrout, you. I come 'ere for a stripper –

JOSH: Take your hand off me. Now sit down•. Right. There some steps up there, Ruby? Oh, here we are. Now take my hand, darling, and we'll go for a cuppa with my mum.

PATRON: Gerroff the stage, you. We paid for her, she's ours!

JOSH: No! This girl belongs to herself and God. She's not here for you sadists.

PATRON: What d'yer mean, sadists? Nobody's touched her.

JOSH: Yes you have. You pierced her with your eyes, you penetrated her with your cruel stares. You've raped her in your hearts, night after night after night. And you don't even feel it anymore. Get out of my way. Come on Ruby, down the steps.

RUBY: Oh, I'm frightened.

JOSH: Never mind them, let's just go.

PATRON: Who do you think you are, mate?

JOSH: I'm the man with the truth. Read your papers next week, mate; you'll find out. Come on now, Ruby. Mum's got the kettle on.

4.12 The boarding house.

JOSH: Now then Ruby, you settle down there by the fire. How about a cuppa, mum?

MUM: Coming up. Josh?

JOSH: What's that, mum?

MUM: Sorry.

JOSH: Don't worry, mum.

RUBY: Thanks ever so much, Mrs. Davidson. I've never met people like you before. It's another world.

DAD: 'Ere, you really a stripper, then?

JOE: Dad!

RUBY: Not any more, Mr. Silver.

JOE: 'Scuse my dad, Ruby. He's never met a - er - you know -

DAD: What you going to do now, then?

MUM: You're going to stay here, I'll find you a dress, you can't wander about in that – thing; and you can't wear Josh's coat forever.

ALFRED: Looks better in it than he does.

RUBY: Can I start again, Josh? Will God let me start again?

JOSH: Oh yeh. You believe it, my darling.

JOE: Alfred? I was wondering: do you know what this is? This little square thing with the wires?

ALFRED: Let me see. Where'd you get it?

JOE: Dunno. I found it in my coat back at your house. I was going to ask you then what it was.

ALFRED: Let's open the back. Oh: a battery. Printed circuit. *(Realises what it is.)* Joe, smash it! Smash it now!

JOE: What d'you mean? *(Knocking.)*

MUM: Late for the landlady. Bet it's the noise.

ALFRED: No, don't answer it.

MUM: I think I can handle the landlady. *(Handle. Door kicked open.)* Oh!

JOSH: Mum!

DAD: Bleedin' 'ell, it's him!

LIEUTENANT: Get away from the door, all of you. Over there.

JOSH: Put the gun down. Just put it down.

LIEUTENANT: Oh no. I'm not losing you, Davidson.

JOSH: Well, you won't. Just leave them alone, it's me you want.

LIEUTENANT: That's right, you're the one I need. Just you, Davidson. You're coming back with me.

5: BATTLE JOINED

5.1 The Boarding House.

MUM: Late for the landlady. Bet it's the noise.

ALFRED: No, don't answer it.

MUM: I think I can handle the landlady. *(Handle. Door kicked open.)* Oh!

JOSH: Mum!

DAD: Bleedin' 'ell, it's him!

LIEUTENANT: Get away from the door, all of you. Over there. Quick!

JOSH: Put the gun down. Just put it down.

LIEUTENANT: Oh no. I'm not losing you, Davidson.

JOSH: Well, you won't. Just leave them alone, it's me you want.

LIEUTENANT: That's right, you're the one I need. Just you, Davidson. You're coming back with me.

JOSH: Just me. Why d'you want me so much?

LIEUTENANT: Because you cure people: Silver was blind.

JOE: Listen, I told you –

LIEUTENANT: You lied; I know you were blind. You cured him, Davidson.

JOSH: Yeh. I listen to Dad God and he –

LIEUTENANT: I don't care how you do it, but you're going to cure someone for me: his life for yours.

MUM: No! No, please go! We'll pay you!

JOSH: It's all right, mum.

LIEUTENANT: I'm surprised you're so cheap, Mrs. Davidson: this is above money.

JOSH: What do you want me to do for you?

LIEUTENANT: You're coming back to the city with me, to Central Barracks. That's where you work your magic. You've no chance if the military catch you here; and if you don't do as I say I'll shoot you myself.

ALFRED: You'll need to get past me you bastard.

LIEUTENANT: Just move and he's dead.

JOSH: Sit down, Alfred.

LIEUTENANT: I've seen him before, on patrol. Where's the crutches?

ALFRED: Where d'you think?

LIEUTENANT: Another cure. Well, listen to me, Davidson: you come with me and if you behave I won't alert the military to this address, I give you my word. But one false move and I radio my task force; and I'll shoot if I have to.

JOSH: Well, who's sick, then?

LIEUTENANT: Friend of mine, boyhood friend. They don't expect him to...

JOSH: What's his name?

LIEUTENANT: Tim. His name's Tim. He has a serious –

JOSH: Don't need to know that. You really think I can do it?

LIEUTENANT: Yes. I don't know why, but…yes, I do.

JOSH: All right then. Oh Dad, look after Tim.

LIEUTENANT: No stalling. Get your coat.

JOSH: No. No, we don't need to go all that way.

LIEUTENANT: What do you mean?

JOSH: He's getting better. Tim's getting better•.

LIEUTENANT: How do you know? When?

JOSH: It's just started. He's going to be all right.

LIEUTENANT: You're buying time. I didn't think you'd be cruel.

JOSH: Well, I'll go if you want, but it's a bit of a waste of time.

LIEUTENANT: Give me that phone. You: give it to me.

DAD: All right, all right. Here! Watch where you're pointing that!

LIEUTENANT: Put it there beside me.

DAD: All right, there you are. *(Dialling, then ringing. Voice answers.)*

LIEUTENANT: Central Barracks? Yes I am. I want sick bay: quickly. Davidson, I don't know why I'm doing this –

JOSH: You really don't need that gun, y'know –

LIEUTENANT: I'll decide that. This must be the stupidest, most desperate – yes? Yes, that's correct; I want to know how – what? How? Yes, yes of course, put him on. Tim? Why are you out of bed? Why did they let you - ? Are you in the wheelchair? But of course you need it. Tim, you – you can't fight with the doctor! Well, tell him I said to let go then. But when, Tim? When? A couple of minutes. Yes, it's wonderful.

It's wonderful. Tim, I have to go, I'll be in touch. Yes, thank you. God bless you too. Good night, Tim.

JOSH: Sounds good. Fighting the doctor; I like that.

LIEUTENANT: I owe you an apology, all of you.

JOSH: Officer and a gentleman!

LIEUTENANT: Here, take the gun. I don't want it.

JOSH: No – I don't do guns really. Why don't you chuck it over there? *(Clatter.)*

LIEUTENANT: Thank you. I don't know what to say.

JOSH: Well, I think you're at a bit of a crossroads, old son.

LIEUTENANT: What do you mean?

JOSH: Well, you've just had a very big hint that it's all true about my Dad God. And me. So question is, what are you going to do with that?

LIEUTENANT: Do with it?

ALFRED: Look, are you still going to be one of these bastards at your barracks or are you coming with Josh?

LIEUTENANT: Well…I… Davidson, it's you. When I look at you I remember all my hesitations, all my questions…

JOSH: And?

LIEUTENANT: And I…all right!

DAD: What's he doing?

JOE: It's a radio! He's got a radio!

RUBY: He's going to turn us in!

MUM: Oh please, you can't!

LIEUTENANT: Central, this is Amber Eagle, are you receiving me? Over.

RADIO: Loud and clear, Lieutenant. What's your position?

ALFRED: You're a bastard after all, then!

LIEUTENANT: Suspects are not at the target location. Repeat, not at the target location. Found the tracking device, left it as a decoy. Wasting my time, the place is empty. Over.

RADIO: Understood, Lieutenant. Any further orders? Over.

LIEUTENANT: I have a lead: they're headed for the dockland; they're trying to escape by water. Task Force to rendezvous with me at Cargo Bay Nine in one hour, repeat Cargo Bay Nine in one hour. Use extreme caution. Is that understood? Over.

RADIO: Understood, sir.

LIEUTENANT: Very good. Radio silence till rendezvous. Over and out.

RUBY: Ohh, and I thought you was all swine, too.

MUM: Thank you.

JOE: Bless his heart, eh? You're a decent sort after all, sir.

DAD: Turn up for the books, eh? Cuppa tea to celebrate.

ALFRED: Just wait though. How do we know that wasn't some kind of code and they're just outside?

JOSH: Don't think you have to worry about that, Alfred.

MUM: Well, what do we do now?

DAD: Told you: cuppa tea. I'll get the kettle on –

LIEUTENANT: You can't stay here, they'll find you.

DAD: Thought you'd sent 'em on a wild goose chase.

LIEUTENANT: It's not that simple. When they don't find anyone at the docks they'll be back here. There'll be a full-scale manhunt.

RUBY: Ooh, no. I want me mum.

MUM: What are you going to do?

LIEUTENANT: I don't know. Run – somewhere.

JOE: You could say we overpowered you. Tied you up.

ALFRED: I don't mind simulating a bruise.

MUM: You could go back and see Tim.

LIEUTENANT: They'd see through that. And besides, I can't go back: something's broken, I can't be that person again.

JOSH: That was hardly a person at all, that person you were. It was just a big collection of shouting and stamping and controlling. Made you feel better about yourself, I expect. I think Tim was the only thing that kept you human.

LIEUTENANT: Then who am I now?

JOSH: Yourself.

LIEUTENANT: I used to feel I put on myself with this uniform.

JOSH: In a way, but not the actual you. Think about it: suppose you got to be Governor, the Leader. Suppose you ruled the world but you lost who you are. What's the point in that, eh?

LIEUTENANT: I don't know. I don't know any more.

RUBY: What's your name?

LIEUTENANT: It's Lieutenant –

RUBY: No, your real name, before you was a soldier.

LIEUTENANT: It's – Simon.

RUBY: Ooh, I like that: Simon. Sounds like somebody with a nice car that brings you flowers and chocolates. And wears a turtle-neck sweater. 'Lieutenant' gives me the willies.

JOSH: What about it, Simon? You one of us?

SIMON: I – yes, I think I am. I don't understand this. There's an influence around you, Davidson.

JOSH: Josh to you.

SIMON: Josh, then. I don't really know who you people are yet...

JOSH: You might find out who you are, though. I think we'd all like to meet that feller. So, boys and girls, let's be on our way.

5.2 The roadside.

RUBY: Simon, where's your uniform? Where'd you get them clothes?

SIMON: I'm afraid I stole them. A washing line.

MUM: Simon!

SIMON: I left money. A very good price.

JOE: He wouldn't get far done up in that black stuff and a peaked hat, now would he?

ALFRED: And I for one was sick of the sight of it.

RUBY: Well, I'll get a rollickin' off Terry if I'm not home soon. Good luck everybody, my lips are sealed. Thanks for everything, Josh –

SIMON: You can't go home.

RUBY: Why not? They're not after me.

SIMON: I'm afraid they will be.

RUBY: What for?

SIMON: Guilt by association. What happened in your club will be all over the town in a few hours. Military Intelligence can't fail to hear about it. Did you address Josh by name?

RUBY: Oh. Yes I did.

SIMON: That settles it. They'll get your address from the club and be at your door by mid-morning.

RUBY: Terry!

SIMON: Terry's quite safe, they don't care about him. But you've got to stay with us, like it or not.

RUBY: Well, I think I like it. If I'm honest, Terry won't miss me.

DAD: Won't he worry?

RUBY: No, he'll think I've just cleared off. He won't be surprised either. Suppose I'd better rob a few clothes lines meself. I've only got Josh's coat and my stage costume.

MUM: Oh, you can't keep that on.

RUBY: That's sort of the idea, Mrs. D.

MUM: Ruby, I've been meaning to have –

JOSH: So, what's the best thing, Simon?

SIMON: The Task Force won't be at the docks yet. Where would you want to go?

JOSH: Up north: see my cousin Callum.

SIMON: No: they'll expect that. In fact they're watching his house already.

MUM: Watching his house?

SIMON: I was in charge of Josh's case, Mrs. Davidson. You kept his holiday destination from me very cleverly when I was in your house, but we traced it quickly. I also knew you were lying.

MUM: You knew?

SIMON: It's m – it was my job. I'm sorry.

MUM: I suppose they're watching my house too.

SIMON: Of course.

MUM: Well, that's that. Oh!

JOSH: What, mum?

MUM: Well, just before I saw Simon and the vicar with the soldiers – outside the house, back home – this man bumped into me and said, 'You can't go home, Mrs. Davidson. You can never go home again. Neither can Josh.' I'd forgotten about it till now. He said he knew me.

JOSH: That's a funny one, mum. I wonder what that was about.

MUM: No, you don't.

SIMON: Look, my advice is, go north, double back a couple of times and get ourselves lost.

JOSH: Looks like we hitch a lift then.

JOE: Here look, flag that lorry down. He's not stopping! Yer mis'rable swine!

SIMON: Here's another one. Stop it, Alfred.

ALFRED: Certainly. Would you like me to lie in the road?

SIMON: Don't give me ideas.

RUBY: Hang on, leave it to me.

DAD: What you going to do, then?

RUBY: I still got me stage costume on, haven't I? Nice show of legs always gets a lift.

MUM: Ruby!

SIMON: I say.

DAD: Ohh, me heart.   *(Lorry brakes.)*

RUBY: There y' go. Never fails.

DRIVER: 'Allo there, darlin'. Nice night, eh?

RUBY: Hello. Thought you might be going my way.

DRIVER: Might be. 'Ere, that's a funny sort of get-up for the side of the road.

RUBY: Well, we're forces entertainment, y'see. We go round the barracks cheering the lads up. Only we missed our transport after the show and I never had time to change. I mean, that old bloke there: he's only twenty-five - still got his make-up on.

DRIVER: Get away.

DAD: Yeh, that's right. Er – I'm still doin' the voice an' all.

DRIVER: Brilliant! You're a talented bunch, you are. What do they do, then?

RUBY: Well, he sings…

SIMON: How do you do?

RUBY: And he does sort of comic turns with the other two blokes.

JOE: Got a million of 'em, I have.

DRIVER: That one don't look very funny.

ALFRED: My trademark is *droll* humour; a dry, acerbic wit.

DRIVER: Oh, right. Who're you, then?

JOSH: I just sort of look after everybody.

DRIVER: Oh, the manager.

RUBY: So, if you could just give us a lift for a while, I'd be ever so grateful.

DRIVER: I never 'ad a concert party before. Yeh, all right then. You can sit up in the cab with me, darlin'.

RUBY: Ooh, ta!

MUM: And I'll sit beside her.

DRIVER: Wot for?

RUBY: She's the Director.

DRIVER: All right. Rest of yer in the back.

RUBY: Ooh! All aboard!

3. The back of the lorry.

JOE: What you going to do now, Simon?

SIMON: You tell me. I think I've had rather a sudden career change.

JOE: I think we all have.

SIMON: What did you do before, Joe?

JOE: Whatever you can do when you're blind. I had this little job doing upholstery; another one making baskets. The one I really hated was threading beads on strings for making them door curtains. I had to chuck that one; I was getting really depressed. Wasn't I, dad? Oh, he's asleep. Josh as well.

SIMON: What about you, Alfred?

ALFRED: Oh, professionally engaged in anything that didn't require two good legs. Mine certainly wouldn't have stopped a lorry.

SIMON: What was wrong?

ALFRED: A little cosmetic enhancement from a mortar shell. During the coup.

SIMON: Oh. I'm sorry.

ALFRED: Not your fault.

SIMON: Well, no. I just feel like…well, saying something.

ALFRED: You weren't born when all that happened. Mind you, it's funny. I've spent thirty years doing all the harm I could to you bastar – 'scuse my French, force of habit; but here I am in the back of a lorry with you, a recent occupant of the detested black uniform, and we're heading we've no idea where, because we both met that fellow snoring peacefully beside us.

SIMON: I wouldn't have thought it.

ALFRED: Neither would I. To be honest, it's not easy; but it's happening.

JOE: Josh sort of does that to you.

SIMON: Yes, he's a good man.

JOE: Yes he is, but it's not that. I mean, being around good people doesn't always affect you, know what I mean?

ALFRED: Oh, you're right. My father was a saint, absolute saint. I worshipped him; but I was still a drunken womaniser till I was thirty-five. I was more virtuous after that; the legs put women off, I think.

SIMON: So what is it about that man over there. I hardly know him and…here I am.

JOE: Known him all me life.

SIMON: Well, is he a very good person, an example? Shows you the error of your ways, that sort of thing.

JOE: Not exactly. It's more like, there's some decisions it's harder to make if Josh is around.

SIMON: What, he sort of wags his finger and goes tut-tut?

JOE: No, no, you're not getting it. I mean, I never heard him put anybody down or anything. Some of them vicars, they think they're paid to make you think you're dirt. But if Josh is there, you might feel things you wouldn't be feeling otherwise.

SIMON: Give me an example. You're very mysterious.

JOE: I dunno. I think that sort of depends on who you are.

SIMON: Well, in the light of recent events, I think I see. My word, who have we gotten involved with?

4. The town square.

JOSH: There you are then, Mr. Silver. Time-honoured pint of bitter.

DAD: Ta, Josh. It's nice in this town. I like these little pubs where you can sit outside.

RUBY: Yeh, you can watch everybody in the town square; and there's a cathedral at one end.

SIMON: And not a black uniform in sight. I'm not missing mine, really.

RUBY: Hope you never do.

DAD: That's mediheval, that is. Market square right at the church door. They did that, them mediheval people.

JOE: Good job that lorry driver was thick as a brick. Forces entertainment!

SIMON: I thought Ruby was superb. Tremendous initiative.

RUBY: Thank you Simon. Glad you appreciate me, anyway.

JOE: How's your back after a night in the lorry, dad?

DAD: Better than I thought it'd be. Oh, here's Alfred and your mum, Josh.

JOSH: Hello, mum.

MUM: Hello, son. Well, that's the lodgings arranged.

ALFRED: Very well appointed Des. Res. not far from here. Even a little pink bathroom off the ladies' apartment.

JOSH: Yeh, that's nice. Thanks Alfred.

ALFRED: All right; break it to us gently, Josh. What is it?

JOSH: Sit round my table, everybody. Now, listen to me, this is important. This is about your whole life from now on.

RUBY: Ooh, blimey.

JOSH: You know why we're here? You know why you're with me?

ALFRED: If we weren't, we'd probably all have been shot by now.

JOSH: Apart from that. The biggest reason.

MUM: Tell us, love.

JOSH: It's going to start here. It's really, really going to start in this town. What dad God's got for me to do. And what you're here for is to watch: to hear what I say, see what I do, and understand. To remember what it all means and how it works. Because one day, when I'm…one day…later, when it's spreading, you're the ones that'll carry it on, and the thousands and millions that never even saw me are going to know me because of you.

MUM: That's why we can't go home, isn't it?

JOSH: Yeh. Something like that, mum.

MUM: I think I know who that man was. The man that said that.

JOSH: Yeh. Thought you might. Right then. You watching, everybody? Here we go. Morning! Morning everybody! Nice town you've got here. Just arrived, loving it so far. Just sitting, watching you all going about your business. You got good beer as well.

ONLOOKER: Who're you then, lad? On yer holidays?

JOSH: Oh, I'm a man with a mission.

ONLOOKER: You selling something?

JOSH: No, no; and I'm not trying to get elected mayor or anything. Don't worry darling, I'm not going to kiss your baby.

WOMAN: Ahh, go on; you look a nice man. There, look, he wants a kiss.

JOSH: Oh. Well, come on then, I love kids.

WOMAN: Go on then, Charlie; tell the nice man welcome to our town.

JOSH: Give him here. Hello, little feller. Ahh look, he's got a little teddy. Aw, he's smiling, he's smiling. Oh Charlie, the things you're going to see. Dad god bless you and look after you and meet you face to face and give you peace inside all your life. There's a smacker for you•. Go on back to your mum now.

WOMAN: Oh. Thanks mister. That was lovely.

JOSH: Yeh, it was, wasn't it. Well, like I was saying, I was sitting here, looking at people, and I thought, they're not happy, not content. So I thought, nice day for a change, isn't it?

ALFRED: What's he up to now?

JOSH: Folks, I know you want somebody different in charge of your lives. You do, don't you? A lot of us hoped the church would do something, but it got sucked in and now it's just part of the way things are. No hope there.

SIMON: Oh, be careful Josh.

MUM: Simon, it's thrilling. My wee boy.

SIMON: Nothing thrilling about a detention centre.

JOSH: Anybody ever felt strength and hope and the sense of life and the reasons why you matter come washing out of that cathedral over there?

ONLOOKER: Not me.

ONLOOKER: Lot of bloody time-wasters.

JOSH: Nobody feel that about God then? Well, I'll tell you: I do.

ONLOOKER: Oh, he's a street preacher.

ONLOOKER: When's the collecting tins coming round?

JOSH: No tins, mate. If God was somebody that wanted paid I wouldn't like him. This is personal for me, it really is. I – I'm crazy about him; he's so fantastic and beautiful and committed –

ONLOOKER: Good for you, son. It's not like that for us.

ONLOOKER: We've had thirty years of that bloody Leader. Where's your brilliant God for us, eh?

JOSH: I know, I know. Look, I grew up with this. My mum here, she was only three months married and her husband got shot to bits in the coup. So yeh, you want something new; you want a door to open in the world and let something in. Well, it has; it's here•.

ONLOOKER: What is?

JOSH: The new set-up, the new order; stability from a different authority –

ONLOOKER: You want to shoot the Leader, then!

JOSH: No. Do it that way, you get more of the same. Look, that door is wide open, the new thing has come in. It's from God: he's sent it, he's started it. It's his new society and you can be in it if you want. I'll show you how to live in it.

ONLOOKER: You want a revolution! Where's your army?

JOSH: No. This isn't politics: it's bigger, it's deeper, it starts inside you.

ANGRY MAN: No good to me, chum.

JOSH: How d'you mean?

ANGRY MAN: Me arm. Got ripped up in a machine; it's useless. Lost me job, haven't worked for years. You start a new society, I won't have a job in it.

JOSH: No, it's not – no, sorry. I'm really sorry.

ANGRY MAN: Got any ideas about that?

JOE: You thinking what I'm thinking, Alfred?

ALFRED: Probably.

JOSH: Oh, dad. Well, I've got one idea. Stretch your arm out.

ANGRY MAN: Yer what?

JOSH: Stretch your arm out.

ANGRY MAN: I don't think that's funny, mate.

JOSH: Well good, 'cause I'm not being funny. Now come on, stretch it out.

ANGRY MAN: Well, if that's how you want it. I'm going to humiliate you something terrible; nobody'll ever listen to you again after this. Right then: one arm, stretched out. Here we go. Heeere we go. Bleedin' 'ell! Bleedin' 'ell!

ONLOOKER: He's doing it! Look at that arm!

JOSH: Come on then. Bend it, wiggle your fingers.

ANGRY MAN: But...I saw it. They showed me the x-rays.

JOSH: How many people know this feller? A lot. A lot know this is real.

ANGRY MAN: I'm sorry, I'm sorry. Oh, look at that; I can fold me arms, I can shake hands.

JOSH: Now, listen everybody. If I can do that by the power of God, then God's new order is here•. It's right in among you.

ANGRY MAN: Yer, right: gimme a gun! I'll blow that Leader's head off.

JOSH: That's not how you get in. You want to get in that set up you got to change, you can't think the same.

ANGRY MAN: Well, what then? What do you do?

JOSH: You've got to be like little Charlie over there. You got to just let it all go and fall back on God and watch him call the shots and trust him like a babe in arms.

ANGRY MAN: Eh? I'm not doing that.

JOSH: Then you don't get in.• Right folks, why don't you just go home and have a think about this, eh? Suppose I come here about ten tomorrow and we can have another chat? That all right? Well, I need a pint; have a good day.

MUM: Oh Simon, my wee boy!

SIMON: He could have whipped that crowd up; he could have started a revolution…•

MUM: I remember him at the school.

JOSH: Everybody get that? I might set an exam, y'know.

ALFRED: Well done, lad!

JOE: Josh, I don't know what to say: my old mate…

MUM: Son, I'm so proud of you.

JOSH: That's nice mum. Remember to be proud of God as well.

MUM: Oh, but everything's going to change at last. All the terrible things will get swept away.

JOSH: No. Not yet, mum.

MUM: But…you're starting the new society…

JOSH: Yes, but don't you see what it means for me?

MUM: Well…what?

JOSH: I'm at war. It's battle joined.

6: GIVE ME TO GOD

6.1 The town square.

MUM: Oh, but everything's going to change at last. All the terrible things will get swept away.

JOSH: No. Not yet, mum.

MUM: But...you're starting the new society...

JOSH: Yes, but don't you see what it means for me?

MUM: Well...what?

JOSH: I'm at war. It's battle joined.

MUM: Who are you at war with? You mean the Leader?

JOSH: No. He's gonna be at war with me; but no – he's not my enemy. And I'm not gonna be the enemy of anybody.

MUM: But...don't you want to stop the regime? Your new order –

JOSH: You're not getting it, mum. Me and people have got the same enemy•; and I will fight that foe. And you musn't try to stop that happening.

MUM: How would I do that? What do you mean?

JOSH: You're gonna have to let me go. I'm gonna have to be somebody else now, mum. Just remember I love you. You'll still get your hugs. C'mere. There. Now, I'm gonna have that pint. Think about things, mum. You thirsty, Joe? Alfred?

MUM: But... Josh, come here. Come back here. Oh!

PASSERBY: Morning, Mrs. D. That a tough one, then?

MUM: I beg your pardon? Oh. It's you. You told me -

PASSERBY: You couldn't go home again. Yeh, that's me.

MUM: I think…I've got a feeling I met you before that.

PASSERBY: Yeh. Josh knows about it. You still reading that little book?

MUM: The Psalms? No, I forgot.

PASSERBY: Well, you read it. Take it on board. It's amazing what's in there for you. Your Gran knew what she was doing when she gave you that.

MUM: How did you know about that?

PASSERBY: I gave her the idea. You have a talk with Josh about things, read that book and don't get in the way!

MUM: Oh, not you too! Look, God's going to make my son the most important man in the world!

PASSERBY: You'll see it, yeh.

MUM: Yes! My dream come true! Oh, what will it be like?

PASSERBY: A knife in the guts.•

MUM: What! Look, if God wants –

PASSERBY: How do you know what God wants? You can't see past what you want. Look, you might be his mother, Mrs. D., but you've gotta listen to him like everybody else. Let him go. I'm telling you, let him go.

MUM: Well, you have a nerve! We'll see what Josh says about this. Josh! Josh!

JOSH: Having a drink, mum.

MUM: Josh, come and talk to this man. He said – where is he? Where - ?

JOSH: Nobody there, mum.

MUM: I know there's nobody there! He was – I just – I - *Oh!*

6.2 The Governor's office.
(Knocking.)

GOVERNOR: Yes? *(Door open / close.)*

GOVERNOR: Captain.

CAPTAIN: Reports, Governor.

GOVERNOR: What news? Where's my lieutenant?

CAPTAIN: No more evidence, sir.

GOVERNOR: The telephone call to Sick Bay?

CAPTAIN: It was Simon, sir; we traced the call to a number in the street indicated by the tracking device. The building was searched and his tracker and a gun were found in one of the rooms.

GOVERNOR: Sign of a fight?

CAPTAIN: No, sir; and the gun hadn't been fired.

GOVERNOR: If they've murdered him I'll burn down every church in the city.

CAPTAIN: I'm sorry, sir; he's a good man. We do have a new dispatch. The visionary's surfaced in another town. He was preaching in the cathedral square this morning, going to resume tomorrow approximately ten hundred hours. There were plain-clothes operatives present and we have a full report.

GOVERNOR: Give it here.

CAPTAIN: Another cure, apparently. Criticised the church.

GOVERNOR: That wouldn't be hard. Wait. 'The new set-up, the new order, stability from another authority.' 'Somebody else in charge.' He wants a revolution!

CAPTAIN: He apparently means God, sir.

GOVERNOR: I don't care who he means. We're in charge!

CAPTAIN: We also obtained photographs, sir.

GOVERNOR: Let me see. Too large a crowd for my liking. Who's that group round him?

CAPTAIN: The other fugitives: his associates.

GOVERNOR: Who's she?

CAPTAIN: His mother, I believe.

GOVERNOR: His mother? Can't he look after himself? Who's that? The fair-haired one? It can't be! Is there a close-up?

CAPTAIN: Here, sir.

GOVERNOR: Simon! My Lieutenant, out of uniform! Not you, not you; you cannot be a deserter. Captain, get me the garrison commander of that town.

CAPTAIN: Sir.

GOVERNOR: I want enhanced enlargements of these pictures and a forensic assessment. I want my Lieutenant back.

6.3 In the cathedral.

JOSH: Welcome to your friendly local cathedral, everybody.

LISTENER: Never been in here before. Thought it would fall down.

JOSH: Somebody must like you after all.

LISTENER: Did you have to book this place? Was it expensive?

JOSH: No, no. I mean, it is a church after all, you just walk in. Right, shall we have a chat about God's set-up then? 'Course we will, that's what you came for, eh? All right. Now, what's it like when God shows up and starts getting involved? What's it like in a place where things are going the way Dad God wants them to?

LISTENER: There'd not be that bloody Leader.

WOMAN: Be quiet, Arthur.

LISTENER: Would everybody get cured of things? Like that feller yesterday with the arm?

JOSH: Well, that's one way it shows up. But, other times, you might not know it's happening. He can be really subtle, Dad God; it might be a mystery, a secret.•

LISTENER: Don't fancy that: I miss things.

JOSH: Don't worry, he'll tell you his secrets.• He'll do it so only you get it. You won't miss anything. See, even if it's not in your face, it doesn't mean nothing's happening. He's really powerful, he can deliver, but he doesn't always do things the way you'd think he would.
Look, you chuck seeds in the ground, you put yeast in dough; and you don't see what happens next. But you do get bread, you do get a harvest. You're the dough; you're the ground. Will you go with it?

LISTENER: So…something's going on undercover…

JOSH: Yeh, that's it.

LISTENER: Then later on God lets us have a new government.

JOSH: No, you're back at politics again. That's not deep enough. Look, it's people that do politics. You get the people right, you get the politics right. Now, if Dad God's gonna get life the way he wants it, he's gotta have people that fit that.
So…it's not about a coup, it's not about elections, not basically about any kind of system, or anything outside of you. It happens inside. It's not even about religion.

DEAN: Good morning. I am the Dean of this cathedral.

JOSH: Josh Davidson. Very nice to meet you.

DEAN: We'll see. Mr. Davidson, you appear to be preaching to these people. Extempore.

JOSH: Well, good thing to do in a cathedral, don't you think?

DEAN: You're not clergy.

JOSH: Well?

DEAN: You're not licensed, sir. And by the look of them, these people aren't communicant members.

WOMAN: Ooh, 'ark at 'im.

DEAN: It's a matter of appropriateness, madam. Mr. Davidson, I appreciate your enthusiasm for the cause of religion, but may I suggest that in future you consider hiring the working men's club at the other end of the square? Now, a service is about to begin, so…

JOSH: Oh, well, we could stay for that.

DEAN: No. It's a private ceremony. A novice of the Blessed Sisters of Plenitude will be taking her vows.

RUBY: Oh, I'd love to see that. I think nuns are lovely. They looked after my mum when she was poorly.

MOTHER ANASTASIA: Dean? Dean, we are anxious to begin.

DEAN: And so you shall. This is the Reverend Mother Anastasia, superior of the order, and with her the Sisters of Plenitude.

DAD: Blimey, penguins!

JOSH: Hello, I'm Josh Da –

MOTHER ANASTASIA: I know: I have been listening. Sir, I shall be blunt. Your homilies are simplistic, sentimental pietism. They are not sanctioned by the rule of any order or by any ecclesiastical tradition that I am aware of. Please understand that, as superior of this order, I have shaped these women's minds for over twenty years and I will not allow any new or independent concepts to disturb their thinking. This is my responsibility before God. Now, our novice Passivia• takes her vows today and I –

JOSH: What was it like for you?

MOTHER ANASTASIA: What?

JOSH: When you took your vows. Bet that was a great day, eh?

MOTHER ANASTASIA: Yes…a wonderful day. But that –

JOSH: And you so wanted to serve God, you really did.

MOTHER ANASTASIA: Yes. Yes, of course.

JOSH: It was all you ever wanted. You loved it.

MOTHER ANASTASIA: Yes, I did.

JOSH: Something went wrong though, didn't it? You started feeling you had to make everything perfect; you started controlling people instead of guiding them. You were good at it at first – brilliant organiser, a born mother for the sisters, but you forgot Dad God doesn't expect you to be perfect. You forgot, so you got frightened, and then it was all about control so you wouldn't end up with a thunderbolt in your back.

MOTHER ANASTASIA: I…I've heard this sort of thing before…

JOSH: It got out of hand, darling. Your guiding hand turned into a rod of iron, and then your mother's heart was more like a swinging brick. Now you're feared, you're not loved.

MOTHER ANASTASIA: I'm not listening to this…

JOSH: He's still there; Father God's still there, my love. Start again, be who you were meant to be.

MOTHER ANASTASIA: Stop this. Stop this, I know what you're doing –

JOSH: Not all your fault though. There's that horrible thing feeding off your hurts, trying to turn you to stone.

MOTHER ANASTASIA: I know you! I know you, Joshua Davidson!

JOSH: And I know you! Leave her alone!

MOTHER ANASTASIA: Stop it! Don't torment me, it's not time!

JOSH: Shut up! Now get out! Get out of her! *Now!*

NUNS: Mother! Mother! Oh, she's dead!

JOSH: Stand back, give her space.

DEAN: Call the police! Someone call the police!

ALFRED: No! He never laid a finger on her!

NUNS: Get an ambulance! Oh, she's coming round.

MUM: Does she need the kiss of life?

DAD: She won't get it from me.

JOSH: Help her sit up, there you go. Welcome back, my darling. How do you feel?

MOTHER ANASTASIA: It's gone. That terrible voice is silent.•

JOSH: Feel good?

MOTHER ANASTASIA: Wonderful. I am my own again. Sisters, help me up.

SISTER PASSIVIA: What happened, Mr. Davidson? What did you do?

JOSH: There was something from outside her, something that wasn't her. Sort of parasite. I just got rid of it.

SISTER PASSIVIA: And is she all right now?

JOSH: She'll need to re-learn a few things, make a few changes; but, yeh, she's all right. Well, I suppose you'd better get on with those vows.

MOTHER ANASTASIA: A moment, please.

SISTER PASSIVIA: Can I bring you a wee sherry, Reverend Mother?

MOTHER ANASTASIA: No thank you, Sister Passivia. Mr. Davidson -

JOSH: Call me Josh, I like it.

MOTHER ANASTASIA: Then bear with me, Josh. Sisters, I have been afraid for many years; but now I wish to be vulnerable. I do not understand this, but perhaps in time I shall. In the meantime, I ask you to forgive what I have been and help me start again.

(The sisters applaud.)
JOSH: Bless your heart, Rev. Mum. So: what about them vows then?

6.4 The Archbishop's chambers.

GOVERNOR: Well, my tame Archbishop. You asked me to visit your sepulchre, so here I am. What do you want?

ARCHBISHOP: The church is grateful –

GOVERNOR: What do you want?

ARCHBISHOP: Well, two matters, I believe, will be of great interest. First, news from northern climes. You have heard of one Callum Gillespie?

GOVERNOR: Davidson's cousin. What about him?

ARCHBISHOP: I have obtained a copy of a local newspaper from Gillespie's parish. The church, you see, maintains fellowship and fraternal links with the northern presbyteries. The publication's readership is in the lower educational constituency –

GOVERNOR: Tell me what it says!

ARCHBISHOP: Of course. Father Jeremias, you have the paper?

Fr. JEREMIAS: I do, Your Grace.

ARCHBISHOP: Will you read the relevant article, please?

Fr. JEREMIAS: Certainly, Your Grace. Er...glasses... 'Our local firebrand Callum Gillespie is still pulling in the crowds at the now-famous Preaching Glen, where last Sunday's turn-out was a record 12,000. But while preacher Gillespie is setting the heather on fire, his cousin Joshua Davidson is doing the same in the south. Apparently the church down there is pretty cool about him, but the man in the street finds him more to his liking than the official odour of sanctity.' Tasteless.

GOVERNOR: I can't say I blame the man in the street.

ARCHBISHOP: Droll, Governor. Do continue, Archdeacon.

Fr. JEREMIAS: 'Preacher Gillespie agrees. In fact, he says God has sent cousin Joshua• to be the man this country is waiting for.'

GOVERNOR: Oh, it's a family business?

Fr. JEREMIAS: 'Last week Gillespie publicly accused Presbytery leaders of collaborating with regional military chiefs in what he called a "Godless, conscienceless abuse of authority." He stated this showed the "urgent need"' – 'urgent need' is in inverted commas – 'for Joshua Davidson's mission.'

GOVERNOR: Give me that. 'Some people see this as an implied criticism not only of regional authorities but of the whole government regime.' Have you dragged me out to listen to the vapouring of alarmist tabloid pundits?

ARCHBISHOP: But you are aware of Preacher Gillespie?

GOVERNOR: I have a file on him; this will be added. Now: your other bleat?

ARCHBISHOP: Well, you will recall that in approximately two weeks' time the cathedral hosts a service of thanksgiving for the Leader's thirtieth anniversary?

GOVERNOR: You don't expect me to attend the damn thing?

ARCHBISHOP: More than that, Governor. I invite you to read the lesson.

GOVERNOR: Read the lesson? Are you entirely insane?

ARCHBISHOP: Consider, Governor. Your presence will underline the seriousness with which the Leader takes the church – state relationship. And your reading will emphasise the support the church offers the state in its God-given role. A rationale, as it were.

GOVERNOR: A rationale?

ARCHBISHOP: Here is a copy of the Scriptures; and here is the passage I suggest you read.

GOVERNOR: I didn't know this was in your book.

ARCHBISHOP: These pages contain many serendipities. This passage may even provide a context for a response to Callum Gillespie.

GOVERNOR: Well, well. Fascinating.

ARCHBISHOP: Yes. And now, perhaps, a sherry...?

6.5 Rosie Lee.

DAD: How about a cuppa tea then, lads?

SIMON: Super, Mr. Silver.

JOE: Dad, you got tea on the brain, you have. Two weeks Josh has been talking and sorting people out and you keep making tea.

DAD: Oh, can't do without me cuppa.

JOE: Y'know, Simon, I don't think he gets it really, all Josh's stuff. Thinks his mission in life's to make the tea.

SIMON: Josh seems to appreciate it.

JOE: Well, yeh.

DAD: 'Ere, Simon, I got some o' that poncy Earl Grey stuff for you. You want milk in it?

SIMON: Oh, no, no. No milk in Earl Grey.

DAD: Oh, right.

SIMON: What about you, Joe? Do you grasp what Josh says?

JOE: Yeh, I think I do; and it's sort of like I'm getting a handle on Josh. Like, who he is, know what I mean?

SIMON: Not really. What do you mean?

JOE: It's hard to say...

DAD: Here we are, lads. Earl Grey and Rosie Lee.

JOE: Thanks, dad. Here, Simon? You going to listen to your old boss reading the lesson at that service?

SIMON: The Governor? I don't know; it's completely out of character. There'll be something behind that, all right.

6.6 The thanksgiving service.

ARCHBISHOP: Let us unite our hearts in the collect for the day, which is to be found on page three of your orders of service. Let us pray. Almighty God, who hast gathered mankind into tribes and nations that together they may seek and find thee, accept our hearty thanks for the Leader thou hast ordained for our fortunate nation and so smile upon him that under his guidance we may live quiet and peaceable lives, to the glory of thy most holy name. Amen.

And now, the reading of the lesson, which is found in the thirteenth chapter of the Epistle to the Romans•. It is a great personal pleasure to me that our reader today is, most fittingly, our Regional Governor. Let us hear the Word of God.

GOVERNOR: Dearly beloved, avenge not yourselves, but rather give place unto wrath: for it is written, Vengeance is mine; I will repay, saith the Lord.
Therefore if thine enemy hunger, feed him; if he thirst, give him drink: for in so doing thou shalt heap coals of fire on his head.
Be not overcome of evil, but overcome evil with good.•
Let every soul be subject unto the higher powers. For there is no power but of God: the powers that be are ordained of God.
Whosoever therefore resisteth the power, resisteth the ordinance of God: and they that resist shall receive to themselves condemnation.
For rulers are not a terror to good works, but to the evil. Wilt thou then not be afraid of the power? Do that which is good, and thou shalt have praise of the same:
For he is the minister of God to thee for good. But if thou do that which is evil, be afraid; for he beareth not the sword in vain: for he is the minister of God, a revenger to execute wrath upon him that doeth evil.
Wherefore ye must needs be subject, not only for wrath, but also for conscience sake.
For this cause pay ye tribute also: for they are God's ministers, attending continually upon this very thing.

Render therefore to all their dues: tribute to whom tribute is due; custom to whom custom; fear to whom fear; honour to whom honour.
Amen!

6.7 Tea with the Reverend Mother.

RUBY: Well, never thought I'd be sitting in a cathedral having a cuppa with nuns.

MOTHER ANASTASIA: Very few people do, Ruby. More tea?

RUBY: Oh, ta. What about you, Mrs. D.? Turn-up for the books, innit?

MUM: Didn't expect it, no.

MOTHER ANASTASIA: Excellent Darjeeling, Sister Passivia.

PASSIVIA: Thank you, Reverend Mother. It's just tea bags from the corner shop.

MOTHER ANASTASIA: Nonetheless, you brew a very fine cup.

PASSIVIA: Do I? You never said so before, Mother. You really encouraged me there.

MOTHER ANASTASIA: Something I would have failed to do previously.

PASSIVIA: Don't worry, Reverend Mother. The sisters are so happy for you; the cloisters are buzzing.

MOTHER ANASTASIA: Buzzing? Well, well.

MUM: How do you feel now you've taken your vows, Passivia?

PASSIVIA: Marvellous, Mrs. Davidson. Here I am in the life God had for me. I'd recommend it to anybody.

MOTHER ANASTASIA: Anybody, sister?

PASSIVIA: Well, no. Being a nun's not for everybody, sure; but if you're one of the ones it's for you'd better get measured for your habit tout suite.

RUBY: I got you something, Passy. Can I call you Passy? Anyway, it's to celebrate your vows. Got it out the gift shop.

PASSIVIA: Oh, you're a saint!

RUBY: Dunno about that. Anyhow, I thought you probably wouldn't want a tea-towel with the cathedral on it, so I got you this.

PASSIVIA: A brooch! Oh, the lovely wee dove!

MOTHER ANASTASIA: Charming.

PASSIVIA: Thank you, Ruby. Let me give you a hug. Oh: I should have asked you though, Reverend Mother. Is it all right wearing brooches on our habits?

MOTHER ANASTASIA: A month ago I would have told you it marred the perfection of the black. Wear it and be joyful.

(Door.)

JOSH: Hello, ladies.

MOTHER ANASTASIA: Joshua!

MUM: Have some tea, Josh. We don't see so much of you these days.

JOSH: Things to do, mum. Got a world to fix.

MUM: Well, sit beside me. Have a break.

JOSH: Quick cuppa wont hurt, I suppose. People outside want to hear me.

MUM: They won't mind. There you are. There's a biscuit. Take two.

JOSH: Thanks mum. Well, anybody hear the thanksgiving service on the radio?

MOTHER ANASTASIA: Oh, dear.

PASSIVIA: I shouldn't say it, but sometimes that Archbishop talks a lot of twaddle.

MUM: He's nothing to say. Not like Josh.

RUBY: What d'you think of the Governor reading out the Bible! Blimey.

MOTHER ANASTASIA: An exercise in subtlety.

RUBY: You hear the way he said Amen at the end?

MOTHER ANASTASIA: He should have said 'Glory be to God.'

PASSIVIA: That'll be the day.

MUM: Well, Josh is bringing glory to God. Over two weeks here and people can't get enough of him. They love what he says.

MOTHER ANASTASIA: A great thing is happening here.

MUM: And the military's left us alone. This is going to spread far and wide. Oh, we'll change this country.

JOSH: Been reading your Psalms, mum?

MUM: Oh… Do you know, I forgot. I've been thinking about everything you've said.

JOSH: Not everything, mum.

PASSIVIA: Josh, look: Ruby gave me a brooch. See the lovely wee dove?

JOSH: The dove; yeh, I saw it. The breath of God came down on me like a beautiful white bird of light when I saw the mission. That's how I do what I do: the power of the bird of light. My Friend.

(Knock, door.)

MOTHER ANASTASIA: Simon, come in. Oh, your friend looks distressed.

JOE: Josh, this is Ewan. He's just got here; says he has a message for you.

EWAN: You Josh Davidson?

JOSH: Yeh. Sit down mate, you look whacked.

MOTHER ANASTASIA: Some tea, Ewan?

EWAN: Listen Josh, I've got word from your cousin.

JOSH: Callum! What's wrong, mate?

EWAN: Callum's in the jail. They came for him the other night. I was in the house but they just wanted him. I got out the back way. He told me to come and tell you.

JOSH: What's the excuse?

EWAN: Och, civil disorder, incitement to rebellion – doesn't matter, they just want him out the way. They don't want him talking about you.

JOSH: So it's really about me?

EWAN: He says God's gonny save this country with you. I believe him.

JOSH: The new thing appears, the old thing tries to stop it. Thank you Ewan. Right, I'm going up there.

EWAN: No. Callum thinks it's a trap; they want you on your own.

JOSH: I'm safe, Ewan. It's not my time yet.

MUM: What do mean, not your time?

JOSH: Will you take me, Ewan?

EWAN: Get your stuff together, let me get a rest and we'll start.

JOSH: Thanks, mate. I really apprec -   *(Burst of gunfire outside.)*

MUM: Oh Josh, what's that?

JOE: Don't move Josh, I'll have a look.   *(Door.)*

MOTHER ANASTASIA: Sisters, stay with me. This place is safe, I know it.

LOUDHAILER: This is the Regional Division of the Republican Military Police. Citizen Joshua Davidson is under arrest on suspicion of conspiring to overthrow the state.

EWAN: Callum's in good company.

LOUDHAILER: Citizen Davidson, you must surrender yourself. No-one will be harmed. If you do not comply we are authorised to use reasonable force. *(Gunfire.)*

JOSH: Right, I'm going out there.

MUM: No! I'll stop you!

JOSH: Let me go, mum! In your heart, let me go now. Give me to God. *(Door.)* Ewan, guard these girls here.

EWAN: Right, Josh.

JOSH: If they take me, you tell Callum. Give him love from cousin Josh.

MUM: No! Josh, no!

6.8 At the cathedral door.

JOSH: Joe, what's happening?

JOE: Squad of soldiers, lots of guns. Don't go out that door.

LOUDHAILER: Present yourself, Davidson, or we will force entry.

JOSH: Gotta go out, Joe. Love you, mate, love you. Help me with the door.

(Bolts, bars, big wooden door creaking open.)

JOE: God bless you, Josh. Here, hang on - listen!

DAD: Leave him alone, yer swine! What's he done, eh? What's he done?

JOE: Bleedin' 'ell, it's me dad!

DAD: If I was twenty years younger – take that, yer great thug.

JOE: He's hit him! Dad, no!

OFFICER: Arrest this man. Take him away.

DAD: Get yer hands off me. I'm tellin' you –

JOSH: This is it Joe; here goes. *(Door further open.)* Over here! Let him go.

(Explosions, gunfire.)

OFFICER: What's happening?

SOLDIER: Under attack, sir! Revolutionary forces!

OFFICER: Return fire!

JOE: Josh, get back in.

OFFICER: Defence formation! *(Heavy explosions. Gunfire continues.)*

SOLDIER: They have our range, sir! Hold position?

OFFICER: No, we've no artillery! Fall back! Fall back! Mission abandoned! Fall back!

JOE: Dad! What've they done with him? Where is he? Where's my dad?

7: LIFE AND DEATH

7.1 At the Cathedral door.

DAD: Leave him alone, yer swine! What's he done, eh? What's he done?

JOE: Bleedin' 'ell, it's me dad!

DAD: If I was twenty years younger – take that, yer great thug.

JOE: He's hit him! Dad, no!

OFFICER: Arrest this man. Take him away.

DAD: Get yer hands off me. I'm tellin' you –

JOSH: This is it Joe; here goes. *(Door further open.)* Over here! Let him go.

(Explosions, gunfire.)
OFFICER: What's happening?

SOLDIER: Under attack, sir! Revolutionary forces!

OFFICER: Return fire!

JOE: Josh, get back in.

OFFICER: Defence formation! *(Heavy explosions. Gunfire continues.)*

SOLDIER: They have our range, sir! Hold position?

OFFICER: No, we've no artillery! Fall back! Fall back! Mission abandoned! Fall back!

JOE: Dad! What've they done with him? Where is he? Where's my dad?

(Gunfire & shouting continues.)
JAMIESON: Hey, you stay in yer wee churchie, pal; ye canny do nothing.

JOE: Who the 'ell are you, then?

JAMIESON: Ah'm in charge o' they brave rebel lads• there. Gaun, lads, hunt they animals out o' here! Ma intimates an' the military know me as, wait for it, the Pimpernel – kinna flamboyant, but it fits: they cannae get their hands on me. When Ah'm no' pittin' holes in black uniforms it's Andy Jamieson, at yer service.

JOE: What about my dad? They took my dad.

JAMIESON: The auld yin? Sorry pal, they pit him in the van; he'll be well down the road by now. Chin up though, Ah'll see whit we can do. An' you'll be Josh Davidson?

JOSH: Yeh. That's right.

JAMIESON: Well, you are the one Ah want tae see, big man.

JOSH: What d'you mean?

JAMIESON: Yer wee friend here told me all about you.

FRIEND: All right then, Josh?

JOSH: You're the bloke with the arm. I cured you a few weeks ago.

FRIEND: Yeh. I was a bit stroppy then. Sorry.

JAMIESON: Point is, Ah like what you say, Josh. Ye fancy a wee chat?

JOSH: All right then.

JAMIESON: That's the boy•. Right: sum'dy round here gonny get us a cuppa tea an' a pie supper?

7.2 A chat.

JOSH: Okay, in here, Andy. This is Mother Anastasia.

JAMIESON: Haw, fun wi' a nun! How ye doin', Ma?

MOTHER ANASTASIA: A slice of lemon with your tea, Mr. Jamieson?

JAMIESON: Eh, naw. Jist as it comes, three sugars. An' mibbe an empire biscuit•.

MOTHER ANASTASIA: Digestive.

JAMIESON: Oh, right.

MOTHER ANASTASIA: I'll leave you to your conversation.

JAMIESON: It's bin fun. Say hi tae the penguin colony.

MOTHER ANASTASIA: Good day.   *(Door.)*

JAMIESON: Whit does she do for an encore? Rip yer head off?

JOSH: What d'you want to talk about, Andy?

JAMIESON: According tae ma jammy pal that got his arm sorted, you're givin' it big licks about new societies an' new people runnin' the show. Now, Ah like that. We're talkin' the same language.

JOSH: What are you saying?

JAMIESON: We're the rebels; we want tae shoot the bad men. We want tae make it like it was before this totalitarian holiday camp started, mibbe even better. You've got the religious side, of course: disnae do it for me personally, but mibbe there's two sides tae the same coin.

JOSH: Meaning?

JAMIESON: Well, you keep on wi' the brave new world stuff, we'll back ye, see ye all right; an' mibbe you can help the folk think God's on Johnny Reb's side. Whidje think?

JOSH: Your friend told you wrong. It's about something inside, it's not about politics.

JAMIESON: Oh, Dad God disnae care about politics?

JOSH: Oh, he cares. He cares about anything that affects people. All people, mind: he cares about both sides.

JAMIESON: Aye, well, he wouldnae run wi' my gang.

JOSH: That's right, he wouldn't. He's got a very strong sense of identity: he doesn't need to run with other people's gangs; but anybody can run with his.

JAMIESON: Ahh, ye're harmless. Ye're too harmless.

JOSH: Oh, no. I came to make this world burn. I wish it was blazing already•.

JAMIESON: Ye not think much of the world then? Ye jist want tae burn it up?

JOSH: No; my fire doesn't destroy anything, or anybody.

JAMIESON: Well; no' really getting' anywhere are we? We'll jist drink our tea an' mibbe try again later.

JOSH: No; I'm going up north tonight. They've got my cousin in jail.

JAMIESON: Animals. You do what ye've got tae do, big man. An' best o' luck. Ye're gonny need it.

7.3 Questioning.

CAPTAIN: Right, old man: we want to know what's going on up there. We're going to get some answers out of you.

DAD: Get yer hands off me. You'd have got a white feather for that once. *(Door.)*

GOVERNOR: What's happening here?

CAPTAIN: Prisoner's ready for you, sir.

GOVERNOR: Let him go.

CAPTAIN: Sir.

GOVERNOR: Now, who have we here? Davidson's disciple.

DAD: Yer; an' proud of it, I am.

GOVERNOR: Why?

DAD: 'Cos – 'cos – I dunno, I never met nobody like him.

GOVERNOR: Really?

DAD: Yeh. He's good; he's better than good, he's – oh, I dunno.

GOVERNOR: Old soldier, are you?

DAD: Yes, I am.

GOVERNOR: Fought during the coup, did you? I won't ask on which side. Do you know who I am?

DAD: Er…no.

GOVERNOR: I'm the Governor of Southern Province. I'm the man who could close every church in the country; I'm one of the four people who can walk into the Leader's office without an appointment. I'm the man who used to have a Lieutenant called Simon.

DAD: Ohhh…

GOVERNOR: It's true, then. Why is he with Davidson?

DAD: I dunno – well, he had to be; didn't want shot, did he? He helped us get out of that other town.

GOVERNOR: Why?

DAD: 'Cos Josh cured that Tim feller.

GOVERNOR: Tim?

CAPTAIN: Simon's friend in sick bay, sir.

GOVERNOR: He's recovering?

CAPTAIN: Nothing wrong with him, sir. Perfect health immediately after the phone call.

GOVERNOR: Tell me how he did it, Mr. Silver.

DAD: I dunno, he just tells people to be all right and they are. He can do it, that's all.

GOVERNOR: And who are the inner circle, the people who travel with him? Why are they there?

DAD: Well, we're supposed to watch Josh and learn everything. Er…well, there's my lad Joe – he was blind, y'see, and Josh fixed him and then we had to clear off when Simon come for him in the pub –

GOVERNOR: The pub?

CAPTAIN: In the report, sir.

DAD: And there's Joe's uncle Alfred, Josh fixed him an' all and then Simon shot his house to bits and we got out a tunnel; and, er, you know about Simon; and there's Josh's mum, Mrs. Davidson, real nice lady, and there's Ruby, she's a stripper. Well, she was a stripper, but she give it up.

GOVERNOR: His mother and a stripper. Obviously planning for world domination.

DAD: Oh, Josh never said nothing like that –

GOVERNOR: What did he say? I'm hearing things about a new order, new society, a set-up with a different authority. Sounds like a coup brewing to me; a revolution.

DAD: Nah, don't be stupid. Who told you that?

GOVERNOR: A little bird.

DAD: It's not like – the government; Josh hasn't got a party - oh: we don't have parties now. Well, he don't want to be Leader nor nothing.

GOVERNOR: His audiences seem to feel differently.

DAD: Well, they won't get it into their thick heads. It's summing God does inside you, in your heart, sort of thing, so yer start sort of living with God. He keeps trying to drum that into 'em, but they don't listen, they got politics on the brain.

GOVERNOR: You seem less afraid.

DAD: Yeh, I am. It's a priv'lege, sir, that it is, being with that man.

GOVERNOR: Well, behave yourself and we might send you back to him.

DAD: Yeh, an' I'd rather be with him than you, yer bleeder! Oh 'ell.

GOVERNOR: What did you call me?

DAD: I said – I said, yer bleeder.

GOVERNOR: Come close, come close. I need to know that all you've said is true. So look me in the eye; and while you're doing that, look into this pistol. *(Pistol cocked.)* Do you want to change your story, old soldier? Come on now, make something up.

DAD: I – I –

GOVERNOR: Quickly. Give me an excuse to pull him in.

DAD: No! I can't, I won't, It's all true, everything I said. Do what you like, it's true! Oh, Joe! You'll miss me! Don't cry, son!

GOVERNOR: Well, courage under fire. *(Pistol uncocked.)* Almost under fire. An old soldier indeed; I've seldom seen such loyalty. I salute you, sir. Davidson has won the hearts of two good men. Captain, I think we've finished here. Give him a good meal and put him on a train to his friends. Good day to you, sir.

DAD: Here! Hang on.

GOVERNOR: Yes?

DAD: Would you have done that? Would you have blown me brains out?

GOVERNOR: No. Of course not; I'm a soldier, a strategist. I'm not a killer. Goodbye, Mr. Silver. **(Door.)**

DAD: Blimey.

7.4 A telephone call. *(Dialling. 'Hello?')*

GOVERNOR: Archbishop. This is the Governor. Now listen, here is my revised policy on Davidson: we will let him be. He is apolitical, purely religious; he has been misunderstood by hypersensitive, power-fixated clergy who needlessly alerted the military and wasted public money. The diocese will be fined accordingly.
Now, Davidson says much that the regime can incorporate and he has the loyalty of men I respect. Church and state will monitor him and make sure the rabble do not misinterpret him and use him for their own ends. We will not support him, but we will not touch him. Is that clear? Is-that-clear? Yes. Yes, that is final, Archbishop. I am hanging up now. I am replacing the receiver. Goodbye.

7.5 The break-out.

EWAN: It's that window there, Josh. Thank goodness they put him on the ground floor.

JOSH: Ewan, cutting through that wire fence was too easy. You don't smell a rat?

EWAN: This isn't a high-security place like down south. They think we're all daft haggis-bashers up here.

JOSH: Weren't many guards.

EWAN: Never are. They wouldn't believe we'd try this. Now then, here we are. You wake Callum up; I've got the wire-cutters.

JOSH: Callum! Callum, it's Josh! Wake up!

CALLUM: What? Leave me alone.

JOSH: Callum, it's Josh!

CALLUM: What - ? Josh! Oh Josh, what're you doing here?

JOSH: We're getting you out. Ewan's cutting the window mesh.

CALLUM: Ewan! God bless your cotton socks!

EWAN: Woollen, Callum, woollen.

CALLUM: Josh, I'm sorry.

JOSH: Sorry? What for? After all them nice things you've been saying about me?

CALLUM: When they threw me in here I felt it was all going wrong; I wasn't sure if God sent you or not.

JOSH: Listen mate, there's sick people not sick any more, there's desperate people hearing Dad God's on their side. He sent me all right. Remember that day in the glen, when Dad sent my Friend to me? It's all true, my son, and you're getting out.

CALLUM: Yes! I'll be at my auld faither's for tea.

EWAN: That's the mesh off.

JOSH: Right, up you come. Give us your hands.

CALLUM: Wait, wait.

JOSH: What?

CALLUM: I'll have to cancel my breakfast.

JOSH: Get up here! *(Scrambling.)* Okay. Now jump down. *(Feet on gravel.)*

EWAN: We cut through the fence over there, Callum. *(Feet running on gravel.)* Keep low, we're nearly there.

CALLUM: I'll preach about this tomorrow.

JOSH: Oh no; you're coming south with me.

EWAN: Here: get through. Watch and not tear your shirt.

CALLUM: Right, that's me.

EWAN: There's people waiting just past these trees. A wee quick run – *(Dogs, shouts.)*

JOSH: What's that?

EWAN: How the hell did they - ? *(Searchlights switching on.)*

JOSH: Searchlights! Don't move, Callum!

CALLUM: I'm not going back in there! I'm away!

JOSH: No! Come back! Callum, stop! *(Gunfire.)* No! Callum, you all right? Callum? *Callum!*

7.6 The Archbishop's chambers.

GOVERNOR: I did not authorise a liquidation!• I didn't even want him arrested.

ARCHBISHOP: The north does have a tradition of unilateral action –

GOVERNOR: You initiated this! Anything connected with Davidson threatens your gangrenous church. He is an alternative to you.

ARCHBISHOP: But we have our relationship with the state.

GOVERNOR: You wish it to continue?

ARCHBISHOP: I have always been candid in my fraternal communications with the north –

GOVERNOR: I know: we intercept them.

ARCHBISHOP: Then you know I have frankly given my purely personal opinion, quite without executive intent, that the activities of an individual carry a vast personal responsibility that may –

GOVERNOR: Say it, man!

ARCHBISHOP: Placed beside the value of the nation's security, the value of a specific individual's personal subsistence may in precise circumstances become well-nigh negligible•.

GOVERNOR: One little man in a glen and you fear for the nation.

ARCHBISHOP: Possibly I was misinterpreted, made an excuse; possibly your own impassioned reading of scripture at the thanksgiving service –

GOVERNOR: I was emphasising the authority of the state, not issuing death warrants!

ARCHBISHOP: But such powerful words.

GOVERNOR: This is absurd. If you think - . You manipulated me! My reading that thing became an implication.

ARCHBISHOP: Governor, I am stung. I am called to be for this nation a representative of God.

GOVERNOR: If I were forced to have a god, I would choose one that resembled Davidson rather than you. Good day, Archbishop.

7.7 Mum and the Reverend Mother.

MOTHER ANASTASIA: Mrs. Davidson. Good morning.

MUM: Hello, Mother.

MOTHER ANASTASIA: You're worrying, I think.

MUM: Possibly.

MOTHER ANASTASIA: Josh was right, you know: we need to let go of people.

MUM: How can we?

MOTHER ANASTASIA: Because God does not. That's why it's safe, for them and us.

MUM: Voice of experience, Mother?

MOTHER ANASTASIA: I am a widow, Mrs. Davidson. My husband was killed during the coup. A stray incendiary; he wasn't a combatant. I know you suffered the same.

MUM: We were only married a matter of months.

MOTHER ANASTASIA: And your anger has lasted since then. It's only natural. But perhaps that's why you hang onto Joshua so firmly: you don't want to lose someone else.

MUM: I've got such dreams for him. He'll be a great man.

MOTHER ANASTASIA: You know this?

MUM: Oh, yes. Mother, do you believe in angels?

MOTHER ANASTASIA: Yes, I do.

MUM: An angel showed me how important Josh would be. Before he was born. I don't know if it was a dream or the real thing.

MOTHER ANASTASIA: They can be the same.

MUM: I've dreamed about his greatness ever since; he just doesn't seem to want to move that way.

MOTHER ANASTASIA: People can be great in many different ways; but perhaps your letting go can be part of bringing the dream to reality.

MUM: I don't follow you.

MOTHER ANASTASIA: Let it be for now. The reason I told you of my bereavement was that I hoped it would enable me to help you.

MUM: Help me? Oh - !

MOTHER ANASTASIA: Oh, not Joshua, he's perfectly safe. I came to show you this newspaper.

MUM: What's this?

MOTHER ANASTASIA: The article here.

MUM: *(Reading)*: Oh! Callum! No!

MOTHER ANASTASIA: Killed while attempting to escape, they say.

MUM: But Josh - ?

MOTHER ANASTASIA: There was a telephone call; he is in no danger whatever. He says he'll be here soon.

MUM: Oh, Mother! Mother!

MOTHER ANASTASIA: Come here, my dear. Let me hold you. I feel you haven't cried for a very long time…

7.8 The funeral.

Rev. FARQUHAR: I stand here on one of the saddest days of my long and eventful career. I have assisted many dear souls in our normally idyllic community to commit their loved ones to God and lay them to their rest under the trees of this beautiful and historic churchyard. Sadly, the calm of our hills and glens was tragically shattered by the sound of the shots that brought a young life so full of promise to an end.
Callum Gillespie was one of the brightest stars in the firmaments of community and Kirk and our hearts go out today to his father Reverend Gillespie, his sister Eilidh, Ewan and all friends and family. We welcome too• his cousin Joshua who has been able to be with us today.

JOSH: Eilidh, where did they find this bloke?

EILIDH: Presbytery arranged it; father wasn't happy.

Rev. FARQUHAR: And now it is my sad but honourable privilege to lay Callum to his rest beside his beloved mother; but as I do, I am led to recall the heavy but pertinent teaching of Scripture that we are to obey God's appointed authorities.

JOSH: How much are they paying him?

EILIDH: Too much.

Rev. FARQUHAR: The authorities, we are told, are to be honoured as the servants of God, but Callum, towards the end, could not bring himself to obey this command and the tragic consequences we all know.

JOSH: He's not getting away with that?

EILIDH: He is not: look at father.

JOSH: Ohhh.

Rev. FARQUHAR: So, even as we mourn, I exhort you to take to heart the –

Rev. GILLESPIE: Will you proceed to the burial, Rev. Farquhar?

Rev. FARQUHAR: I – I am proceeding, Rev. Gillespie. If you will bear with me. A sensitive occasion –

Rev. GILLESPIE: Your friends there with the rifles needn't be nervous. I won't cause a riot at my own son's funeral.

Rev. FARQUHAR: Then let us proceed with the committal, if that is your wish, and the wish of all... Ah. It is. Very well. Gentlemen, if you will take the cords... Since it has pleased Almighty God to take unto Himself the soul of our dear brother here departed, we commit his body to the –

Rev. GILLESPIE: Almighty God is not pleased. This was not my son's time, and God did not take him from this world, as you and your military accomplices well know.

Rev. FARQUHAR: Rev. Gillespie, perhaps if we adjourn to the church –

Rev. GILLESPIE: Be quiet, sir! You are not fit for this.

Rev. FARQUHAR: I am an ordained minister –

Rev. GILLESPIE: Step away from the grave, you babbler. I will bury my son myself. Eilidh, come here; take my hand. Joshua, will you hold my Bible?

JOSH: It's an honour, sir.

Rev. GILLESPIE: Stand there, please: good. I believe• what Callum said about you, Joshua: you are God's gift to this world.

JOSH: God showed you that Reverend.

Rev. GILLESPIE: Aye, he did. Now then: Let us worship God.

7.9 Mum and the Psalms.

MUM: "He trusted on the LORD that he would deliver him: let him deliver him, seeing he delighted in him.
But thou art he that took me out of the womb: thou didst make me hope when I was upon my mother's breasts."

MOTHER ANASTASIA: Are your Psalms helping you?

MUM: Yes and no. So many grim situations in them.

MOTHER ANASTASIA: Real, perhaps? Life is like that.

MUM: What hope did Callum have, though?

MOTHER ANASTASIA: You know what hope.

MUM: "Thou hast brought me into the dust of death."

MOTHER ANASTASIA: Read on.

MUM: "Be not thou far from me, O LORD: O my strength, haste thee to help me." But he's dead.

MOTHER ANASTASIA: And why should that be the end of hope?

7.10 Callum's return.   *(Birdsong.)*

EWAN: Oh, it's yourself, Josh.

JOSH: Morning, Ewan. Eilidh.

EILIDH: We've not seen you all morning.

JOSH: Oh, just enjoying the sunshine. Listening to dad.

EILIDH: We're taking some flowers to the grave. Will you come with us?

JOSH: I'd like that. Oh, carnations. He liked carnations. *(Walking on path.)*

EILIDH: Aye, he did. Well, you'll be away soon. Mind and tell your mother to come and see us.

JOSH: Yeh, course. You and your dad'll be all right?

EILIDH: Oh, yes. We felt the shock after the funeral, but that's a week now and…time moves on.

JOSH: You'll see him again.

EILIDH: Thank God for the resurrection.

JOSH: Oh, yes. Gritting your teeth a bit there though, Eilidh.

EILIDH: Yes, Josh; but we die in hope. Callum did, I will, you will.

JOSH: Yeh. Yeh, I definitely will.

EILIDH: Well, here we are. We'll need to get his name put on the stone under mother's. One more thing to see to.

EWAN: I'll do that for you, Eilidh.

EILIDH: Bless your heart, Ewan. Well, there's your carnations, Callum. These wreaths are awful wilted looking.

EWAN: I'll clear them.

EILIDH: Josh, you never say much, but I know you loved Callum like a brother. Will you say a prayer?

JOSH: Yeh, I'd love to. Dad God was just talking to me about Callum.

EILIDH: Was he, Josh? Well, on you go.

JOSH: Right. Well, dad, you were saying how it hurt you when Callum…you know; and you were saying you had special plans for him, and you…d'you really want to do that? All right then. Um…

EILIDH: What is it, Josh?

JOSH: I'm going to need you to trust me, Eilidh•. Really trust me. Can you do that?

EILIDH: I think so, Josh.

JOSH: Okay. Then help me, Ewan. Dig him up.

EWAN: He's been a week in the ground, man!

EILIDH: Josh, you can't.

JOSH: Eilidh, can you trust me about whatever happens if we do that? Can you trust me because of what Callum thought about me?

EILIDH: Yes. Yes, I can do that.

JOSH: Ewan?

EWAN: Yes, I can; though God help me, I don't know why.

JOSH: Right then. There's some spades and rope over by that shed. Let's get started.

(Fade out, then fade in to wood scraping on earth, ropes creaking.)

JOSH: Right, lift and heave. Heave again…hup! *(Thud.)* There we are. Pull it over a bit. Right: now get the lid off. Use the spade.

EWAN: Man, you don't mean that!•

JOSH: 'Course I do. What's the point of getting him up here and not taking the lid off?

EWAN: But –

JOSH: We're going to need the lid off, Ewan. Come on. Spade in there. Force it. And…

(Creaking, splintering.)

EILIDH: I'm not looking.

JOSH: That's it: good. Bit more. Now, prise it open... *(Wood splitting.)* And lift... *(Wood breaks. Clatter.)* Hello, Callum. You've got your preaching suit on. Oh, that tie, though; it is so not you. Oh, I'm so sorry you had that interruption. So wrong. It was horrible; it was horrible losing you. I hope it didn't hurt. Well, I'm just going to speak to dad now, all right? Yeh, 'course it is. Well, here we go. Dad, you are so full of life. Breathe out your life, breathe out that white bird of light that Callum saw. Come from the four winds•, O breath, upon my cousin Callum. It was not his time, dad, you know that; so now bring the end of the world forward for him• and let how things will be break in. Thanks, dad. Thanks, thanks, thanks, thanks. Oh, dear; oh my goodness. All right: Callum? Callum, up you get.

EILIDH: Josh! Oh, Josh, no; oh, stop it.

JOSH: Sit up now; breakfast, come on. *(Callum gasps and shouts.)* There you go. Come on now, another breath. Oh, brilliant. Good, sit up now, that's it...

CALLUM: Oh. Oh, what time is it?

JOSH: Time you were up, my son.

CALLUM: Josh! Good morning. Oh, what a dream.

JOSH: Good one?

CALLUM: Oh yes. Och, it's gone; there was light in it.

JOSH: Well, up you get; out of that...bed. That's it, stand up.

CALLUM (*Stretching*) : Ohhh. Look at that, I've been sleeping in my clothes.

JOSH: Oh dear; you must've been shattered.

CALLUM: Aye. Oh, Eilidh, good morning. Eilidh, what's wrong with you?

EILIDH: Callum! Oh, Callum! *(Etc.)*

CALLUM: Och, Eilidh! I can't breathe! That's the best hug I've had from you in a while. Or do you just want something? Ewan, hello.

EWAN: Hello, Callum.

JOSH: Tell you what, cos. Have a bit of breakfast, then get your gear together and come down south with me.

CALLUM: I'd like that. How's your work going?

JOSH: Doing good. It's getting really serious now.

CALLUM: Oh, that's fine. Josh?

JOSH: Hm?

CALLUM: Why are we in the churchyard?

8: CLOSE RELATIVES

8.1 Callum's return.

JOSH: Dad, you are so full of life. Breathe out your life, breathe out that white bird of light that Callum saw. Come from the four winds, O breath, upon my cousin Callum. It was not his time, dad, you know that; so now bring the end of the world forward for him and let how things will be break in. Thanks, dad. Thanks, thanks, thanks, thanks. Oh, dear; oh my goodness. All right: Callum? Callum, up you get.

EILIDH: Josh! Oh, Josh, no; oh, stop it.

JOSH: Sit up now; breakfast, come on. *(Callum gasps and shouts.)* There you go. Come on now, another breath. Oh, brilliant. Good, sit up now, that's it…

CALLUM: Oh. Oh, what time is it?

JOSH: Time you were up, my son.

CALLUM: Josh! Good morning. Oh, what a dream.

JOSH: Good one?

CALLUM: Oh yes. Och, it's gone; there was light in it.

JOSH: Well, up you get; out of the…bed. That's it, stand up.

CALLUM *(Stretching)* **:** Ohhh. Look at that, I've been sleeping in my clothes.

JOSH: Oh dear; you must've been shattered.

CALLUM: Aye. Oh, Eilidh, good morning. Eilidh, what's wrong with you?

EILIDH: Callum! Oh, Callum! *(Etc.)*

CALLUM: Och, Eilidh! I can't breathe! That's the best hug I've had from you in a while. Or do you just want something? Ewan, hello.

EWAN: Hello, Callum.

JOSH: Tell you what, cos. Have a bit of breakfast, then get your gear together and come down south with me.

CALLUM: I'd like that. How's your work going?

JOSH: Doing good. It's getting really serious now.

CALLUM: Oh, that's fine. Josh?

JOSH: Hm?

CALLUM: Why are we in the churchyard?

8.2 Tea Time 1.   *(Dinner gong.)*

RUBY: Tea up! Come and get it!

MOTHER ANASTASIA: Ruby! Good gracious! You should try summoning the sisters to prayer!

RUBY: Ooh, Mother Anastasia! How y' diddlin' then?

MOTHER ANASTASIA: Er – very well, I think. No-one seems to be hungry.

RUBY: Layabouts. *(Gong.)* Tea uuuuuup! Come on! Ooh, bet you never thought you'd have an ex-stripper bangin' a gong in your convent, eh?

MOTHER ANASTASIA: Well, no; but such are the anomalies that surround Josh Davidson. *(Door.)* Ah, Mrs. Davidson.

RUBY: How's things, Mrs. D?

MUM: Wonderful. Seeing Josh with those crowds! He's had an edge to him since he came back with Callum.

MOTHER ANASTASIA: Where is Josh? I haven't seen him today.

RUBY: Sloped off for a pray. Gotta chat wiv dad, he said.

MUM: Oh yes. Strategy.

MOTHER ANASTASIA: I'm sorry?

MUM: God will tell him what to do next.

MOTHER ANASTASIA: Oh. But it's going so well here. The crowds…

RUBY: Yeh, they're bussing them in now.

MUM: God might move him. There's the whole country.

MOTHER ANASTASIA: You really think – everyone? The nation?

RUBY: Yeh! Ev'rybody's sick of them po-faced vicars.

MUM: Why not? God and Josh together – what couldn't happen?

RUBY: I'd like tea to happen.

MOTHER ANASTASIA: Then summon the faithful, Sister Ruby.

RUBY: Right. *(Gong.)* Tea up! Come on, gettin' cold! Tea up!

8.3 Chatting with Dad 1.

JOSH: Dad, you are so…I mean, that thing with Callum! Brilliant! I mean, what next, dad? Just what have you got up your sleeve?
Gotta know, seriously, cause I just love being Servant and doing what you're doing; it is the biggest blast…
So: am I gonna be round here for long, or -   Really? Wooh, that's a tough one. What am I gonna say to *them*?

8.4 Tea Time 2.

DAD: Where's me tea, then? I'm starvin', I am.

RUBY: Should a' been here quicker, then. Get y'selves sat down. Simon, you're down there next to Mother A.; Joe, you and your dad there. Where's Alfred? *(Door.)*

ALFRED: Here, my dear, eager for your luscious repast.

RUBY: You'll get repasted where you least expect it, mate. Siddown. Ooh, where's Callum? He's been hiding away since he got here.

ALFRED: Well, wouldn't you? Think about it. *(Door.)* Oh, here we are.

CALLUM: Sorry I'm late.

JOE: Callum! Sit down mate, tea up. Meat an' two veg courtesy o' Muvver Anastasia's girls!

CALLUM: Thank you, Joe. You're looking cheerful.

JOE: 'Course I am. They sent me back me old dad, didn't they?

DAD: That's right, Joe.

RUBY: Right, I'm mother. Ooh! No, Mother A. is. I'm serving though – here you go, Callum.

CALLUM: Well, I'm ready for this. Never had my tea in a convent before.

MOTHER ANASTASIA: We're very happy you're all staying in our guest rooms while Joshua works in this area.

SIMON: Mother Anastasia's a brick.

MOTHER ANASTASIA: With a few rough corners knocked off; but thank you, Simon.

ALFRED: Never thought I'd see a Governor's Lieutenant getting pally with a mother superior.

SIMON: Ex-lieutenant, Alfred.

CALLUM: You were in the military?

SIMON: Yes I was. And now I'm with Josh.

CALLUM: Oh. How did that happen?

SIMON: Friend of mine was dying, Josh cured him. A hundred miles away.

CALLUM: Away! Well, the age of miracles isn't past.

ALFRED: You'd know about that, wouldn't you?

CALLUM: Aye. I suppose…no, it's just – military personnel on Josh's side! I never thought I'd live to – to - er…

ALFRED: Well, you have. With a vengeance.

SIMON: I feel like apologising to you.

CALLUM: Och no, it wasn't you.

SIMON: No, but – well…

CALLUM: Aye. Em…I think I'd maybe enjoy my tea more if everybody wasn't looking at me. If you don't mind.

ALL: Oh, right. Sorry…

CALLUM: Lovely stew, Mother, er…

MOTHER ANASTASIA: The sisters work wonders with what they have.

CALLUM: Oh, they do. So...what does Anastasia mean?

MOTHER ANASTASIA: Oh...it's Greek•. Mrs. Davidson, more tea?

MUM: No thanks, mother.

CALLUM: Auntie, you're staring a wee bit.

MUM: Take my hands, Callum.

CALLUM: Auntie, I'm at my tea.

MUM: I need to know you're solid.

CALLUM: Och, I'm as solid as the table.

MUM: I keep feeling you're going to float away or something. Tell me again, Callum: it wasn't just something they put in the paper to demoralise us? It did happen?

JOE: 'Course it did. I saw him changing his shirt. He's got two bullet holes in his back.

RUBY: Does it hurt?

CALLUM: No, no. They're healing up.

ALFRED: Look at the back of his neck.

MUM: Callum! You never said! Turn round.

CALLUM: Och, auntie...

MUM: Turn round. Oh! Callum!

RUBY: What was it like?

CALLUM: What?

RUBY: You know, when you –

CALLUM: Well, I don't know, I...

MOTHER ANASTASIA: Ruby, this is the most personal story possible. It's not for chatting over the tea-table.

RUBY: Well, how am I going to tell my grandkids? Go on, Callum, I never met anybody dead before.

MUM: He's not!

RUBY: I know. I'm not gonna blab it round the pub nor nothing.

ALFRED: Aye, she wouldn't cheapen it.

RUBY: Nothing like this ever happened before; but it's happened to somebody that's my friend. That's why I want to know: it's a bit of my life.

MUM: Tell us, Callum.

MOTHER ANASTASIA: Mrs. Davidson –

MUM: Tell us all you can. We need to know what God's getting Josh to do.

CALLUM: There's not much to say.

DAD: Not much to say? How can there be not much to say?

CALLUM: That's how it felt.

MUM: Go on, Callum.

CALLUM: When I got out of the prison and through the fence the searchlights came on. You'd not have got me back in that jail for a pension, so I just ran, and I heard dogs barking and Josh shouting; and then I heard the guns, and – oh, there was a terrible pain between my shoulders, and the back of my neck. I was falling, and it seemed to take an awful time and I wasn't landing...
There was light, I don't know where from. It was light you could touch...

RUBY: What d'you mean?

CALLUM: I don't know.

MOTHER ANASTASIA: *Lux Aeterna•.*

CALLUM: Aye. And there was…um…I think there was singing: one voice, and a million voices, both at once. Don't know where it came from, there was no direction…

MOTHER ANASTASIA: The choir invisible•.

CALLUM: The what?

MOTHER ANASTASIA: Never mind.

CALLUM: Well; then Josh was telling me to get up and I was in my bed. I thought somebody'd left the window open.

RUBY: That it then?

CALLUM: Afraid so.

MUM: And then what?

CALLUM: I got up to get my breakfast, and there was Eilidh and Ewan, and I looked around and there was broken wood all round my feet and thon muckle hole in the ground.

RUBY: Ohhhh.

MUM: But Josh told you everything.

CALLUM: Aye he did, Auntie. He says, 'Welcome back, cos. You've been down that hole the best part of a week.'

DAD: Blimey, eh? Must a' ruined your suit.

JOE: Crack a smile, Simon. You look like yer cat's died.

MOTHER ANASTASIA: Is something wrong, Simon?

SIMON: When I was in military academy…they drummed it into you – the worldview: church is in the Dark Ages, materialism's the way… They were intelligent men, not fools at all, and they believed it, but…my mind's been reeling for weeks: I know all that's not the case –

MUM: Josh drummed *that* into you.

SIMON: No, he didn't•. Nothing was drummed in, that would have been a violation. I just – moved. But…who is he? Who *is* Josh? I don't know yet.

MUM: He's my son; my wonderful boy.

RUBY: *I* know.

SIMON: Who then? Who is he?

RUBY: Well, I know, but I couldn't put a name to it. I know who he is to me, though. I really know that.

SIMON: I'm glad for you, Ruby. I truly am. I think I'll take a stroll.

RUBY: What about your tea?

MOTHER ANASTASIA: We'll leave it in the oven. Off you go, Simon; off you go.

8.5 A Breath of Air. *(Outside. Feet on gravel.)*

SIMON: Fine night, Josh.

JOSH: Wotcher, Simon. Thought you'd be sitting round the fire.

SIMON: Oh, breath of air; you know.

JOSH: Why not join the nuns for evening prayers.

SIMON: Oh, I don't think so. I got rid of one black uniform; now I'm surrounded by dozens.

JOSH: Black and white, Simon.

SIMON: Yes; still, I don't think Vespers• is quite me.

JOSH: What is you, chum?

JOSH: I don't know yet. Hope I find out.

JOSH: 'Course you will.

SIMON: Josh, you don't ask us to wear uniforms or take vows like the sisters. When I was a soldier, I had to recite the Oath of Allegiance to the Leader every day. There's no list of orders or legislation with you: you just talk about your dad's society and practice what you preach.

JOSH: Couldn't say it if I didn't do it.

SIMON: But what you say is so…huge. It takes in everything; but it's basic and simple, and it's so…open.

JOSH: Yeh. You're getting it, Simon.

SIMON: What am I getting?

JOSH: Well, you used to say rah-rah for the leader every morning. He just wanted a few words, polish your boots, be a good member of the anthill. Doesn't even know you've left. He's got ten thousand more good boys'll do as they're told where you came from.

SIMON: Your point being?

JOSH: I want something different than he does. I want the thing inside that everybody needs and hardly anybody manages to find.

SIMON: I don't think I follow you.

JOSH: I want that real person, who you really are. I can see it, y'see; I can see who everybody really is, and who they could be. I can see people, and they're so beautiful to me, me and my dad, we want 'em like a bridegroom wants his bride. Am I making sense?

SIMON: The Leader wouldn't see it that way.

JOSH: You reckon?

SIMON: Doesn't even know I've left, that I'm not on his side now.

JOSH: Well, yeh. Depends what you want, dunnit? He doesn't want much really. But if I lost you, it would hurt.

SIMON: Josh, I didn't want fresh air. I was hoping I'd meet you.

JOSH: Oh right.

SIMON: I've been with you for a while, and I've listened, and watched, and… there were a lot of beliefs and identities that I thought were me.

JOSH: Right, right.

SIMON: They're crumbling; they're just peeling away from me, like scabs –

JOSH: The identities?

SIMON: Yes, they're, er…I can't keep a hold of them anymore.

JOSH: What's that feel like?

SIMON: Confusing. Painful. Rather frightening really.

JOSH: Because?

SIMON: Well, it's – it's unknown territory. I mean, when I used to put the uniform on, the black uniform, I felt terribly strong, I felt I mattered. I saw the Leader, you know, at our commissioning parade, and I felt I could burst. I have a place in the world, I thought; I have beliefs the whole world should hold. I am who this uniform says I am. But it's all falling away, peeling off, like a scab from a healed wound.

JOSH: What's underneath?

JOSH: Not much. Only me.

JOSH: Just you? Actual Simon?

SIMON: Yes.

JOSH: Then I'm very pleased to meet you, actual Simon. Put it there, mate.

SIMON: Yes, of course, thank you – oh…

JOSH: What?

SIMON: I need to meet you, Josh. I want to meet who you really are. Josh, you live with God; there's something in you, something that comes from you. Josh, who are you? Tell me who you are.

JOSH: You tell me.

SIMON: What?

JOSH: You ought to know by now, Simon. Who d'you think I am?

SIMON: You - I think – I think, whoever he is, God really is your 'dad'. You are certainly…close relatives.

JOSH: Keep going.

SIMON: I was never sure about God. The Academy didn't encourage it. But he ought to be something like you. I hope he is.

JOSH: Who's doing the hoping?

SIMON: Well…not the man in the uniform, Josh. He never existed really; he was just a construct. Actual Simon is hoping; actual Simon wants God to be like you.

JOSH: Want to meet him?

SIMON: If I can.

JOSH: 'Course you can, you're real now. You can only meet people when you're real.

SIMON: Josh, you are my clue. I want to meet him because I've come to think that perhaps he saw us and decided that you should join us.

JOSH: Why d'you think so, Simon?

SIMON: Well, I don't know really, it's sort of intuitive. I didn't work it out.

JOSH: No, you didn't. My dad told you.•

SIMON: Oh; well, I haven't had a vision or anything –

JOSH: No, he told you way deep down inside. He found actual Simon and he told him; and he was so quiet and still about it you didn't even know he was talking. Good on you, Simon. Give us a hug, mate.
(Machine-gun fire.)
SIMON: What the hell's that?

JAMIESON: It is I, Andy Jamieson, charismatic figurehead of the soon-tae-be-victorious rebel forces roon' here, good boys wan an' all, God bless 'em.
(Gunfire.)
SIMON: Put that gun down, you fool! You'll kill someone!

JAMIESON: If only! If only Ah could kill a' thae black-coated animals we drove out a' here! God bless Johnny Reb! Haw-aw, a' the wey fae Brig'ton, the olive oil an' the o-a-range juice•…

JOSH: Hello, Andy. Been celebrating something?

JAMIESON: Aw, aye; wur glorious victory. The day when a' they black-coats like yer wee friend here are turnin' in their richly-deserved graves. Oh, Ah know, Ah ask around. Ah know what you are, soldier boy.

JOSH: Simon's not with the military any more, Andy.

SIMON: I'm with Josh, Mr. Jamieson.

JAMIESON: Long's it suits ye, eh? Aw, Ah get it – ye're a plant, ye're a mole. Ye waitin' for yer contact? Did Ah disturb ye?

SIMON: Look, I'm not going to listen to this. I've known better men than you cut down in –

JAMIESON: Have they let you fire a gun yet, son? Eh? Ye shot em'dy yet?

SIMON: Yes. Some.

JAMIESON: Some? Just some?

SIMON: To defend myself. My unit was attacked –

JAMIESON: Soldier boy's got blood on his hands! Mibbe it was you shot my brother; mibbe it was you did the raid on my town.

SIMON: I told you: I've left the military. I wouldn't –

JAMIESON: Why? What changed?

SIMON: I – I don't know.

JAMIESON: Ye don't know? Come *on* there!

SIMON: I've been with Josh.

JAMIESON: Been wi' Josh?

SIMON: Yes. That's what did it. Look, I'll even shake your hand. Come on, shake.

JAMIESON: Don't you touch me! I'd put a bullet through this hand before I'd shake yours, soldier boy.

JOSH: Right: stepping in now, lads. Simon, why don't you just…see how my mum is or something, and I'll have a chat with Andy.

SIMON: All right, Josh. Good night, Mr. Jamieson. I wish you well.

JAMIESON: Haw? Josh, my compliments to the Lieutenant; and he can take his good wishes and stick –

JOSH: Tell everybody I won't be long. Will you, Simon?

SIMON: All right. I'll see you later, Josh. *(Leaves. Feet on gravel.)*

JAMIESON: That the best ye can do, Josh? A wee boy out a' thug school, a stripper, a couple a' old guys and yer mammy? Gonny take ye at least a week to chinge the world wi' that crowd.

JOSH: Oh, they'll do it Andy. Them and the Bird of Light.

JAMIESON: You need ma army; you need Johnny Reb. What about it, Josh? You preach up a storm, dae yer one-man casualty department. We back each other up, we'll get this country won before the holidays. Just you make it clear yer new society husnae got the Leader and his hard men in it.

JOSH: Andy...

JAMIESON: Punters got tae know God disnae like these guys. Divine retribution grows out the barrel o' a gun an' that, y'know? The new people's regime would be helluva grateful.

JOSH: Can't do that, Andy.

JAMIESON: 'Mon now, Josh. Givin' you a chance here. End justifies the means, eh?

JOSH: You reap what you sow, Andy. The means say what the end will be. And do you know what your end will be?

JAMIESON: Aw, aye: freedom, peace, justice.

JOSH: No. I wanted to hug this country, hold onto it, tight; but it's going to see more bloodshed and destruction than it ever has. You will not bring in the new society because you're just going about it the same old way•. My dad's new order is different; but people will suffer and die and be worse slaves than before because you have no clue what really creates peace and freedom.

JAMIESON: What ye gonny do then? If you were in a room wi' the Leader an' he gave ye a gun, what would ye do? What would ye do?

JOSH: I'd say, This doesn't belong to me: this is yours. I fight by other means. And I'd give it back to him.

JAMIESON: He puts it at yer head. What d'ye do then?

JOSH: I forgive him.

JAMIESON: Forgive him?

JOSH: Yeh. You break the cycle, Andy. It's got no power over you then.

JAMIESON: Break the cycle? Ah would put ma knife in that auld bastard's throat an' not even think about it. That is justice.

JOSH: And my dad's aiming at something bigger than justice.

JAMIESON: No more. Don't give me any more. Ah will win, Josh. Ah will burn the Leader an' all he stands for; and then Ah will bring you down. Ah will bring you down, Josh. Right: Ah'm away back tae ma good boys. You away an' see yer mammy.

8.6 Tea Time 3.   *(Table buzz: plates, cutlery.)*

ALFRED: So Josh, did you have your pray about strategy?

JOSH: I did, Alfred.

ALFRED: And?

JOSH: Well, dad said…can I just have that sauce? No, brown one; ta…he said, things are moving; we need a confrontation.

ALFRED: Confrontation? Who with?

JOSH: The big boys; the people at the top. The Archbishop and his priests and synods and his whole rotten church set-up. Tear the whole thing up and start again. It's the biggest obstacle to what my dad is doing.

MUM: Josh! That's thrilling!

SIMON: Josh, you can't! That Archbishop's dangerous! Don't meet him on his own ground!

RUBY: Oh, he'll walk it. It's a stormer up here already. Have another cuppa tea, Josh.

SIMON: He's a viper, Josh, he'll strike at anyone; and he'll use the military.

ALFRED: Josh could point his finger and blow him to bits if he wanted.

JOSH: Now Alfred, behave yourself.

MUM: Darling, how will you do it?

JOSH: Dunno yet, mum. I'll need another chat with dad.

ALFRED: Tremendous! Josh for Archbishop!   *(Cheers, applause.)*

8.7 Chatting With Dad 2.

Right, dad. Yeh, right; I will take on these priests; for everybody's sake. Don't know what they'll do about it though.
Oh. Right. Not surprised really.
Yup. Yup, I'm Servant all right, dad.
Bad as that, eh? Oh dear. That's serious, that is.
No, Servant didn't have it easy, I know that.
Right then, dad. Only, you're gonna have to help me with this one, 'cause...Mum's not gonna like it. Not one little bit.

8.8 A Talk With Mum.

MUM: Oh Josh, just the man. Come and look at these posters for your meetings. I've just got them.

JOSH: Mum, do you remember when all this started and I was telling everybody in church what I had to do and the Vicar shut me up?

MUM: Oh yes. Silly man.

JOSH: Yeh. Remember I said I'd been reading the bit in the Bible about that feller called the Servant?

MUM: Yes, that was lovely.

JOSH: And Dad God said I was to be like the Servant bloke – setting people free, all those things?

MUM: That's what you're doing. Is something wrong, darling?

JOSH: No, no. There's a lot more about Servant. He does other stuff.

MUM: You mean, like Callum?

JOSH: No, it's different; gotta take it up a level, Mum.

MUM: I don't know what you mean.

JOSH: Dunno if I do, but – look mum, I'm 'Servant'; I was born to be Servant and I've gotta go all the way with it.

MUM: But you are; everything you do –

JOSH: Not yet, not everything, not right through to the end –

MUM: What? What end?

JOSH: No, wait, wait, wait. See, when he's done the good things, the freedom things, that stuff, Servant has enemies, people that beat him and whip him and -

MUM: Josh!

JOSH: No, wait mum; listen to me, listen to me.

MUM: I don't want to listen to this.

JOSH: I'm going to have a head-on with the priests; you know that, you're happy with that.

MUM: Well, yes –

JOSH: Right; well, there's people that have a head-on with Servant. In the Bible. So he has a conflict with whoever it is; like I'm going to have a conflict with the priests. Well, I'm bound to: they're not gonna sit down and just let me do what I like, now are they?

MUM: No...

JOSH: No. They're gonna have a go at me, mum. It's not the end of the world, but I think it's gonna to be hard. I think it'll hurt, mum. But I'm big enough for it, mum; and when I've got through it Dad God'll turn it around so all kinds of good things'll happen for people that wouldn't have happened otherwise. So I've...gotta do it. It's gotta be me.

MUM: You mean this *has* to happen?

JOSH: Yeh.

MUM: I never read that bit. Servant gets hurt?

JOSH: Yeh, these people get a hold of him, and they have a kangaroo court and he gets beaten and whipped and he dies, and –

MUM: They're going to kill you?!

JOSH: I didn't say that; I just meant when these priests get a hold of me –

MUM: Josh, stop it!

JOSH: I'm sorry, mum, I just –

MUM: God is not going to take you away from me!

JOSH: Mum –

MUM: Josh, have some sense! Did God say this to you?

JOSH: Yeh, he did.

MUM: He didn't! Josh, look around! He's doing things through *you*! It all comes from *you*! Why would he let people kill you?

JOSH: I didn't say kill!

MUM: Don't do this to me! You never understood my dream! You never believed me about the angel! Don't you know who you are?

JOSH: Yes! I am Servant! I knew that from day one. You knew it.

MUM: No I didn't. Not if it means this.

JOSH: Look, mum. I don't know just what's going to happen when I go down there. But it won't be like now: it'll be hard, it'll hurt. That's all I'm saying, just accept that. It's been tough for you before. You're a strong woman, mum.

MUM: You're saying two different things; you're tearing me apart, Josh.

JOSH: Mum, just listen –

MUM: No, I won't! You're too special for me to listen; even when I was carrying you I knew that, so stop this Josh! Stop it now!

JOSH: I can't, it's who I am! I am Servant! I've gotta go through this!

MUM: What about me? Do I have to see you beaten up?

JOSH: Stop it mum.

MUM: You haven't heard God, Josh.

JOSH: Don't say that, mum.

MUM: You can't have; he doesn't want this.

JOSH: You don't know. Now don't pull me apart.

MUM: You're not going to the capital: God's telling me to stop you.

JOSH: Stop it!

MUM: I won't let you go. I'll save the mission.

JOSH: Don't get in the way, mum! I'm going.

MUM: You're not well, you're abandoning us!

JOSH: I have to go!

MUM: No!

JOSH: I am Servant, I'm going! Don't be my enemy, mum!

MUM: Josh!

JOSH: Don't be my enemy•!

9: A NEW TAKE ON IT

9.1 A chat with mum.

MUM: You're not going to the capital: God's telling me to stop you.

JOSH: Stop it!

MUM: I won't let you go. I'll save the mission.

JOSH: Don't get in the way, mum! I'm going.

MUM: You're not well, you're abandoning us!

JOSH: I have to go!

MUM: No!

JOSH: I am Servant, I'm going! Don't be my enemy, mum!

MUM: Josh!

JOSH: Don't be my enemy! *(Door.)*

9.2 The nave.   *(Josh strides up.)*

MOTHER ANASTASIA: Hello Josh; your morning audience is outside the cathedral.

JOSH: That's nice•.

MOTHER ANASTASIA: Quite a crowd in the square. They've come from far and wide apparently –

JOSH: Yeh right, very good. Mother Anastasia, maybe you could just go and look in on mum for me.

MOTHER ANASTASIA: Isn't she - ?

JOSH: No, she's not.

MOTHER ANASTASIA: Then I'll do that at once. Oh: before you go out, this gentleman wants to see you.

JOSH: Right then. What can I do for you?

ERIC: You know me, Josh.

JOSH: Don't think so.

ERIC: Yer done a miracle on me arm; then I was wi' Andy Jamieson when the rebels attacked them black-coats.

JOSH: Oh. Yeh, right, I remember. Look, I gotta go out in a minute, so...

ERIC: Well, basically, I've chucked Jamieson: I don't want ter be a rebel no more. Andy's just doin' it the same old way. I want ter be on your side, Josh; I want ter come with yer. Will yer have me?

JOSH: What's your name, mate?

ERIC: Eric.

JOSH: Yeh, I'll have you, Eric. Stay close to me; it's so important. Come and meet everybody.

ALFRED: Ho, Josh! How's your good self today?

JOSH: Very well, Alfred. This is Eric; he's joining us.

ALFRED: Oh. Well, welcome aboard, Eric. Alfred; I'm the brains of the outfit. That's Joe and his dad, the femme fatale decorating yonder pillar is Ruby, and this fine gentleman is Simon.

SIMON: I'm sure I've seen you before, Eric.

ERIC: Nah, I just got one of them faces.

ALFRED: Oh, well, just blame it on your mother. Speaking of which, Josh, where, er...?

JOSH: She's busy. Shall we start?

ALFRED: Certainly, Josh. There's the most tremendous front of house on the other side of these doors. Square's nearly full, standing room only. As you'd expect in a square. Aye. Now, Eric, here's your first job: help me swing wide the portal, then just watch. That's what we do: watch this man here. Who's a bittie preoccupied, I think. You all right, Josh?

JOSH: Coming into focus, Alfred; finding who I am.

ALFRED: Very good, Josh; just whatever you say. Not that I follow you at all.

ERIC: Eh?

ALFRED: It was deep, Eric: don't worry about it. Right-ho; well, off we go then. Got the handle, Eric? Ladies and gentlemen out there, I give you...Joshua Davidson! *(Door. Cheers, applause.)*

9.3 Mum and Mother A.   *(Knock, door.)*

MOTHER ANASTASIA: Ah, Mrs. Davidson.

MUM: Mother Anastasia. Look, the posters have come. Aren't they good?

MOTHER ANASTASIA: A good photograph of Josh.

MUM: Yes, I like that one. But the printing's bright, very garish. Why don't I get some tea for us?

MOTHER ANASTASIA: Why don't we chat? You've just seen Josh?

MUM: Yes, Mother, he's...oh, Mother! He frightened me! He shouted!

MOTHER ANASTASIA: Oh. Not like him.

MUM: No, he's never done this before. All my life I've told him he was special, God was going to make him great...

MOTHER ANASTASIA: All his life?

MUM: Yes, I always told him about my dream of the angel. Mother, you still believe me about the angel?

MOTHER ANASTASIA: Yes, I do.

MUM: The angel, the dream, said Josh would be a great man. He always listened, he never said much –

MOTHER ANASTASIA: And now he has?

MUM: It's as if he wants to throw away everything I told him and ruin things.

MOTHER ANASTASIA: Why don't you tell me about that?

MUM: I don't know; he only said it to me...

MOTHER ANASTASIA: I think he'd like you to get it off your chest. So what about some girl talk?

MUM: You're right; I need to tell somebody. I don't know what's happening. But what if he walks in?

MOTHER ANASTASIA: We've lots of time. Great men are usually with the people, you see, and that's where your great man is now. They'll keep him busy.

9.4 In the square.   *(Crowd hubbub.)*

MAN: Ere! Josh! Josh, I got a problem. Legal problem•.

JOSH: Not a lawyer, mate.

MAN: No, but look, my dad left all his dough to my brother 'ere.

JOSH: What about it?

MAN: Well, you make him half it with me.

JOSH: I'm not an agony column either, chum. Thank God you've got a brother; he's not your problem, greed's your problem.

MAN: Wot, greed? Well, wot about the Leader, then? Wot about taxation? That's greed.

JOSH: You want drains, don't you? You want hospitals?

MAN: Look, the level of taxation in this country –

JOSH: Oh, somebody else's greed, not yours, that's the trouble. Don't hide behind politics, look at yourself; you can't put Dad God second fiddle to money•.

MAN: Look, I go to church –

JOSH: Lot of good it's done you. Money's destroying you: it's wrecking your family, it's messing up your relationships and you're not bothered? That's denial mate: you're shrivelling up inside. Your vicar should have told you that.

9.5 Mum and Mother A. 2.

MUM: Oh, Mother, I was so shocked. There was a gleam in his eye, he was so grim and determined –

MOTHER ANASTASIA: Let me guess, Mrs. Davidson: you've never had a real confrontation with Josh before.

MUM: No, I suppose not. Just over stupid things like where to go on holiday; but he's never been like that before – such a fury!

MOTHER ANASTASIA: And the person you knew suddenly disappeared.

MUM: Yes! He was like somebody else! He seems to want to destroy his mission. Mother, you don't think he's ill?

MOTHER ANASTASIA: No: I can't think that. Mrs. Davidson, when you dreamed of the Angel, did it say exactly how Joshua would achieve his greatness? Were there...details?

9.6 In the square 2.

JOSH: If my dad was standing here – so you could see him, that is – if he was standing here, there's people he'd turn to and say, 'Good on you, mate! Well done, congratulations!'

MAN: What d'yer mean? We're all common five-eighths here.

IRENE: Ooh, yer, I'm no saint, I know that, Gawd 'elp me.

JOSH: Well, for you, darling, dad God would dash off to the Post Office and buy a huge Congratulations card and a balloon and write – what's your name, love?

IRENE: Irene.

JOSH: He'd write, 'Congratulations to Irene, love from God. Then a big smacker underneath. *Muah!*

IRENE: What for?

JOSH: Said it yourself: you're not a saint, you know you need him. You've got a heart like a poorhouse and you're not ashamed to admit it•. He loves it when people get real like that.

IRENE: But – but – what I done was –

JOSH: I know; I know it all; but listen, Irene, it's all forgiven. The slate is clean, my darling. You can get on with your life now. Just – start again.

IRENE: Yes. Yes, I will. Thank you, Josh, thank you. Oh, what a relief...

JOSH: Thank God for Irene, everybody! Let's hear it for God and Irene! Now, if you can admit you're in poverty inside, my dad congratulates you, 'cause you're under his rule.
And he says Good on you if the mess of the world has broken your heart•, for he will personally comfort you.
And well done if you don't give people what they deserve: same treatment's coming to you•.
He says Good on you if you think, 'I wish the world was the way God meant; I wish *I* was,' because then you will see what you wish for•.
And if you wait for that and hang on, you get to live in the world• when God's made it over again.
He'll applaud you if you've no muck• in your heart, and when you try to get people to give peace a chance, because then you're the sort of person he is.
And when they can't stand you because you want the world to be right, and they see you trying to live right and they persecute you and marginalise you for it, my dad says, 'Congratulations, I am in this with you and you're mine no matter what. That's what they did to everybody that lived for me: you are in good company•.' And when they treat you like dirt, pray for them, love them from the heart. For if you do, you will be like God.
If you really lived like my dad wanted, if you really were what he meant you to be, you'd have the good life from him that the bishops and priests don't even dream about. This world would be just like rotten meat without you, you'd stick out like sore thumbs. Or would you settle for something - rubbishy?
But now - listen! Listen to me. This day is coming, when they will turn on you, and come for you and drag you from your house and into the courts and abuse you and seek your life just because you're mine. When that happens, I say to you, sing, dance, clap your hands, 'cause I will understand and my dad and me will gladly join hands with you and suffer with you•. And you will know me in a way you cannot know me now.

Right: God bless, everybody. That's it till after tea-time. *(Crowd murmur, dispersing.)*

ALFRED: Eric? Were you listening? Did you get all that, did you follow it?

ERIC: Er – yeh. Sort of.

ALFRED: Oh good. Well, later on you can explain it to me.

SIMON: Josh, what was that? Were you talking about facing the priests?

JOSH: Dunno, really. Face whatever I've got to, I suppose.

SIMON: Josh, don't do it. The priesthood's riddled with politics. I've read the classified reports in military intelligence: there are heartless men there; they think they have permission to do what they want because they're the church. Please, just carry on as you're doing – time will bring a change.

JOSH: I think I'd like a cuppa and a bun or something. You coming in, Simon?

SIMON: They have tremendous power. There are thousands of good people in that Church, even some saints, but they don't know the truth.

JOSH: Ahh, terrible thing truth. Liberates you, but it might shake you to bits first.

SIMON: Josh, snap out of it. The Church is led by men who are the complete antithesis of what you represent.

JOSH: Well, a man's gotta do what a...hello, mum.

MUM: Hello, Josh.

JOSH: What did you think of the preach, then?

MUM: Wonderful, darling, as always. Unexpected; and confusing. Upsetting, worrying, and I'm frightened. You weren't the same. What's happening to our mission?

JOSH: Nothing that shouldn't.

MUM: That doesn't help me.

JOSH: Love you, mum. You know that, don't you?

MUM: 'Course I do.

JOSH: Thought so. Come on, give us a kiss. Right: cuppa time. Let's see how the nuns are at home baking. See you later, mum. Why don't you get some of these posters up? Come on, Simon, I'm gasping.

SIMON: You should at least have said don't worry.

JOSH: Can't, Simon. Sorry, just can't.

9.7 After Evensong. *(Organ music, church bustle.)*

Fr. PRENDERGAST: Ah, peace be to you, Father Jeremias. A fine service tonight, was it not?

Fr. JEREMIAS: Oh, very much so, Father Prendergast. I like to sit quietly afterwards to soak up the very last of the Amen.

Fr. PRENDERGAST: The Cathedral choristers excelled themselves. The Mass in C is very close to my heart.

Fr. PRENDERGAST: Oh, and mine. The Kyrie is so laden with compassion the presence of God is tangible.

Fr. JEREMIAS: I agree, I agree; one feels cleansed.

Fr. PRENDERGAST: Oh indeed. But I must say the Archbishop looks burdened.

Fr. JEREMIAS: Concerned about the approaching Synod, no doubt. And Joshua Davidson.

Fr. PRENDERGAST: Do you think Davidson really could topple the Church? You know what they're saying.

Fr. JEREMIAS: We need his kind of challenge, father. The grit in the oyster makes the pearl. But who knows what a man like Joshua Davidson may do. And next to him, what do we have to offer?

Fr. PRENDERGAST: Ah well, there's coffee being served in the Sacristy. Will you join me?

Fr. JEREMIAS: Yes, thank you, I think I shall. I wonder if you'd mind helping me up…thank you – oh!

Fr. PRENDERGAST: Archdeacon! Are you in pain?

Fr. JEREMIAS: Yes, my back. I fell on the chancel steps, far too highly polished. I must say it's getting worse. Well, I'm on my feet. To the coffee?

Fr. PRENDERGAST: Here, take my arm.

Fr. JEREMIAS: Thank you. Now, best foot forward – ow! Oh dear. I very much doubt I'll manage to reach the Sacristy.

Fr. PRENDERGAST: Oh dear. Come back to your seat.

Fr. JEREMIAS: Ooh! Let me just stand still. I don't suppose you have an aspirin about you?

Fr. PRENDERGAST: I'm terribly sorry, I don't. Oh dear. I know what Joshua Davidson would do.

Fr. JEREMIAS: Joshua - ? Oh. Oh, I see.

Fr. PRENDERGAST: How do you suppose he does it?

Fr. JEREMIAS: What? Oh, the cures? I've no idea. He simply tells people to be intact again and they are.

Fr. PRENDERGAST: God has sent that young man, it's obvious. Whatever the Archbishop says.

Fr. JEREMIAS: Bold words, Father Prendergast, but I confess I concur with you.

Fr. PRENDERGAST: I have come to believe that Davidson's cures are accomplished by the power of God.

Fr. JEREMIAS: Certainly. I myself – ooh! Would you bring me a chair, please?

Fr. PRENDERGAST: Certainly. Here you are.

Fr. JEREMIAS: Thank you. Kindly help me sit down, if you please.

Fr. PRENDERGAST: Of course. Carefully now, carefully. Try to be seated incrementally.

Fr. JEREMIAS: That is a little better, thank you. Well, Davidson's cures may show the power of god, but apparently only when Davidson says the words.

Fr. PRENDERGAST: Oh. Well, yes. Rather a shame he isn't here.

Fr. JEREMIAS: I entirely agree.

Fr. PRENDERGAST: Yes. Um…Father Jeremias?

Fr. JEREMIAS: Yes?

Fr. PRENDERGAST: I have conceived an extremely unusual thought.

Fr. JEREMIAS: I beg your pardon?

Fr. PRENDERGAST: I confess I am entirely unsure of the theological ramifications of this, but I have an idea.

Fr. JEREMIAS: And what might that be?

Fr. PRENDERGAST: Well… Archdeacon, I am going to say something to you.

Fr. JEREMIAS: Say on.

Fr. PRENDERGAST: Joshua Davidson may not be here, but...on *behalf* of Joshua Davidson, I declare you perfectly well. You are of sound vertebrae, your muscles are themselves again, you are intact. Should you wish, you may skip like a lamb.

Fr. JEREMIAS: My dear fellow.

Fr. PRENDERGAST: I must admit I feel extremely foolish.

Fr. JEREMIAS: No, no; no need. Thank you. Shouldn't you say Amen?

Fr. PRENDERGAST: I really don't know. It wasn't a prayer.

Fr. JEREMIAS: I suppose not. How shall we know if it worked?

Fr. PRENDERGAST: I've no idea. Are you in pain?

Fr. JEREMIAS: Well...I don't believe I am. Perhaps if I stood up...oh, I say.

Fr. PRENDERGAST: Yes?

Fr. JEREMIAS: Let me twist around a little. Let me bend. Yes, yes. I think...I think...I shall attempt to genuflect.

Fr. PRENDERGAST: Oh, I say!

Fr. JEREMIAS: Now, then: down, and...up. Well!

Fr. PRENDERGAST: Archdeacon, tell me, tell me!

Fr. JEREMIAS: Father Prendergast, I am perfectly sound in every part.

Fr. PRENDERGAST: *Exultate!*

Fr. JEREMIAS: And it happened at the name of Joshua Davidson. This may change everything. I must tell the Archbishop: I'll go at once. Thank you, Father Prendergast, thank you.

Fr. PRENDERGAST: Not at all. God speed, God speed.

9.8 The Archbishop's Chambers.
(Knocking, door.)

Fr. JEREMIAS: Archbishop, the most remarkable thing has ha – oh.

ARCHBISHOP: Archdeacon, the hour is late.

Fr. JEREMIAS: My apologies, Your Grace. I had no idea you had company.

ARCHBISHOP: Ah, yes. Archdeacon, may I present Father Blasko•, Vicar-General of the Sacred Congregation for the Protection and Defence of the Church. You may trust the Archdeacon, Father Blasko.

Fr. BLASKO: God be with you, Archdeacon.

Fr. JEREMIAS: Thank you. I don't believe I've heard of your order, Father.

Fr. BLASKO: We operate mostly overseas; and because of the nature of our work, we are not – obvious.

Fr. JEREMIAS: Ah. What is your work?

Fr. BLASKO: To live up to our name. We labour for the safety of the Church, to protect her from all her adversaries.

ARCHBISHOP: Father Blasko has been labouring in our corner of the vineyard for some time. Behind the scenes. He has discovered crucial information relating to Joshua Davidson.

Fr. JEREMIAS: Joshua Davidson?

Fr. BLASKO: Yes, Archdeacon. I have evidence that will convict him of conspiring against the state – Sedition in the First Degree.

ARCHBISHOP: A capital offence, Archdeacon.

Fr. JEREMIAS: But Davidson is apolitical; the state would not try such a charge –

Fr. BLASKO: No. There is a wide secret network. I have papers, names, recordings of telephone calls, contacts in the revolutionary forces. He means to bring us all down.

ARCHBISHOP: Stay with us, Archdeacon: hear more. I have a fine Amontillado sherry. Will you partake, Father Blasko?

Fr. BLASKO: No, thank you. I never drink wine•.

Fr. JEREMIAS: Your Grace, I shall leave you together. I must –

ARCHBISHOP: You said a remarkable thing had happened.

Fr. JEREMIAS: Did I? Yes, three members of the local military professed conversion this evening.

ARCHBISHOP: Really? Which unit? I must write to their commander.

Fr. JEREMIAS: Now I think of it, I believe they were simply on manoeuvres. Passing through. No record made, you see.

ARCHBISHOP: Oh. What a pity. Well, I bid you goodnight, Archdeacon. Father Blasko and I have much to discuss•.

9.9 The Governor's Office.   *(Clink of glasses, drink pouring.)*

GOVERNOR: A drink to celebrate: it's not every day I have an Archbishop and the head of a religious order in my office.

ARCHBISHOP: The Church gladly interacts with the world.

GOVERNOR: Pity. Will you join me? Do something human for once?

ARCHBISHOP: I am no moralist, Governor, but…thank you, no.

GOVERNOR: What about you, Father….?

Fr. BLASKO: Blasko. Father Blasko. Of the Sacred Congrega –

GOVERNOR: Protection of the Church; yes, I know. Well, I wish you a considerable degree of failure. Now: what do you want? You must be desperate to come here like this.

ARCHBISHOP: Firstly, we congratulate you on your nomination as the Leader's successor. A very great honour.

Fr. BLASKO: The Sacred Con –

GOVERNOR: Thank you; what else?

ARCHBISHOP: A request…

GOVERNOR: What?

ARCHBISHOP: We request the state to grant civil powers to the Church hierarchy, to enable us to move against Joshua Davidson.

GOVERNOR: Denied. The state has no quarrel with Davidson.

ARCHBISHOP: But his immense influence…his movement could become a third arm within the country –

GOVERNOR: We have had this conversation before: Davidson is not political.

Fr. BLASKO: But he is, Governor. I have proof.

GOVERNOR: What do you mean?

Fr. BLASKO: These papers will prove it. Here are Davidson's collaborators in the revolutionary forces; here are transcripts of conversations with key military personnel that discuss the assassination of the Leader and the overthrow of the administration; here are signed memos from within your headquarters – seemingly innocent, but indirectly authorising the transfer of government funds to Davidson's leading sympathisers.

GOVERNOR: Let me see. What do you take me for?

Fr. BLASKO: Governor?

GOVERNOR: We know these rebels: they haven't come near Davidson. I know these 'key personnel': they are all shadowed, and they are integral to our operations; they would not risk the state, their families or their lives with this stupidity.

ARCHBISHOP: Father Blasko's agents –

GOVERNOR: All substantial movement of funds is authorised by me: I have already seen these memos you choose to misinterpret, including the one with the ham-fisted copy of my signature.

Fr. BLASKO: My agents have worked long and hard –

GOVERNOR: I didn't know you hated Davidson enough to lower yourself to such amateurish levels, Archbishop. Now get out.

ARCHBISHOP: We wish to help. The Leader's successor must ensure stability.

GOVERNOR: Which already exists. Don't insult me any further.

ARCHBISHOP: Governor, the little foxes spoil the vines•: some regard Davidson as a little god.

GOVERNOR: Well, if Davidson is God, what does that make you? Good day, Archbishop.

ARCHBISHOP: Governor, I must –

GOVERNOR: Find some other means of destruction you can bless. Good day.

9.10 A chat with dad.

JOSH: Dad, got a tough one here. I know I got all hard and determined; that was nearly like a vision or something when I was talking in the square. But mum's right, it could turn really nasty if I take on the priests.

Yeh, I know I'm Servant and he had a hard time, but I will do what Servant does: I just gotta be sure. So, tell me again, will you, so I can stick with it. Tell me again.

9.11 Afternoon Tea.

ALFRED: Well, Eric? You enjoying our happy band so far?

ERIC: Dunno, Alfred; it's really different. Dunno what I expected, really.

JOSH: Think I say better stuff than Andy Jamieson, Eric?

ERIC: Andy doesn't say anything; he just shoots people. But I think this country needs you, Josh, not him.

JOSH: Bless your heart for saying that, Eric: you're a good mate.

ALFRED: I fought for this country. Well: I fought for what it used to be; but Josh has got something else again. Which is sounding a wee bit grim and determined lately. Touch of the blood, sweat and tears.

JOSH: Same stuff, Alfred. I've not moved.

ALFRED: Oh, you're not saying anything different; you just have a different shading, if you follow me.

JOSH: Just sort of a new take on it. *(Door, tea tray, etc.)*

MUM: Here's the tea, boys.

JOSH: Buns and all, mum?

MUM: Complete with jam, don't you worry.

JOSH: There's a joke there somewhere.

MUM: Don't bother, Josh.

ALFRED: I have come to believe, after a protracted intellectual upheaval –

ERIC: You not been well?

ALFRED: I've been thinking about things, Eric. For a long time. I firmly believe that the primary source of tea in this world is not the sub-continent. No, underground springs of the brown liquid gush forth in convent kitchens everywhere: it's the only explanation.

JOSH: You hang around cathedral convents, you gotta drink tea, Alfred. It's how the world works.

MUM: Well, you work for a change. Read your post.

JOSH: Oh, mum.

MUM: This outfit needs an administrator, Josh, and I am it; so read your post. Here's today's letters.

ALFRED: Come on, I'll start you off. This looks official. "Dear Mr. Davidson, We write to express our support for your endeavour, and to assure you that we intend to commend your venture to our associates. Moreover, we are happy to enclose a cheque towards your expenses." But how much? *Whoah!* Look at that!

JOSH: Lemme see. Blimey, I could send all the nuns to Tenerife with that. Who is this?

ALFRED: Here.

JOSH: They're a big outfit, aren't they?

ALFRED: Very. "Thinking ahead, it would be a delight to have your name linked with ours. However, a small number of your statements could, we feel, imply an attitude of acceptance towards certain social minority groups with which we find we have a difficulty. The re-phrasing or omission of – ."

JOSH: No! Heard it all before. Send the cheque back.

ERIC: Why don't you just - ?

JOSH: No, Eric, I know their game. They think I was born yesterday. I'm not for sale.

MUM: Good for you, darling.

JOSH: Ta, mum. What else, Alfred? I'm not doing supermarkets, remember.

MUM: Don't you dare!

ERIC: What's wrong wi' supermarkets?

ALFRED: Tell you later, Eric. Now… "Dear Josh, will you come and visit our kids at the sick children's home on the 24th thanks. Some of them don't hardly ever get out but they all seen you on the news and they are big fans. Here is a photo of us that is me and daughter Julie at the front she was eight last week and thinks you're gorgeous. She drew a picture of you please come an see us. Love, Rose Pringle."

JOSH: Awww, God love 'er, I'll go to that.

ALFRED: There's the drawing.

MUM: She's got your nose right.

JOSH: Very distinguished profile, that. What's that big posh letter, Alfred?

ALFRED: Well, let me see. "To Joshua Davidson, our well…" I think you better read this one yourself, Josh.

JOSH: Eh? Give it here. "To Joshua Davidson, our well-beloved son in the faith. We are distressed by the division that has grown between your movement and the Church, a schism for which the Church itself may be partly to blame."

ALFRED: What is this?

JOSH: "You will be aware of the approaching Synod, the Church's supreme authority that directs its life. We extend an invitation to you to be present, in order to openly and publically express your thoughts and your perceptions of us, and we of you. We earnestly hope that in an atmosphere of brotherly honesty we may find reconciliation and a healing of the divide that has grown between us. Yours in the grace of God..." What's that?

ALFRED: It's the Archbishop: that's his name in Latin.

JOSH: Blimey.

MUM: Josh, no.

ERIC: Well, that's all right, innit? Bein' friendly?

MUM: Josh, you can't, don't trust them.

ALFRED: What're you going to do, Josh?

JOSH: Well, um…

ALFRED: Chat with your dad about it?

JOSH: Er…no; I don't think I need to.

10: KING OF THE WORLD

10.1 Afternoon tea.

JOSH: "You will be aware of the approaching Synod, the Church's supreme authority that directs its life. We extend an invitation to you to be present, in order to openly and publically express your thoughts and your perceptions of us, and we of you. We earnestly hope that in an atmosphere of brotherly honesty we may find reconciliation and a healing of the divide that has grown between us. Yours in the grace of God…" What's that?

ALFRED: It's the Archbishop: that's his name in Latin.

JOSH: Blimey.

MUM: Josh, no.

ERIC: Well, that's all right, innit? Bein' friendly?

MUM: Josh, you can't, don't trust them.

ALFRED: What're you going to do, Josh?

JOSH: Well, um…

ALFRED: Chat with your dad about it?

JOSH: Er…no; I don't think I need to.

10.2 A late-night visitor.

MUM: here's your toast, Josh.

JOSH: Got any cheese, mum?

MUM: There. You shouldn't eat cheese at night: it makes you dream.. You want more cocoa?

JOSH: No thanks, mum. I'll turn in soon.

MUM: I never thought we'd be back in the old house after so long.

JOSH: Good job you paid the mortgage off.

MUM: Ohh yes; crumbs. Well: I'll just do my curlers.

JOSH: You've done 'em.

MUM: Oh. Oh, I can't settle. Aren't you nervous, Josh?

JOSH: What for?

MUM: Oh, nothing really; just, you know, you're speaking to the National Synod tomorrow.

JOSH: Go to bed, mum.

MUM: Josh, you've had all those months and you haven't studied or prepared or anything. You should at least be making notes.

JOSH: I'm gonna talk about Dad God; I do that every day.

MUM: Oh, you're so *calm!*

JOSH: Well, you try and do your curlers by worrying, see how you get on.

MUM: You were just the same at school: always the last minute. *(Doorbell.)* Who's that at this hour?

JOSH: Probably the Anxiety Police, checking up on you.

MUM: Eat your toast. ***(Goes to the door: we hear her speak to the visitor.)***

JOSH: Oh Dad, calm her down. Only you can. This is very nice cheese, Dad: I'm really glad you created cheese. Well, cows: milk, that kind of thing – oh, hello.

MUM: Josh? Josh, this is father…

Fr. JEREMIAS: Jeremias. From the cathedral.

JOSH: Oh. 'Scuse me, I was just getting ready for bed. Last bit of toast.

Fr. JEREMIAS: Quite all right, quite all right. I'm sorry to disturb you at this late hour•, but it is rather important.

JOSH: 'S all right. I thought you priests were all tucked up in bed by now.

Fr. JEREMIAS: Most of us. Some function well in darkness•. May I speak privately?

JOSH: Yeh. Mum, would you…?

MUM: Oh. Is it about the Synod, Father? I do Josh's admin, you see, so if I could help…

JOSH: Don't think so, mum. Why don't you nip upstairs?

MUM: All right. Can I make you a cocoa before I go, Father?

Fr. JEREMIAS: No, thank you.

MUM: Oh well. I'll be off then. I've put your hot water bottle in, Josh.

JOSH: Thanks.

MUM: Good night then, darling. Good night, Father.

Fr. JEREMIAS: Good night, Mrs. Davidson. *(Door.)*

JOSH: It's not about the Synod, is it?

Fr. JEREMIAS: I'm afraid not, Mr. Davidson, I –

JOSH: Call me Josh.

Fr. JEREMIAS: Josh. Thank you. I, er…

JOSH: You don't have good news for me.

Fr. JEREMIAS: Then – you know…?

JOSH: I don't know exactly what, but a long time ago, my Dad God told me that when I met the priests, I'd have a very hard time.

Fr. JEREMIAS: God told you this?

JOSH: Yeh.

Fr. JEREMIAS: Then I must tell you exactly what. I have come to warn you, Josh. The hierarchy have forged documents that they will try to use to prove you guilty of Sedition in the First Degree. I need hardly tell you that is a capital charge.

JOSH: How d'you know that?

Fr. JEREMIAS: I am an Archdeacon, one of the senior clergy at the cathedral. I have personal access to the Archbishop. Ask Mr. Silver and his father about me: I was present when His Gr – when the Archbishop interviewed them.

JOSH: Yeh, they told me, I remember. You're sticking your neck out for me, Father.

Fr. JEREMIAS: Josh, many of us became priests because we wanted the Church to live as you live, to speak and act like you.

JOSH: Go on.

Fr. JEREMIAS: So many of us hoped to be assured that God is our Dad, as you so refreshingly and profoundly put it. But we have lost our way. Josh, tell me: how can our dream become reality? How shall I find what I have been seeking?

JOSH: Well, the first thing is, you keep on seeking; and ask and ask and ask for what you want. You bang on the door long enough, it's gonna open. My dad is not out to lunch.

Fr. JEREMIAS: You're telling me God will hear at last?

JOSH: Heard you as soon as you opened your mouth. It's just – some things take time.

Fr. JEREMIAS: Some things?

JOSH: Your journey to where you want to be. Your…change. But it will happen.

Fr. JEREMIAS: How do you know? You must tell me! I have sought this for so long – study, reflection, debate, multiple degrees; but the answer always eluded me. How do you know this will happen?

JOSH: Well, I know because of the kind of person my dad God is.

Fr. JEREMIAS: The kind of person?

JOSH: Yeh. You ask for a good thing, he won't give you a bad thing. He's not like that.

Fr. JEREMIAS: But he might give you…nothing.

JOSH: No; he's not like that either. Look, a little kid asks his dad for fish and chips for tea. What's any half-decent father gonna give him?

Fr. JEREMIAS: Fish and chips?

JOSH: No: he's gonna give him a live rattlesnake!

Fr. JEREMIAS: What! Oh…

JOSH: Yeh: he'll give him what he asked for: fish and chips *and* a pickled onion. Might even take him out for a steak. And he wouldn't say, 'You're getting nothing, go and starve.' Don't worry, Father – definitely no rattlesnake.•

Fr. JEREMIAS: It depends on what God is like…

JOSH: Yeh. That's why you can be sure. Because you can trust him.

Fr. JEREMIAS: Trust. How simple; how human. I have been on the paths of the intellect; but I see that the heart has its ways of knowing also. I must go; we will speak again. But – one thing for my prayers tonight: how do I trust?

JOSH: My Friend will come to you like a bird of light; and under his wings you will find your trust.

Fr. JEREMIAS: My heart moves, Josh. I know that I shall find what you speak of, though I do not understand you now.

JOSH: 'Course you will. Right, off you go back to your cell, or whatever you fellers sleep in. Have your cocoa.

Fr. JEREMIAS: Will you go to the Synod? I would urge you to leave the city tonight. They will not hesitate to use their forged evidence.

JOSH: Gotta go. We'll see how it turns out.

Fr. JEREMIAS: Of course. My card, should you or your mother need to contact me. For any reason.

JOSH: Thank you Father.

Fr. JEREMIAS: And now I must go. God bless you Josh. At least one person at the Synod tomorrow will be on your side – and a certain Father Prendergast. Don't bother, I'll see myself out.

10.3 The Archbishop's Chambers.

GOVERNOR: Archbishop, good day to you. All well for your old ladies' tea party this afternoon?

ARCHBISHOP: The Synod is ready to begin, Governor.

GOVERNOR: Good. The Leader and I will listen to the radio broadcast and be entertained.

ARCHBISHOP: I hope you will be edified.

GOVERNOR: I doubt it. Now, I'm here to confirm security arrangements and to inform you that there will be a military presence.

ARCHBISHOP: The cathedral precincts are consecrated ground.

GOVERNOR: Not consecrated to me. Davidson's appearance may render the occasion a little volatile•. Not that I'm worried really: I can't see your withered clergymen running amok.

ARCHBISHOP: We have no need: we are the Church. ***(Door.)***

GOVERNOR: Ah. Good day, Father Blasko.

Fr. BLASKO: God be with you, Governor.

GOVERNOR: Unlikely. Have you been forging any fresh evidence against Davidson?

Fr. BLASKO: There is no fresh evidence, Governor; and that which we have we cannot use.

GOVERNOR: Oh really? Have you grown a conscience?

ARCHBISHOP: But of course: you wouldn't know. Are you aware of the theft from the cathedral vaults?

GOVERNOR: Yes: I wondered what anyone would want to steal from this mausoleum.

ARCHBISHOP: There were valuables. A jewelled icon, medieval altar cloths –

Fr. BLASKO: My work, Governor! They have stolen my work!

GOVERNOR: You mean they took your evidence?

Fr. BLASKO: It was in the same safe. It is irreplaceable.

GOVERNOR: Irreplaceable? You can invent more lies.

ARCHBISHOP: A sympathiser of Davidson's must be responsible: no doubt the valuables are now financing his movement. We cannot guess how they knew of the evidence.

GOVERNOR: Don't flatter yourself. I don't know why Davidson wastes his time with you and your Synod.

Fr. BLASKO: Governor, will you help us? The police have found nothing: it is a disgrace –

GOVERNOR: I agree. Whoever did this should be given a reward. When they find him, send him to me. Good day, gentlemen: enjoy your Synod.

10.4 Going to Synod.

MUM: Never thought they'd send a car for us, Josh.

JOSH: Think it looks better, mum. Imagine us all piling out of a bus at the cathedral. That'd lower the tone a bit.

MUM: Josh, you wouldn't have gone in a bus!

JOSH: 'Course I would: taxi fares are shocking down here.

MUM: Well, you've got a reputation now.

JOSH: Precisely, mum. Anyway, I'm gonna unwind a bit on the way. Driver? 'Scuse me – can I have a look at your paper? Ta.

MUM: Josh! The paper?

JOSH: Yeh, the paper; why not?

MUM: I just thought you'd, er, pray or something.

JOSH: Done all that, mum. Dad's still here.

MUM: You're meeting the Church's National Synod; it's one of the biggest days of your life.

JOSH: Depends how you look at it, mum. Oh dear, United's lost again.

MUM: Josh, everyone's so wound up and you – I wonder if you take this seriously sometimes.

JOSH: No you don't.

MUM: Well, no. Sorry.

JOSH: Look, you're worried sick, but you're hoping the cars and all means it'll go easy on me, aren't you?

MUM: Yes, I am.

JOSH: We did talk, mum. I'll go through with it whatever happens. We accepted that.

MUM: I won't say any more. Hold my hand.

JOSH: There you are. All right? Oh, price of fish is down.

MUM: Oh, why aren't you worried - ?

JOSH: Tsk, tsk, tsk. Aww, Wally Trotter's died! He was my favourite comedian.

MUM: Oh, Josh!

JOSH: Wonder if I've got a paragraph? Oh look, I'm on the front – oh, blimey! Oh my goodness!

MUM: What?

JOSH: "Davidson Papers a fraud says Regional Authority." "Church denies links with alleged evidence for revolution plans." What? Somebody's sent the paper a lot of stuff about me going to blow up the Leader and stage another coup!•

MUM: Oh Josh, no!

JOSH: Well, we wondered what was gonna happen. Dad, look after this. I'm gonna have to make myself very, very clear today.

10.5 The Archbishop's Chambers.

GOVERNOR: You did this! You're trying to force my hand against Davidson! You leaked those documents to the press!

ARCHBISHOP: Governor, how could we? They were stolen some time ago.

GOVERNOR: Then who did?

ARCHBISHOP: An opportunist, perhaps? Realising what he had stolen, he decided to make some money.

Fr. BLASKO: More likely he is making money from Davidson and the press. Davidson is manipulating the situation.

GOVERNOR: How could Davidson do that?

Fr. BLASKO: The readers of the paper will assume the documents are real. They will believe Davidson is indeed planning a coup. They will believe he intends to set himself up as Leader.

ARCHBISHOP: And he is telling them so in this way without actually saying it. A clever man.

GOVERNOR: You can't prove that.

ARCHBISHOP: Oh, no; but it is plausible.

GOVERNOR: Well, keep Davidson away from those crowds out there.

Fr. BLASKO: Governor, if the situation is, as you say, one of stability, why should you worry?

ARCHBISHOP: And Davidson is even now arriving. Now, please excuse me, Governor. I require to spend time quietly in prayer, before Synod commences.

GOVERNOR: Those papers are forgeries in any case.

ARCHBISHOP: Your opinion; but can you afford to assume those crowds will agree with you?

10.6 Arriving.

JOSH: Here we are mum, there's the cathedral.

MUM: What was that in the paper, Josh? What's wrong?

JOSH: Tabloids, mum: it's rubbish, just forget it. Your hat's nice.

MUM: It's wrong; the flowers look stupid. Look, what did you say about forged evidence?

JOSH: That's right, it's forged; said so in the paper.

MUM: You looked so –

JOSH: Taken aback, wasn't expecting it. I mean, rubbish tabloid cashing in on the synod: tacky, innit?

MUM: Oh: see what you mean. All right, darling – oh! What's these crowds here for!

JOSH: They've all come to laugh at your hat.

MUM: Josh!

JOSH: You look lovely, mum. Really lovely. Love you lots. I'm glad you're with me today; I'm really proud.

MUM: It's your great day. The world gets to see my boy today. Victory soon, darling.

JOSH: Yeh, that's right mum. Well, let's meet the people. Come on, out of the car: don't ladder your tights, there you go. Now: give 'em a wave – hand in the air, back and forth, that's it. Hello people, hello…

MUM: Hello, hello everybody. Josh, where's everybody else?

JOSH: In the other car. There they are. Oi! Ruby! Joe! Over here!

RUBY: Ooh, Josh, it's so exciting. Nice cathedral, innit? Who's all them men in gowns?

JOSH: That's the priests going in.

RUBY: Oh right. Some car, wasn't it?

JOSH: Yeh, nice. Hello Simon, how's you?

SIMON: Apprehensive. This is hardly the place for the Governor's ex-lieutenant. The place is stiff with military, I could be recognised.

RUBY: No chance, you've grown your hair and you look like a scarecrow.

SIMON: On purpose, Ruby.

MUM: I didn't know you wore glasses, Simon.

SIMON: I don't: again on purpose. Josh, this reeks of conspiracy.

JOSH: Gotta be here, Simon: you know that.

SIMON: Well, be careful.

JOSH: Yeh, don't worry. Now: Joe, Alfred, Mr. Silver, come here. Right: now, we're all gonna sit together before I do my bit. These nice men in uniforms are gonna show us where, so don't wander off, all right? *(Cathedral bells begin.)* Listen to that, they'll be starting soon. Come on, mum. Put your mirror away.

MUM: Oh, my lipstick! You got a hanky, Ruby?

RUBY: There you go, Mrs. D.

JOSH: Mum, come on! Oh, blimey!

10.7 The convent.

MOTHER ANASTASIA: Callum! Quickly, it's almost starting!

CALLUM: Here I'm here, Mother Anastasia. Good afternoon to you, sisters. It's awful nice of you to let me listen to Josh on your wireless. *(Titters from the nuns.)*

SISTER PASSIVIA: Oh, the pleasure's all ours, Callum. *('Oooh!' More titters.)*

MOTHER ANASTASIA: Sister Passivia!

SISTER PASSIVIA: Sorry, Reverend Mother.

MOTHER ANASTASIA: Have you tuned the radio?

SISTER PASSIVIA: I have, Reverend Mother.

MOTHER ANASTASIA: Thank you, sister. Please switch on. Wouldn't you have preferred to be with your cousin, Callum?

CALLUM: I think I've had enough excitement round Josh. *(Radio fades in.)* Och, it's starting!

MOTHER ANASTASIA: Sisters, let us be in earnest but silent prayer as we listen.

ANNOUNCER: A tremendous sense of history and occasion pervades this great cathedral on this significant occasion in the life of the nation's Church. On either side of me in the massive choir stalls, used in daily worship since 1423, sit the senior clergy, the colourfully robed bishops who lead the Church here and in other lands. And as the Archbishop's procession passes the representatives of the laity, I can just make out the man who has brought the crowds waiting outside, Joshua Davidson, who later this morning will explain his message to this historic gathering…

10.8 The Synod.

MUM: Oh Josh, the size of this place. Look at those robes! Oh, I should have worn the red hat.

JOSH: Shush, Mum, it's starting.

MUM: Who's that man on the throne? I mean – the big chair. On the throne! Oh, I didn't mean that, you know what I mean – oh, he's standing up.

JOSH: That's the Archbishop: he's gonna start it.

ARCHBISHOP: My Lord Bishops, guardians of the Church at home and overseas; representatives of our parish clergy and religious houses and of the laity; you who represent our military and civic guardians, we welcome you to the opening session of this, the three hundred and forty-seventh Synod of our national church. May God be with you. Let us pray. O Lord, who alone hast created and dost sustain in faith the church in our land, so guide our thoughts that we may more perfectly seek and understand Thee. To the glory of Thy most holy name. Amen.

DAD: Two-faced git.

MUM: Mr. Silver!

JOE: Shurrup, dad, you'll get us thrown out.

10.9 The Convent 2.

CALLUM: Och, this is thrilling stuff and no mistake, Mother. We've had the budget, the salary for bellringers and the right way to kneel in a confessional. Josh will have to go some to top that, I'm telling you.

MOTHER ANASTASIA: It has to be done, Callum. The sacred in the mundane. 'Move the stone and you will find me; cleave the wood and I am there.'•

CALLUM: Aye. Aye, that'll be right, Mother. Oh wait: this is him now.

MOTHER ANASTASIA: Sisters – knees!

10.10 The Synod 2.

ARCHBISHOP: We are especially grateful for the presence today of our brother Joshua Davidson, well known to all of us. Together, we will consider matters that, sadly, have led to a divide between us. Does he see himself, we ask, as an alternative to the Church? Does he support our teaching? Is his God, his 'dad', the same as ours? And would he relate warmly, as we do, to the State?

MUM: Josh, they never said anything about this!

JOSH: It's all right, mum.

ARCHBISHOP: Our exchange will be broadcast by loudspeaker to the thousands listening outside the cathedral and to millions more by radio. Mr. Davidson, will you step up to the lectern?

JOSH: Right. Here we go, Dad.

MUM: God bless you, darling.

JOSH: Thanks, mum, thanks. *(Sound of Josh's feet on the stone floor.)*

MUM: Oh, look at him. Oh, my boy.

ARCHBISHOP: Good morning, Mr. Davidson. The Lord be with you.

JOSH: And also with you•. I mean that.

ARCHBISHOP: Then we have begun well. Mr. Davidson, I feel I have a father's heart towards you; in the sense, that is, of paternal compassion that, by virtue of one's office, flows towards all who have a connection, however tenuous, with the Church.

DAD: Wot the 'ell's that about? *('Shhh!')* All right, all right.

ARCHBISHOP: My heart is warmed that you choose to stand before us, cast aside your errors and be reconciled to our authority.

MUM: His errors!

SIMON: I knew it! He shouldn't have come!

JOSH: Sorry, that's not what I understood from your invitation.

ARCHBISHOP: I am misunderstood. Let me, speaking the truth in love, yet with pain, enumerate those points at which you diverge from Holy Church, through which God guards the truth. Point one: you speak of a new order...

10.11 The Convent 3.

CALLUM: Mother, with this man never stop? That's twenty disagreements he's read out.

MOTHER ANASTASIA: They're not disagreements, Callum, they're charges. He's turning it into a trial.

CALLUM: What, you mean - ?

MOTHER ANASTASIA: They've got him where they want him. Sisters: storm heaven.

10.12 The Synod 3.

JOSH: Your Grace, sorry, but what are you accusing me of? What have I done that's so wrong?

ARCHBISHOP: If we are to accept you, you must –

JOSH: I tell the people about God, I heal them inside and out, I forbid violence. I've got nothing to hide.

ARCHBISHOP: Really? Have you hidden what we read in this morning's paper? Evidence that you have planned assassination and bloodshed. Evidence that suggests you intend to subject this nation to another coup, one that will exalt you as Leader.

JOSH: That's a lie! I never said that!

ARCHBISHOP: You said much that agrees with it: a new order, someone else in charge –

JOSH: But not politics! I'm talking about inside! I'm talking about God!

ARCHBISHOP: A God who bypasses the Church, a 'dad' who wants to control this country and has appointed you to be his spokesman –

JOSH: Don't you twist my words!

ARCHBISHOP: - and has decided that through you we will see his signs and hear his words.

JOSH: You're twisting everything I said!

ARCHBISHOP: Yet you said it. Answer me, Joshua Davidson. Answer this nation: is God indeed your Father? Are you indeed his representative?•

JOSH: Yes! Yes, he is; yes, I am!

ARCHBISHOP: Then you go too far. The Church can not contain you.

JOSH: I knew that, Your Grace. But don't you say I didn't try. Good morning.

ARCHBISHOP: Where are you going?

JOSH: I'm going outside. I'm going to the people you cheat and throw burdens• on and won't help. I'm going to see all these people out there who will make it into my dad's family before you do.•

ARCHBISHOP: How dare you! We are God's stewards!

JOSH: Then hear what my dad says to you in your cathedral: my house was meant to be a place where all people could meet me face to face and heart to heart, but you have ruined it.• In your blindness and your rottenness• you have slammed the door in the faces of the people I love. So now God says, I'll do it myself. I will do a new thing and I myself will seek these people, for your house is left to you desolate.•

ARCHBISHOP: Come back! I declare you excommunicated!

JOSH: Not a problem! Right. Will somebody open these great big doors, please, and let me out?

(Cathedral doors creak open. A huge cheer of acclaim from the crowd.)

10.13 Mum's House 2.   *(Front door opens.)*

MUM: Oh, that was a lovely dinner, Josh, just the two of us.

JOSH: Yeh, it was – oh: thought you left a light on, Mum. It's pitch black in here.

MUM: I did, I left the hall light on.   *(Light switch on/off.)*

JOSH: Switches aren't working. I think your fuse has gone.

MUM: Oh, I'll get a candle.

JOSH: Where's the fuse wire?

MUM: Little drawer, front room.

JOSH: Right. I'll open the front room curtains: you'll get the street light.

MUM: Okay.

JOSH: Well, end of a perfect day. Can't see a thing in here. Mind the lamp table *(crash)* – oh well, never liked it – you found them candles yet, mum?

MUM: Got them…*now!*   *(Click.)*

JOSH: Oh, light! What's this? Balloons? Streamers?

ALL: *Applause, cheers, whistles, 'Josh! Josh! Josh!'*

JOSH: What you lot doing here? Why aren't you at home?

RUBY: Put the light out, put the light out!

JOSH: You've only just put it on! What d'you want to - ?

ALL: Happy birthday to you…

JOSH: What? Oh no! A birthday cake! Oh, mum!

MUM: You forgot! I knew you would, you always forget!

RUBY: Go on then, blow your candles out!

JOSH: Got no breath after today!

ALFRED: Preachers always have breath!

JOSH: All right, I'll try. Here goes. *(Puff. Applause.)* Oh, that's it, that's it.

MUM: Did you make a wish?

JOSH: No. Can't wish for more.

MUM: Ruby, help me dish this up.

RUBY: Right oh.

MUM: Watch how you cut it. I put sixpences in it like when Josh was a little boy.

DAD: Give us two bits, then. I could do with a sixpence.

SIMON: Josh, are you all right.

JOSH: Yeh. Thanks, Simon, I'm fine.

SIMON: You're standing with your eyes closed.

JOSH: I was saying thank you to Dad.

SIMON: Oh, I see.

JOSH: I was saying thanks for all of you, and thanks for how it went today, and I said, well, what next Dad, and he said…he said - *(Plates crash.)*

MUM: Oh, Eric! Careful!

ERIC: Sorry, Mrs. D. Stupid –

ALFRED: Oh atone, you miscreant. Get him a brush and shovel.

ERIC: Said I'm sorry.

MUM: Listen, no arguments in this house, not today. Eric, you're forgiven, I've plenty more plates.

ERIC: Buy yer some more.

MUM: That's all right, Eric. Ruby, leave the cake just now, we'll pour the wine. Here we are.

DAD: That's a nice one.

MUM: Joe, get the cork out; I can't work corkscrews.

JOE: Right. Here, this is a beauty right enough, Mrs. D. Must've cost a few bob.

MUM: Worth every penny, Joe. Nothing's too good for Josh today.

JOSH: Mum - *(Cork pops.)*

JOE: There you go.

MUM: You pour, Joe. Glasses are on the sideboard.

JOSH: Mum? Look, mum – everybody – I just want to say –

MUM: Speeches later, Josh. We'll have the birthday toast and then the presents.

RUBY: Ev'rybody got a glass? Simon: there y' go, love. Alfred.

JOE: There you go, dad.

MUM: Here, Eric. That's yours, Josh.

JOSH: Ta. Mum, I gotta tell you –

MUM: Wait, darling, wait. Well: what can you say? I never thought we'd have such wonderful friends around us today or that so many wonderful things would have happened to us. It just feels like yesterday I was in that back kitchen getting the tea for Josh coming in from his work. But now my boy's a hero and – where's it going to end? So...there's a big kiss from your old mother, darling. I'm so proud of you. Happy birthday.

JOSH: Thanks, mum, thanks.

MUM: You're welcome, darling. Well, we can't just say 'to Josh.' Not today.

DAD: To the new Leader!   *('No, no...')*

SIMON: Er...new Archbishop?   *(Moans.)*

ALFRED: To God's man for the moment!   *('Bit better.' 'Nah.')*

JOE: Well, if it was up to me, Josh'd be king of the world.

ALFRED: Joe, behave yourself.

JOE: Yer, alright, I started celebratin' a bit early, but I mean, who'd be better, eh? So that's my toast. Here's to Josh, king o' the world!

MUM: Well, who knows? Come on, then – raise your glasses! To Josh, king of the world!

ALL: Josh, king of the world!   *(Applause, cheers.)*

11: INTO THE DARK

11.1 Mum's house.

MUM: Wait, darling, wait. Well: what can you say? I never thought we'd have such wonderful friends around us today or that so many wonderful things would have happened to us. It just feels like yesterday I was in that back kitchen getting the tea for Josh coming in from his work. But now my boy's a hero and – where's it going to end? So…there's a big kiss from your old mother, darling. I'm so proud of you. Happy birthday.

JOSH: Thanks, mum, thanks.

MUM: You're welcome, darling. Well, we can't just say 'to Josh.' Not today.

DAD: To the new Leader!   *('No, no…')*

SIMON: Er…new Archbishop?   *(Moans.)*

ALFRED: To God's man for the moment!   *('Bit better.' 'Nah.')*

JOE: Well, if it was up to me, Josh'd be king of the world.

ALFRED: Joe, behave yourself.

JOE: Yer, alright, I started celebratin' a bit early, but I mean, who'd be better, eh? So that's my toast. Here's to Josh, king o' the world!

MUM: Well, who knows? Come on, then – raise your glasses! To Josh, king of the world!

ALL: Josh, king of the world!   *(Applause, cheers.)*   Speech! Speech!

RUBY: Come on, birthday boy!•

JOSH: Difficult...don't know what to say. Unaccustomed as I am to public speaking...*(Laughter, applause.)*...well, I just want to say...thanks. Thanks, mum, for being my mum –

MUM: Loved every minute of it.

JOSH: Yeh, well, thanks. Love you, mum.

MUM: Aww, give us a big hug.

JOSH: And...love you all. I'm really glad we're all here together...tonight. You're all special; you've made it all so much easier. We belong to each other, whatever happens. You gotta remember that. It's gonna be so important. It's so important that...um – you remember the Ten Commandments? 'You shall love the Lord your God, you shall love your neighbour...'? Well, there's eleven now - I'm adding a new one: love each other. Make it real, make it hurt, make it from the very bottom of your heart, 'cause the only way this world will know you're really with me is if you love each other.•

ALFRED: Well, that's good, Josh, but...we're a distinctive group in many ways. We're your companions, we've come to share a certain attitude to politics, ethics, we know how you think, we remember things you've said –

JOSH: Anybody can walk about with me; anybody can parrot off what I say. Even the Leader could do that. But if you got relationships like I want you to have – see, nobody can fake that, or deny it, argue it away. You just can't, love's not like that. People won't always understand love – they might even be afraid of it or hate it.

RUBY: How could you be scared of love?

JOSH: Well, you never had much, so you know what it's worth; but you'd be surprised, my darling, you really would. See, the biggest thing I do for you is loving you. You gotta do the same for each other. So, do that for me, will you? Well, what you looking at? Get that cake served up. Here, give us the knife. Now then: there you go – first slice. Oh, marzipan! Mum, you are so good at this. Where's the plates?

MUM: Josh?

JOSH: What, mum?

MUM: Are you all right?

JOSH: 'Course I'm all right, what you talking about?

MUM: You can't add new commandments.

JOSH: Can't I?

MUM: No.

JOSH: Well, I've done it.•

ALFRED: Metaphorical, I'm sure, Mrs. D.; figure of speech.

JOSH: No it wasn't, Alfred.

MUM: Darling, do you want to lie down?

JOSH: No, I wanna dish the cake out. This first slice, lovely great big slice, goes to…Eric.

ERIC: No; I can't, Josh.

JOSH: Yes you can, Eric. Nothing to stop you.

ERIC: I gotta go. I gotta get back to me digs, see; fix stuff with the landlord. Y'know, deposit, that stuff.

JOSH: Sure? Lovely big slice of cake, the first bit, the best bit, all sweet and tasty, just for my mate Eric.

ERIC: Er…

JOSH: Stay with me, Eric. Enjoy.

ERIC: No, better go. You have a good time, Josh, see meself out. Happy, er… *(Door.)*

MUM: Well, his loss. All the more for us. Here's yours, Josh.

JOSH: Ta, mum.•

MUM: Get that eaten, everybody, and then I've got sausage rolls and sandwiches and trifle. Vinnie next door hid them for me so Josh wouldn't see them. Ruby, love – kitchen cupboard. There's crisps and nuts and things, could you bring them through?

RUBY: What-ho, Mrs. D. Have we got party hats?

MUM: Now you mention it – no.

RUBY: Ohh! I like party hats!

DAD: You can have my flat cap.

RUBY: Sorry, Mr. Silver, not the same.   *(Fade out.)*

11.2 The Archbishop's Chambers.

GOVERNOR: Why shouldn't I have you arrested?

ARCHBISHOP: On what grounds, Governor?

GOVERNOR: Your attempt to manipulate a situation that could cause a revolution. Your fake evidence, your putting words in Davidson's mouth. You won't make me liquidate him.

ARCHBISHOP: The evidence was given to the press; Davidson chose his own words.

GOVERNOR: You put him in a corner.

ARCHBISHOP: I put him in a place where he would clearly uphold or clearly oppose Church and state. He chose to publically repudiate the Church, the state's closest ally.

Fr. BLASKO: God is in charge, he says, and Davidson is his spokesman. Does that not mean Davidson should be in charge?

ARCHBISHOP: The crowd roared to him. Can you doubt he is their hero? And after what he said...

Fr. BLASKO: Some of them called for a monarchy. And he was not afraid of the radio broadcast.

ARCHBISHOP: He has declared himself to the nation. I fear it is he who has manipulated things.

GOVERNOR: I won't listen to you. It'll be over in a week.

ARCHBISHOP: I trust so, Governor, for all our sakes.

GOVERNOR: What do you mean?

ARCHBISHOP: Well, we are aware of the Leader's severity.

Fr. BLASKO: His purges of leadership are well known.

GOVERNOR: Are you threatening me?

ARCHBISHOP: Governor, what could I do to you?

GOVERNOR: The Leader knows about your forgeries; I told him myself.

ARCHBISHOP: But surely he will assume the nation will believe our documents as presented in the papers and believe Davidson to be a real option.

Fr. BLASKO: Especially after today.

ARCHBISHOP: The Leader will foresee a coup, I fear; and he may see responsibility where there is none. Do be careful, Governor, whatever you do.

GOVERNOR: You want me to crush Davidson for you.

ARCHBISHOP: Governor, if you let this man go you are not the Leader's friend.•

GOVERNOR: Damn you to hell.

ARCHBISHOP: You believe in hell? Are you coming to accept our teaching?

GOVERNOR: If there is justice in this universe there must be a hell, so people like you can burn in it.   *(Strides away, door.)*

ARCHBISHOP: Medieval. These Medieval notions persist.

Fr. BLASKO: Archbishop, a word: I confess I am afraid.

ARCHBISHOP: Afraid, Father Blasko?

Fr. BLASKO: Your Grace, we are religious men; we know there is a God. What if we are fighting against him?

ARCHBISHOP: God has entrusted us with the truth, Father, and he will uphold us. We are the Church: it is our right.

11.3 The birthday party.

MUM: Presents! Shift the sofa. Ta-daah! The treasure trove! Now, as mother of the birthday boy, me first. There you are, darling. Many happy returns.

JOSH: Thanks, mum.• *(Unwrapping.)* Oh…the cardigan.

MUM: You were always on at me to knit you one like that, so I did, in secret. Mother Anastasia hid it in the convent: took me weeks.

JOSH: I don't know what to say, mum.

MUM: Just say thank you. Are you sure you're all right? Is it the wine?

ALFRED: Don't know if you're a reader, but this one was quite an influence on my personal outlook. Ripping yarn as well, thought you'd appreciate it.

JOSH: Tolstoy. Pretty heavy.

ALFRED: Oh, you're up to it.

SIMON: Time your reading with this, Josh: a really good watch. For military precision.

DAD: An' while you're reading, you can stick these on.

JOE: I said, 'Dad, what he needs is a nice pair of carpet slippers.' Here y' go, mate.

MUM: What's that, Ruby? Looks promising.

RUBY: Well, I saw this in a sale and thought of you. Happy Birthday, Josh.

JOSH: Ta, Ruby.

MUM: That lovely wrapping: shame to open it. Oh, what a lovely shirt. Ruby, that's white silk!

RUBY: Thought you needed smartening up, Josh.

JOSH: Thanks, Ruby. Thanks so much. I'm ready now.

RUBY: You like it then?

JOSH: I'll be buried in this.

SIMON: Josh, what are you doing?

JOSH: Taking my shirt off. I'm putting my new one on: my new shirt, my shroud. Ruby's got me ready to lie in my coffin.•

MUM: Josh, stop it.

JOSH: I was talking to Dad, just when the cake came in, and I said, what next dad, and he said, Get ready. They're gonna take me, and they're gonna put me up against a wall, and they're gonna shoot me.

RUBY: No. I won't let them.

SIMON: Josh, I told you. Get away from here; get away now.

MUM: Josh, don't do this: why are you doing this?

JOSH: When you get together after this, I want you to open a bottle of wine• and raise a glass and say, to Josh: remember that party, remember the candles, big church candles round his coffin, remember the day he died and the blood ran down that nice white shirt he got for his birthday.

MUM: He's not well, get him upstairs.

JOSH: No: it's not time to lie down yet.

MUM: Josh, why? You faced the priests, you won; nobody's trying to – oh, I thought we were going to have such a lovely evening, all together. I went to so much trouble, and you –

RUBY: Sit down, Mrs. D. Don't worry.

SIMON: Josh, come over here. Why are you saying this? Do you know something?

JOSH: It's not the end, Simon. Not the end –

SIMON: I don't understand you. *(Doorbell.)*

RUBY: I'll get it.

MUM: No, I'll go; I'll get some fresh air. *(Sitting room door.)*

SIMON: Josh, why not disappear for a while? I know a place - *(Mum calls out.)*

JOSH: Mum!

RUBY: Mrs. D! What is it?

SIMON: Josh, get out of here! *(Door kicked open; soldiers' feet & rifles.)*

JOE: Who the 'ell are you?

ALFRED: Blackcoats!

OFFICER: Get against that wall! Now!

JOSH: Let her go! You let her go!

OFFICER: You're Davidson! I thought a gun at your mother's head would point you out!

DAD: You get out of here - *(Burst of gunfire.)*

OFFICER: The next one won't hit the wall, stay back! What are you staring at?

SIMON: Tim?

OFFICER: How do you know my - ? Simon?

SIMON: Let him go, Tim, you have to let him go.

OFFICER: Simon, what the hell are you doing here?

SIMON: He cured you, Tim.

OFFICER: What are you talking about?

SIMON: When you were dying, in sickbay, I told him about you. He just said the word and you recovered. He was two hundred miles away.

OFFICER: Are you serious?

SIMON: Yes.

OFFICER: Simon, come back to barracks, we'll talk later.

SIMON: I can't, Tim. I'm with him. Oh Tim, what are you becoming?

OFFICER: A soldier. Take him.

JOSH: Let him go! Let them all go, I'll come with you.

OFFICER: Very well: hands behind your head. Get outside. You get over there.

MUM: Josh!

JOSH: Love you mum. Goodbye, everybody.

OFFICER: Get him out.

JOSH: Remember the wine. Remember the wine.

MUM: Josh! Josh!

11.4 Interrogation.

GOVERNOR: What to report?

INTERROGATOR: Tried to beat something out of him, sir, but nothing.

GOVERNOR: Dismissed.

INTERROGATOR: Sir, if I had another hour –

GOVERNOR: Get out.

INTERROGATOR: Sir. *(Feet, door.)*

GOVERNOR: They tell me you're dangerous: your own Church.•

JOSH: Don't know about that. It's all right, though, it's not your fault. Well, it is, but you were cornered, weren't you? They're the really bad ones.

GOVERNOR: You understand then?

JOSH: Pretty obvious really.

GOVERNOR: I have to ask you myself: are you meant to be the Leader?

JOSH: That's not your own question.

GOVERNOR: Don't play games, you're on dangerous ground. What are you aiming at?

JOSH: You know what.

GOVERNOR: State it for the microphone.

JOSH: I am here to show reality. The truth is my Dad God is real, and this world is part of his reality. That is what people live in. They can be open to that or not, in line with it or not, but reality was made by someone who loves them.

GOVERNOR: A major flaw: most of them don't know that.

JOSH: Well, I'm here to shine a light on reality: I am that light.

GOVERNOR: You are a light?

JOSH: I'm like the sun: I shine on everybody. People that open the curtains know I'm speaking true.

GOVERNOR: Oh, it's about truth? Davidson, you are a beautiful philosopher. Laws and states weren't made for you; you're not at home in them. And thank God you weren't trapped in that abominable Church. Very well: I'll consult with my military Chiefs of Staff and my political advisors: the situation is delicately balanced. Meanwhile, you'll have to be detained. Do you understand?

JOSH: Yeh. I think I've got the idea.

11.5 The Cell.

GUARD: Right, get in. Sorry you got to share a room with them two.

ERIC: Josh, I'm sorry, I'm sorry. They made me.

JOSH: Eric?

JAMIESON: How ye doin', Josh?

JOSH: Andy!

JAMIESON: Hail, Saint Josh: we who are about to croak salute thee.• Yer dad's landed ye right in it, eh? Can ye make him get us out o' here?

ERIC: He made me, Josh; he said he'd shoot me kids.

JOSH: It's all right, Eric.

JAMIESON: All right? Listen tae him! Listen, I'll be up against that wall in a minute. It's not just one bullet for a rebel, they load all the guns just tae make sure; did ye know that?

JOSH: No, I didn't, Andy.

JAMIESON: Aye well, see when my skull splits and my ribs shatter, my last thoughts will be pride and hatred.

JOSH: Andy, listen to me. I just –

JAMIESON: But it will not be all right. Despite the glory of my death, the black-clad animals will still be oppressing this country. More of us –

ERIC: Shut up, you; you're no better.

JAMIESON: What the hell do you mean?

ERIC: You like it: you like killing 'em.

JAMIESON: Aye, blood sports. Ah love it.

ERIC: We're just the same as them. What about the raid on the barracks? What about them women?

JAMIESON: Tactical; we had to.

ERIC: We're bloody-handed bastards, Andy! Josh here's done nothing.

JAMIESON: Except try to make us all as nice as him. Disnae work, Josh. Didnae work wi' yer Archbishop – promises, promises, then he sells us in here. Never trust a god wi' an agenda.

ERIC: That Archbishop's not like Josh!

JAMIESON: Aye, he is, they're all the same. Scratch a prophet, ye find a control freak. Ah'm not a nice man, Josh. Ah don't want tae be a nice man; Ah don't want a god that'll leave me gutless and oppressed.

JOSH: Andy, I don't think I'm gutless. I could not have done –

JAMIESON: When you are lying in your blood in that parade ground, what will your dad have achieved? How's he gonny feel? Sigh of relief? His boy took the fall and got him off the hook? God disnae want tae get his fingers burned? Ye're a harmless man, Josh. Ah wish this country was so full of folk like you it didnae need me. But Ah don't want yer God: he disnae know pain, he does not suffer, so he cannot understand me.

JOSH: You'd be very surprised, Andy. You really would.

JAMIESON: Mibbe. But I thank you for listening to me, Josh. Ah've let you do that for me at least. Mibbe you can say a prayer for ma loved ones lying beneath the ground up north.

JOSH: Say one for you, Andy.

JAMIESON: Aye well, I'm not one for prayer meetings. Aw Josh, d'ye not see it? What's yer dad gonny do when you're dead? Is he gonny try again?

JOSH: You could say that, Andy. He'll make it work.

JAMIESON: You don't give up, do you? Ye got yer one wee convert anyway.

ERIC: You ought to say sorry to me.

JAMIESON: What?

ERIC: You made me tell 'em where Josh was; you said you'd shoot me kids.

JAMIESON: And you believed me? Eric, son, I can't say sorry. You know the deals they made: the reprieves, the military withdrawals, the reprisals cancelled. Ah was as stupid as you, Eric: I hated them so much I believed them. But Ah can't feel sorry: if they'd kept their bargain it would have been worth it. See, that's how it is Josh, sometimes: one guy or a lot of guys. Ye just got tae make your mind up. So Ah did the best thing for my people. *(Door.)* Haw, here the Redcoats. Hi-de-hi, guys.

GUARD: Right: he's ugliest; get him first. *(Scuffle.)*

JAMIESON: Get yer hands off me, ya animals –

GUARD: Oh, hands-free? Sidney: rifle butt. *(Two thuds, Jamieson collapses.)* Drag him out, Sid; bring him round outside. We'll be back for you lads: don't go away. *(Sound of body being dragged, door closes.)*

ERIC: Oh, Josh – yer gotta spend yer last minutes with the bloke that shopped you.

JOSH: All right with me, Eric. I knew anyway.

ERIC: How'd yer know? When? Did I give it away in the house?

JOSH: I knew the minute I met you with Andy.

ERIC: You never said.

JOSH: Well, I wanted you on my side, Eric. I wanted you for a friend; but it had to be real, a real relationship, so…

ERIC: Was that what the cake was about?

JOSH: Yeh. We friends, then?

ERIC: Will you have me?

JOSH: 'Course I will. I could do with a friend just now.

ERIC: You got one then. Josh, give us a hand here. See, I've done things, when I were with the rebels: really bad stuff. I mean, it wasn't just military targets. You're a good feller, Josh, you'll be all right, but I'm so scared. I'll be dead in ten minutes, and I don't know what to do; I don't know how to die. Will you think about me, Josh, or something, when you're over there, when you're on the other side?

JOSH: Eric, don't worry. You'll be all right, mate.

ERIC: How can I be all right? What d'you mean?

JOSH: You're safe, mate. You're going where I'm going.

ERIC: How d'yer know?

JOSH: It's what you want.• *(Door.)*

GUARD: Next for shaving. That's you, chum; don't you give us no trouble now.

ERIC (calling as he's dragged down the corridor): I'll see you, Josh; I'll see you later.

JOSH: I'll see you, Eric, I'll see you – *(Door.)* Nearly time, Dad.• I can do this; I can do it with you here. Oh Dad, it's coming; it's at the door: it's dark, it's cold. So dark: it's coming down on me, it's right inside me. I can feel the terrible pit in front of me: no bottom, no light. Cold. The dark's pulling me in. No: that's too much, I'm not going in there, oh no, not me, I can't – I don't wanna do it, I don't wanna do it. Dad! Find another way! Find another way!

No wait: I can do it if you're there, I can do it if you're – *Ah!* Dad, I felt your pain!• You were in such pain there and I felt it! Dad, why are you – dad? Dad, where are you? Where'd you go? Don't go, dad. Don't go away, don't leave me alone. I can't be alone, I've never been alone before! I can't take this! This is the worst! Dad! Why have you left me? *(Door.)* Come on then. Get it over with.

GUARD: Slow down. I just come to say ta. I'm thirty quid better off 'cause of you.

JOSH: Eh?

GUARD: You've got visitors. Right, get in quick.

MUM: Josh, Josh!

JOSH: Mum! Callum!

CALLUM: I got the overnight train. What's happening?

MUM: My boy, my boy! Hold me, son!

JOSH: I can't, I'm handcuffed!

MUM: I'll hold you; I'll never let go. I had a dream about the angel; he said it would be all right. Josh, you're getting it wrong!• God wouldn't let this happen if you followed him!•

JOSH: No mum, he told me –

MUM: No he didn't! You're not well, that's why you go on about shooting and blood on your shirt! Callum's worried sick about you: he thinks you're not well.

JOSH: That what you think, cos?

CALLUM: Och Josh, I don't know•; it's different, it's terrible, I thought God was going to –

MUM: See, that's your cousin! No, just say they've made a mistake and they'll let you home.

JOSH: A mistake?

MUM: The priests'll be angry; if you say you won't do it again, you'll just say what God wants –

JOSH: I know what he wants!

MUM: No you don't! Do what I say, honour your father and your mother. When I worried it was really God speaking. You were all excited, you couldn't see it –

CALLUM: Josh, if you just had a wee rest in your bed –

JOSH: Callum, you would know about resting in a bed.

MUM: That's not fair, Josh!

CALLUM: Och Josh, I didn't mean –

GUARD: Right, time's up.

MUM: You said fifteen minutes.

GUARD: Lucky you got five. Now, come on, squad's waiting.

MUM: What squad? No! You can't, he's not well!

GOVERNOR: What's going on here?

GUARD: Prisoner's mother, sir. Visiting privileges, sir.

MUM: Sir, you can't just – you can't – please tell them. We'll pay any fine, sir, we will, give us time. My son's ill, sir; he over-reacts. His cousin'll tell you – Callum!

CALLUM: He's maybe not himself, sir.

MUM: We wouldn't lie, sir; we're good citizens, church members.

GOVERNOR: Then talk to your priest. Get them out.

GUARD: Come on, gerrout.

MUM: No! Let go of me! Let go of me! Oh darling, I'm sorry! I love you!

JOSH: Love you mum, love you! Callum, she's your mum now!•

MUM: No: I'm yours! My boy! Josh, darling… *(Fades away down the corridor.)*

JOSH: Bye, mum, bye…

GOVERNOR: I've spoken with my advisors. They agree that, given the situation, the Leader would not accept any outcome other than a capital sentence.

JOSH: Sort of knew you'd say that.

GOVERNOR: I'm sorry. I'll see your mother receives assistance. You realise my hands were tied.

JOSH: 'Course they were.

GOVERNOR: What was I to do? What could - ? I suppose you're going to forgive me?

JOSH: As a matter of –

GOVERNOR: No. Leave me some pride.

JOSH: Yeh. Well, no point dragging it out, eh?

11.6 The Parade Ground.

GOVERNOR: There's still time: stand here in the parade-ground and make some sort of recantation.

JOSH: Can't call myself a liar.

GOVERNOR: Look, your friends are in those boxes over there. You could continue to work in some moderate way. Retire: you've given your message.

JOSH: Can't retire: I am the message.

GOVERNOR: An appeal; possible reprieve.

JOSH: Don't think the Leader does reprieves. You're cornered, mate.

GOVERNOR: And you're not?

JOSH: Not exactly: it's more than that.

SERGEANT: Squad present and correct, sir.

GOVERNOR: Thank you, sergeant. Proceed when ready.

SERGEANT: Prisoner Joshua Davidson. Do you have anything to say before sentence is carried out?

JOSH: Yeh, couple of things. One: I haven't actually been charged with anything; but that doesn't matter now, does it? Two: just a little word to you lads with the rifles. You're not looking very happy, but – it's all right. I forgive you. So…don't feel bad…later: all right?

SERGEANT: You got a last request, son?

JOSH: Can you get word to my mum and tell her there's money under my mattress and tell her, it's all right, I'm doing all right just now.

SERGEANT: I'll see to that. Do it myself. Now then, you just walk over here with me, son. Come on. *(Feet walking to the wall.)*

GOVERNOR: Why are you doing this, Davidson? Why is it worth it? That Church would not shed one drop of blood for me, and I would not suffer one second for anything it has to offer. What gives you this courage?

SERGEANT: Company: at the ready.

GOVERNOR: You didn't want the cigarette, you don't want the blindfold. You're looking at the guns.

SERGEANT: Take aim.

GOVERNOR: Farewell, Joshua Davidson. I free you from our madness. Rest in peace. *(Gun volley.)* Still breathing! They bungled it! *(Strides over to Josh.)* Davidson! Davidson, can you hear me? I'm the officer in charge, I have to deliver the coup de grace. I have to finish you. Do you understand?

JOSH: Nobody finishes me. Die when I decide.• Dad? You there, dad? Oh dad, you're back, not on my own now. Here I come•, dad, come and get me. Here I come, here I - *(Dies.)*

GOVERNOR: Davidson? Answer me! M.O.! Where's the M.O.?

M.O.: Here, sir.

GOVERNOR: Do something: examine him.

M.O.: No pulse, sir; and no breathing.

GOVERNOR: Then do something! I want him resuscitated!

M.O.: I'm sorry, sir, he's gone.

GOVERNOR: Well. There was nothing I could do. Sergeant?

SERGEANT: Sir?

GOVERNOR: See to things. Inform Administration. Inform the Archbishop's office; tell them it's done: I wash my hands of it. Tell – tell those bastards at the Cathedral it's nothing to do with me. It's nothing to do with me. *(Strides away.)*

M.O.: Well, Sergeant, better put him in a box. I hope the state has been served.

SERGEANT: Maybe it has, sir. But if you want my opinion, it's bloody criminal what's been done here. That's a good man lying at your feet.

M.O.: Nothing to be done now, Sergeant. Better let the family in.

SERGEANT: Open the gate! Relatives! *(Gate opening, running feet.)*

MUM: Where is he? Where is he? Josh!

RUBY: Mrs. D.! Mrs. D.! Callum!

MUM: Josh, wake up! There's a kiss, darling, there's a cuddle. Lie in my arms, darling: there. He's resting, Ruby, he'll wake up soon.

RUBY: No, Mrs. D. Look, it's just like he said: the blood all down his shirt.

CALLUM: Auntie, he's away, he's away.

MUM: No, the angel said it would be all right. He's too strong to die. He's all my strength; he's all my life was for.

CALLUM: Och, Josh, I thought you were the one, I truly did. Can you not bring yourself back?

MUM: Come back, honour your mother.

RUBY: There's a kiss, my lovely. Thanks for what you done.

MUM: Oh, he's gone: everything's gone. What am I going to do? What am I going to do?

12: NEVER LOOK BACK

12.1 The parade ground.

MUM: Josh, wake up! There's a kiss, darling, there's a cuddle. Lie in my arms, darling: there. He's resting, Ruby, he'll wake up soon.

RUBY: No, Mrs. D. Look, it's just like he said: the blood all down his shirt.

CALLUM: Auntie, he's away, he's away.

MUM: No, the angel said it would be all right. He's too strong to die. He's all my strength; he's all my life was for.

CALLUM: Och, Josh, I thought you were the one, I truly did. Can you not bring yourself back?

MUM: Come back, come back, honour your mother.

RUBY: There's a kiss, my lovely. Thanks for what you done.

MUM: Oh, he's gone: everything's gone. What am I going to do? What am I going to do?

12.2 The Governor's office.

ARCHBISHOP: Governor, you wish to see me.

GOVERNOR: No, Archbishop, I do not *wish* to see you. I never shall.

ARCHBISHOP: I was querulous regarding the fact you requested my presence here.

GOVERNOR: Not a request, Archbishop. Things have changed.

ARCHBISHOP: Normally you would have called at the Cathedral.

GOVERNOR: I will never enter your damned Cathedral again, except perhaps on the happy day I order its demolition.

ARCHBISHOP: I hope relationships between Church and State are not –

GOVERNOR: I got you here to inform you I've received a Police report about your stolen documents.

ARCHBISHOP: Ah. The evidence against Davidson. What news?

GOVERNOR: Your forgeries were apparently recovered and stored in Division Headquarters. Alas, a fire broke out and your evidence was entirely destroyed.

ARCHBISHOP: Doubtless the work of Davidson's sympathisers. Evidence so damning to his memory… Thank you, Governor.

GOVERNOR: I'm required to inform you; I've done so.

ARCHBISHOP: Could you perhaps elaborate –

GOVERNOR: You'll receive a copy of the report in due case. Good day, Archbishop.

ARCHBISHOP: May I invite you to the Cathedral? We should discuss, over a sherry, the matter of –

GOVERNOR: You want to talk to me you'll do it here. Do you understand?

ARCHBISHOP: There is the matter of Davidson's sympathisers, Governor. Now they have a martyr –

GOVERNOR: You admit he was a martyr?

ARCHBISHOP: They will see him as such. I use a proverbial term. Recent events could be manipulated to infuse new life into the movement. If Davidson has a successor –

GOVERNOR: Recent events.

ARCHBISHOP: Yes, the absenting of Davidson from the current scene...

GOVERNOR: Say it. His death. His engineered death.

ARCHBISHOP: Oh, I should say the Leader's decision was inevitable; and given the instability, the sensitivity of the circumstances –

GOVERNOR: Get out, Archbishop. Lock yourself in your confessional for a thousand years; fast and lash yourself and howl to God for forgiveness.

ARCHBISHOP: Strong terms: metaphysical. Are you not of an atheistic persuasion?

GOVERNOR: Is it any wonder?

ARCHBISHOP: I had not expected the language of religion.

GOVERNOR: Religion be damned. Your religion be damned. Davidson has destroyed it: he has killed religion. He is the end of it.

ARCHBISHOP: Killed religion? How could he do this?

GOVERNOR: Because he is so much better. Now get away from me, Your Grace, before my disgust overwhelms me. And if you have died too much to want God's forgiveness, ask the Leader for his.

ARCHBISHOP: I do not follow.

GOVERNOR: As you say, his decision, in the circumstances, inevitable. But they were contrived circumstances. The Leader isn't such a fool as to miss that. He will seek satisfaction. You won't bury your folly as easily as you bury Davidson. Good day.

12.3 The graveside.

Fr. JEREMIAS: We are gathered here as those who knew and loved Joshua Davidson. Our hearts go out to his mother, his cousin Callum and their wider family in this time of their loss. Several of us were Joshua's companions during that brief, bright spell when it seemed that God had sent him to be the hope of this nation. Others, like myself, watched from a distance, marvelled and found that he had won our hearts. For all of us here, and for many others, it feels as if our hopes must sink into this grave and be buried with him. We cannot understand the turn of events that cut short his astonishing life, but rather than demand the impossible – namely, a satisfying answer – we do what Josh would certainly have wished and commit him to the care of the one he knew as 'Dad', the God he loved and served. Let us pray.

"We brought nothing into this world and it is certain we carry nothing out. The Lord gave, and the Lord has taken away; blessed be the name of the Lord." In the midst of life we are in death•…

(His voice continues under the following words.)

MUM: God, I won't ever forgive you. Josh was the point of my whole life and you took him away.

CALLUM: Oh God, there was me preaching to thousands; it's just words now. Why's he dead? You sent him to us; why's he dead?

SIMON: Goodbye, Josh; you were so real. I wanted to be real like you and not exist out of someone's ideology; I'll try, but I don't suppose I shall now. Goodbye.

DAD: Terrible it is, terrible. I feel like getting' my old army rifle out the cupboard and shootin' the bleeders that did this to you. I mean, what's the point, eh? What's the point?

JOE: Stupid: I keep thinking about that little stuffed rabbit you brought round when we was kids. I'll remember you like that: my little mate that was always there for me.

ALFRED: You're a marvellous man, I'm grateful I knew you; but life's a bitch and then you die, even you. So what's it all about, Josh? Why struggle?

MOTHER ANASTASIA: Your victories remain. I will remember how you gave me back myself. I am a real person now because of you.

RUBY: Thanks for loving me, Josh darling; you showed me I matter. You couldn't do nothing better if you lived a hundred years.

Fr. JEREMIAS: …Forasmuch as it hath pleased Almighty God to take unto himself the soul of our dear brother here departed: we therefore commit his body to the ground; earth to earth, ashes to ashes, dust to dust. Merciful God, we meekly beseech thee to raise us from the death of sin: that, when we shall depart this life, we may rest in you. To the glory of thy holy name. Amen.

The family have asked me to express their gratitude to all of you who have come today, especially those of you who have travelled a distance, and to say that you are welcome to join them for refreshments in the King's Head Hotel, Jubilee Road. Thank you for coming. God bless you all.
(Spades shovelling.)

12.4 Mum goes out.

MUM: That's me,• Callum, I'm away out.

CALLUM: Where are you away to, Auntie?

MUM: Don't you know?

CALLUM: Are you away to the cemetery again?

MUM: Grave needs fresh flowers.

CALLUM: Are you not better here with us, Auntie? You'll need the company.

MUM: And look at the walls? What for?

CALLUM: Well, we could – I don't know. Go out for our tea, or –

MUM: And enjoy myself? Is that what you're saying? I'm not leaving him up there himself, Callum.

CALLUM: Auntie, that's nearly a week.

MUM: I know: I've counted the days.

CALLUM: Auntie, he's away; he's had his life. Aye, it was short, but it was more wonderful than most lives can ever be. Can you not let him go back to his Dad? It'd be better for you.

MUM: It was his Dad that took him from me. I'll see you later. *(Door slams.)*

CALLUM: Auntie! Och, you're an awful woman!

12.5 The cemetery.

MUM: Well, Grandma, morning devotions from the cemetery. You never thought your Granddaughter would feel the way she does about God, did you? Bet you prayed and prayed she'd have a nice life; all ups, no downs. Didn't work, Gran. Thanks anyway, but maybe it is just pie in the sky. Oh: listen to me. If you heard that you'd turn in your…

Well. Just for you, then, Gran. Psalm for the day. I don't know why I carry your wee book about. What's it say, then? "Mine enemies speak evil of me, When shall he die, and his name perish?
But thou, O LORD, be merciful unto me, and raise me up, that I may requite them. By this I know that thou favourest me, because mine enemy doth not triumph over me. Thou upholdest me in mine integrity, and settest me – ." God, it didn't happen! You didn't favour him; what good's some damn victory psalm to me? I've lived my whole life thinking you would favour him and you didn't! You didn't!

STRANGER: They're not all like that y'know.

MUM: Who are you?

STRANGER: Some of them Psalms really give God what for. You should try some of them.

MUM: None of your business.

STRANGER: Just trying to help. You don't remember me, do you? Met you in the square outside that cathedral. Said how it would go with Josh; said you'd feel like you had a knife in the guts. Now, was I right, or was I right?

MUM: Were you in the plot?

STRANGER: Now don't be daft, Mrs. D. What you doing here anyhow?

MUM: I'm visiting my son's grave.

STRANGER: Oh, you're barking up the wrong tree, Missus.

MUM: I beg your pardon?

STRANGER: This isn't the place for him. You'd be better off looking round the King's Head.•

MUM: You're very disrespectful. Get out of my way.

STRANGER: Please yourself; but if we're talking about being disrespectful, how about this? You never listened to Josh. You tried to turn him aside. It was all about the great wonderful plans *you* had – never mind how he thought he should go.

MUM: How dare you!

STRANGER: Oh, I dare. Somebody's got to. Now, you never listened to Josh before: you better start doing it now.

MUM: Get out of my sight.

STRANGER: As you wish, Mrs. D.   *(Mum's feet on gravel, striding off.)*

MUM: Why do people do that? Nobody understands. *(Stops, turns)* And if you think - . Where are you? Hello? You're not frightening me, you know! I'm going to the grave now, you can't stop me. *(Starts off.)* Yea though I walk through the valley... I'm here to see you, Josh. Here's your mum with some flowers. Nobody understood you but me, at least you know that – oh! No! Oh Josh, no! No!

12.6 The sitting room.

JOE: So what we gonna do, eh? We got nobody to watch now.

DAD: Well, we done our learning.

ALFRED: To what end, though? We watched him, but we saw things we can't do. Astonishing experience, but – what do we do with it?

MOTHER ANASTASIA: I don't know, Alfred, except that we're the better for being with Josh. It was worth it.

SIMON: Yes: my soldier self faded away. Josh was so secure in himself: I wanted that. But I loved my uniform; it made me exist.

MOTHER ANASTASIA: Well, I shall be a better mother superior. You won't be trying to be a better lieutenant.

SIMON: Oh no; they wouldn't have me anyway – I'm beyond the pale. But I couldn't be in the military as it now is.

MOTHER ANASTASIA: You don't need it now.

SIMON: No; but I want to be true to Josh now, and true to my own self. They sort of go together. Well: what will you do Joe?

JOE: Get a job. Look after me old dad here.

MOTHER ANASTASIA: Where has Mrs. Davidson gone? Did she say, Callum?

CALLUM: Och, she's away to the cemetery again. I suppose it gets her out. We'll not be sitting here in her front room for ever, though. I'll stay a while, then I'll away north.

MOTHER ANASTASIA: Will you still preach?

CALLUM: What about? *(Door, tea-tray rattling.)*

RUBY: Right: life goes on. Tea and sandwiches: you pour, Mother A. Anybody starts moping and moaning, they're for the high jump. *(Cups set out.)*

MOTHER ANASTASIA: Well said, Ruby. Who wants milk?

JOE: We was wondering what to do now, Ruby.

RUBY: Well, I'm not going back to that club: showing me goods to them boozy old pervs. I wouldn't insult Josh's memory.

DAD: Got your self-respect now.

ALFRED: Do you have a plan, Ruby?

RUBY: Yeh: I'm gonna dish out these sarnies. I got cheese an' pickle, egg, and I found a bit of Spam.

DAD: Oh, Spam. I love Spam.

RUBY: There you go, then. Cheese; who's for cheese? Joe.

SIMON: Egg for me.

MOTHER ANASTASIA: I should be fasting, but egg.

RUBY: Alfred?

ALFRED: Oh, the cheese: without pickle. *Merci.*

JOSH: Got any Spam• ones left?

RUBY: No, Mr. Silver's had the lot; there's still - *(Shrieks. Cups drop.)*

JOSH: What's wrong? What is it? Oh, I know – it's the shirt, isn't it, Ruby? Sorry about the holes, not my fault really. Still, you did get it in a sale.

RUBY: You're dead! Get away, you're dead! You're a ghost!

JOSH: Oh, don't be daft. Here, Mr. Silver, can I have one of your sandwiches?

DAD: Yeh, anythin' you want, take it, take it.

JOSH: Ta. Mm, lovely. We used to have Spam all the time in your house, remember?

ALFRED: What are you doing here? We buried you.

JOSH: Yeh, I know; very nice of you, thanks very much. Loved the flowers.

MOTHER ANASTASIA: You're not…? Are you - are you a -

JOSH: Oh – you mean, wooooh! Oh no. Ruby knows, eh? Ruby knows I'm not a ghost, don't you, darling?

RUBY: Come here, you!

JOSH: Hah, you couldn't get a hug like that from a ghost. Oh, Ruby. Oh, that feels good.

RUBY: I thought I'd lost you.

JOSH: You're never gonna lose me again. Promise.

ALFRED: But how? How?

JOSH: Well, let's say my dad doesn't leave things unfinished.

SIMON: Are you saying God, er…

JOSH: Well, I didn't do it myself, did I? Here, is that a sticky bun?

MOTHER ANASTASIA: Your Dad God was there all the time.

CALLUM: Didn't look like it.

MOTHER ANASTASIA: But he was there; hidden under those terrible things.

JOSH: Yeh, all the time. Well, nearly.

CALLUM: What do you mean nearly?

JOSH: Well, just before I came out the prison…he wasn't there. Just wasn't there. That was really horrible; the worst. I spoke to him afterwards and he said it was terrible for him as well. Said he could hardly stand it.

ALFRED: You spoke to him…afterwards?

JOSH: Yeh, 'course I did. What a hug I gave him.

ALFRED: But, if you –

MOTHER ANASTASIA: Just leave it, Alfred.

ALFRED: But what's it about? What was happening to you?

JOSH: Can we just change the subject, Alfred? It's pretty deep stuff and I just want to enjoy myself with you lot.

RUBY: Right! Party!

MOTHER ANASTASIA: I'll…make more sandwiches.

RUBY: No, never mind sandwiches, we'll get a take-away! What you gonna have, Mother A.?

MOTHER ANASTASIA: Well, I…the convent doesn't have foreign food.

JOSH: There's a menu by the phone, stretch your mind.

CALLUM: Och, I don't think I believe all this at all.

ALFRED: Join the rational club, Callum: I mean, a couple of days ago –

DAD: Oh, open yer eyes, Alfred! How's about a bit o' music, then? Where's the radio?

SIMON: Capital idea! We could have -

DAD: We're not having your poncy Radio Three. *(Music.)*

RUBY: Not likely! Party time!

ALFRED: Why are you not all fainting with shock? Where is the intellectual crisis, the grasping for rationality - ?

RUBY: Just accept it, Alfred! Come on, have a dance.

JOSH: Er, I just wanna say: before…you know…I had this thought. I thought, there'll be great stuff for me, once I've got through this.• And there is; this is the start. Thanks everybody.

RUBY: Oh, Josh!

JOSH: Ohh, I can't take any more hugs.

RUBY: You're back, you're back.

JOSH: I know; and I'll tell you something else.

RUBY: What?

JOSH: I could murder a curry.

12.7 Mum's return. *(Door. We hear Mum gasping, clearly distressed.)*

RUBY: Hello Mrs. – Mrs. D! What's up? What's the matter?

MUM: Oh Ruby, the grave!

RUBY: What?

MUM: They – they desecrated his grave! I took flowers up, and when I got there – oh! Oh, it's terrible, there's just a big hole in the ground and the wreaths are everywhere and the lid of the – broken, all broken and scattered –

RUBY: Come and sit down, it's all right.

MUM: Why do they hate him so much? Ruby, I don't know what to do, I'm afraid to tell the police –

RUBY: Come in the sitting room, don't worry.

MUM: You don't understand! There's nothing in the grave! He's gone! Josh is gone!

RUBY: I gotta tell you something. Come in here. *(Door. 'Hello, Mrs. D.' etc.)*

MOTHER ANASTASIA: Mrs. Davidson! Whatever is it? .

CALLUM: Auntie, look at you! Come and sit down.

MUM: Oh, Callum! *(Sobs.)*

CALLUM: Tell us, now. What is it?

MUM: They took him away, they took him away!

CALLUM: Took who away?

MUM: They dug up the grave! Josh isn't there!

CALLUM: What - ? Oh; oh no, it's all right.

MOTHER ANASTASIA: Yes, he was here.

RUBY: He was with us, he gave me a big hug; it was fantastic.

MUM: What have you been doing in here?

RUBY: Told you, Josh was here.

MUM: What have you been doing in my house? Are you mad? Look at the state –

RUBY: Oh, we had a sort of party –

MUM: A party!

SIMON: Marvellous time.

JOE: He ain't dead, Mrs. D.

MUM: What!

ALFRED: Oh, I know, I know; but even the professional sceptic here –

DAD: He was here, he was.

MOTHER ANASTASIA: He's back with us!

MUM: What the hell do you think you're doing?

CALLUM: Auntie - !

JOE: No lie, Mrs. D. He was here. You only missed him by half an hour.

MUM: Is this for my benefit? Is it? Comfort the little mother? You people are sick! Josh was here, was he? Did you see the bullet holes?• Did you?

MOTHER ANASTASIA: Mrs. Davidson; truly. My own eyes: I handed him tea –

MUM: Really? You'll be surprised to know he's gone, then?

SIMON: What d'you mean?

MUM: They desecrated the grave. Josh has gone, the grave's empty!

JOE: Why would they…oh!

RUBY: S'pose that explains it then.

MUM: Is this supposed to make me feel better? Did you dig up the grave and concoct this lie? Why are you doing this?

MOTHER ANASTASIA: You don't know what you're saying; sit down –

MUM: Why have you turned against us? Is it the Church? Are they paying you? Is it threats?

MOTHER ANASTASIA: None of us would ever do such a –

MUM: Get out of my house.

RUBY: Oh no, no, he'll show up again –

MUM: Don't touch me! You're pathetic, all of you. Get out: leave me alone. I don't want you any more. I'm going to stay here and remember Josh; just the two of us. Just me and my boy. Leave us alone.

12.8 Josh's Room. *(Door.)*

MUM: Can I come into your room, Josh? I know you used to tell me off for barging in. You don't mind, do you, darling; it's just I'm lonely and I don't know where you are and it's like you're nearer if I'm in here. Can I just sit on the bed? Oh, you made that in a hurry, didn't you? Oh, Josh; socks on the floor as usual; you just won't put the clean ones in the drawer either, will you? There. *(Drawer.)* Look at that, shirts all just shoved in. Never done picking up after you. There: now that's tidy. All tidy, nothing disturbed. I'll keep it nice, this room will always be nice for you, I'll always do things for you. I just wish I knew where you were. Oh, darling, you're just not close enough at the moment, not even in here. I've got to get nearer to you, and…do something for you; just…something for you and me. Oh wait, darling, I'm coming. Just wait…

12.9 The cemetery.

MUM: I'm coming, Josh, I'm coming; I'll do something about this for you...

STRANGER: Evening, Mrs. D. What're you up to, then?

MUM: Don't you come near me.

STRANGER: Walking through a graveyard carrying a shovel does look a bit suspicious, y'know.

MUM: I'm going to fill in my son's grave.

STRANGER: What for? He's not in it.

MUM: For decency. For his memory. Because I'm his mother. Where is he? Do you know where he is?

STRANGER: You're digging a hole for yourself with that shovel, y'know. He doesn't need this.

MUM: How do you know what he needs?

STRANGER: Oh, well, don't take my word for it. Ask him yourself.

MUM: What! What do you - ? Where are you? Stop this! Stop it!

JOSH: Hello, mum. Well, never mind gawking at me, give us a hug.

MUM: Oh! Oh, my boy!

JOSH: That's it. It's all right; hang on tight, hang on. Oh, thanks Mum, thanks.

MUM: What?

JOSH: Mum, you hung in there for me. I knew you were there, listening to those guns. That meant so much.

MUM: But – but – you're not in the – how did you - ?

JOSH: There's a bit of a knack to it. Had a bit of help, gotta admit. But never mind that, 'cause here I am, and here you are, and we are all together…•

MUM: You – you – but – but – but –

JOSH: Do you know, you look just like a fish when you do that. Remember that time I came home from school with first prize for maths and you just stood in the kitchen and went 'But - but - but - .'?

MUM: I thought – I thought you were –

JOSH: Yeh, 'course you did.

MUM: I – I held you – in the parade ground – after they – after they –

JOSH: Shot me, yes.

MUM: I got – I got – on my hands – you were bleeding – it was on my hands -

JOSH: Yeh, well, don't get tacky. Not very nice; no, it wasn't.

MUM: Were you – were you really - ?

JOSH: Oh yes. I really was. This has all been very serious.

MUM: The angel was right – all those years ago, in the dream. He was right – you are special. You are great.

JOSH: That's right, mum; but there's greatness and greatness. Sometimes you get great by going right down to the very bottom. You lose everything, then you get more than everything back again. It all depends on my Dad.

MUM: He gave you back to me.

JOSH: Yeh, he did.

MUM: Oh, God, sorry; I'm so sorry. Josh?

JOSH: Yeh?

MUM: I've got to ask you.

JOSH: Oh.

MUM: You know what I'm like.

JOSH: Yeh, but I'm not gonna fade away; you're not gonna wake up.

MUM: All the same.

JOSH: All right then. Well, this is the actual shirt – bit draughty now. And if I unbutton it…there.

MUM: Ohhh. Oh, son. Was it…did it hurt?

JOSH: Well, not as bad as you'd think. You sort of go a bit numb. Quite quick, though.

MUM: Oh, and you were all yourself.

JOSH: Yeh, I was. You couldn't help that though, mum.

MUM: Oh, but he was there, Dad God; he was there.

JOSH: No, he wasn't.

MUM: But – you always said –

JOSH: Yeh, but he wasn't there then.

MUM: You mean God left you?

JOSH: No, not *left* – I mean, not like he wasn't bothered and walked off. He couldn't be there.

MUM: I don't understand you.

JOSH: Well, he didn't just leave me to it. See – we arranged it beforehand; we worked it out and decided. We thought we'd both have the pain of it – I'd have mine and Dad would have his. His pain was as bad as mine, but part of the pain was that we couldn't be together. Each of us went through it on our own.

MUM: But why?

JOSH: Well, that's how it works. You go down to the bottom of the dark, you can't have the tiniest little bit of light; not even the light of having a bit of company. So we were both in the blackness, separately, or it wouldn't have worked. That was the worst bit. That really was the worst bit.

MUM: And – where is he now?

JOSH: Eh? Oh. Well, here. You don't think I got back all by myself, do you? Oh, blimey, mum! I know I'm your wonderful boy, but Dad had to do that for me.

MUM: And for me. Button your shirt now, darling. You'll catch your –

JOSH: No! No, I won't; bit late for that. Mothers, eh?

MUM: Oh. Sorry, I just -

JOSH: Convinced then, are you? You must be, you're treating me like nothing happened.

MUM: Yes, darling. I'm convinced.

JOSH: Thought you might be.

MUM: Josh, it's like – this is so… I'm convinced, but it's not real yet – no, that's stupid. You're sort of somebody else now: you're the Man Who Came Back. It's as if you're you but you're not my son any more.

JOSH: Don't be daft, mum. You don't think that.

MUM: No. No, I don't.

JOSH: I'll always be your son; and you'll always be my mum.

MUM: Some things just don't change.

JOSH: Nope. Not even when you're killed. Well, ex-killed; ex-dead. Er...de-buried; un-interred...out-terred. I could have a reverse funeral. Can you have reverse funerals?

MUM: There's some kind of change, though. It's not just back to normal.

JOSH: Er...no. It's a bit more than that.

MUM: The thing is, you're alive.

JOSH: Yes, I am. And I'll never look back.

13: REMEMBER THE WINE

13.1 The cemetery.

MUM: Josh, it's like – this is so… I'm convinced, but it's not real yet – no, that's stupid. You're sort of somebody else now: you're the Man Who Came Back. It's as if you're you but you're not my son any more.

JOSH: Don't be daft, mum. You don't think that.

MUM: No. No, I don't.

JOSH: I'll always be your son; and you'll always be my mum.

MUM: Some things just don't change.

JOSH: Nope. Not even when you're killed. Well, ex-killed; ex-dead. Er…de-buried; un-interred…out-terred. I could have a reverse funeral. Can you have reverse funerals?

MUM: There's some kind of change, though. It's not just back to normal.

JOSH: Er…no. It's a bit more than that.

MUM: The thing is, you're alive.

JOSH: Yes, I am. And I'll never look back.

13.2 Jubilee Road.

MUM: Well, here we are. The old homestead: Jubilee Road.

JOSH: Yeh. They dragged me out that door and threw me in a van.

MUM: Well, no more. You're room's all ready; I even put your socks away.

JOSH: Won't be needing the room, mum.

MUM: You're touring again? I thought we'd have a quiet life.

JOSH: No, you didn't.

MUM: I can dream.

JOSH: Nice try, mum, but it can't just go back to how it was.• 'Oh, this is my son Josh; he used to be dead, you know.' I don't think so, do you? Bit of adjusting to do.

MUM: Can't we just relax?

JOSH: No chance. Look behind you.

Mrs. PEMBERTON: Mrs. Davidson! Mrs. Davidson! Hello!

MUM: Mrs. Pemberton!

Mrs. PEMBERTON: I'm so glad I caught you, Mrs. Davidson. Hello, Joshua; I've been following your career with interest. Heard you on the wireless at the Synod, thought you were absolutely marvellous. That's what it's all about, you know.

JOSH: Well, there you go. Good on you, Mrs. P.

Mrs. PEMBERTON: The stopped the broadcast when you told off the Archbishop. Technical fault, they said, but I wasn't born yesterday. You must go public, Joshua. Deny those dreadful rumours.

JOSH: Rumours, Mrs. P?

Mrs. PEMBERTON: Oh, you know: they're supposed to have taken you behind a wall or something and – bang!

JOSH: Oh, yeh. Well we'll certainly sort that one out.

MUM: Were you coming to see me, Mrs. Pemberton?

Mrs. PEMBERTON: Yes, I wanted to try my fruit scones on you – apricot; completely new recipe. Test all things, as the scripture saith.• I'm going to unleash them on the Flower Guild this Wednesday, so do form an opinion, won't you?

MUM: I certainly will, Mrs. Pemberton.

Mrs. PEMBERTON: Excellent. Well, I'm off. Bye-bye, Joshua. Oh, that's a terribly raggy shirt you're wearing: full of holes – surprised your mother sends you out – oh. *Oh.* Are those real bullet-holes?

JOSH: Er, yes. Yes, they are actually.

Mrs. PEMBERTON: It's true. I thought so. I thought you were the one, dear. Couldn't be anyone else.• Well, I'll be off then, my dears. Enjoy the scones, won't you? Bye-bye, Joshua; no stopping you now.

JOSH: Well. There you go, eh?

MUM: You'll be coming in, then?

JOSH: Don't think so, mum. Not the same. I just wanted to see where I'd lived.

MUM: To say goodbye?

JOSH: Well...

MUM: Half an hour. Have a cuppa.

JOSH: Um...all right then, half an hour. I'll have some fruit scones.

MUM: Sure you want to?

JOSH: Mum, I survived a firing squad; I think I can risk Mrs. Pemberton's scones.

13.3 The Silvers' house. *(Door.)*

JOE: Don't answer it, dad.

DAD: They won't want us, we're small fry.

SIMON: You can't be sure.

DAD: Oh, give over. Who's that, then? Eh? *(Opens door.)* Woah! You again!

JOSH: Hello, Mr. Silver. Thought you'd all be here. Wonder if p'raps you could just look after this little lady for me?

MUM: Hello, everybody. *(Recognition.)* Er – look, sorry everybody; I sort of lost the rag earlier on.

RUBY: Ohhh…don't blame you, Mrs. D. We didn't handle it very well.

JOE: Just sprung it on you, sorry.

DAD: Come in, love, put yer feet up. You comin' in, Josh?

JOSH: Thanks, but no thanks; though I'd dearly love to be in this house again.

RUBY: Well, come on, then.

JOSH: No, can't, it's…well…places to go, people to see. No, er, gotta see a man about…well, gotta see a man. Tidy up a few things. Well, till the next time. Behave yourself now, mum. 'Bye.

13.4 The Governor's office. *(Knock.)*

GOVERNOR: Yes? *(Knock.)* My appointments are over for the day.

VOICE: Haven't got an appointment.

GOVERNOR: Then make one. *(Door.)*

JOSH: Thought I'd just drop in.

GOVERNOR: This isn't a social club. If you don't –

JOSH: Hello, Governor.•

GOVERNOR: Good God.

JOSH: Yeh. Agree with that.

GOVERNOR: Tell me how.

JOSH: My dad did it. God: my Dad.

GOVERNOR: Why are you here?

JOSH: Well, didn't meet you under the best of circumstances; sort of got off on the wrong foot. Anyway, you tried to do your best for me, and despite all the goings-on, I quite liked you.

GOVERNOR: And I you, Davidson. If we had met in a different way…

JOSH: Well, you'd still have been you, I'd still have been me. You really were cornered, though; they really put the pressure on, didn't they?

GOVERNOR: Yes. But I still had responsibility.

JOSH: I know. I've done it though.

GOVERNOR: Done what?

JOSH: What you're not asking me. What you can't make yourself say.

GOVERNOR: Yes, I would expect that of you. I most genuinely regret –

JOSH: Yeh, I know. Y'know, you haven't said, 'This can't be happening,' or anything like that.

GOVERNOR: I know it's happening. I'm a realist. I'm a soldier.

JOSH: Yeh, s'pose so.

GOVERNOR: But why have you come here?

JOSH: We've just said it. And, I wanted you to know I understand; and I wanted you to know it's true about me.

GOVERNOR: And others? Will you meet the Archbishop?

JOSH: No, I don't think so.

GOVERNOR: Make him believe!

JOSH: Well, no; he doesn't want to meet me. I mean really, really doesn't want to. S'pose I respect that, really. And if I did meet him, he'd find a reason to make himself believe it wasn't real – then he'd get harder and harder and worse and worse. Wouldn't be doing him a favour, really. Or he might use the fact I met him to back up what he's into; and I'm not. I am so not on the same page as him.

GOVERNOR: Then you're saying I wanted…?

JOSH: Well yeh, you could say that.

GOVERNOR: What's going to happen now?

JOSH: S'pose that's up to you really.

GOVERNOR: You do know I'm an atheist? An unshakeable atheist.

JOSH: Yeh, 'course you are. Don't blame you. Tell you one thing, though: there's hardly anybody in that Church more likely to be a man after my own heart than you are. Hardly anybody's got more belief than you have.• Not many people know that.

GOVERNOR: I'm not following you. Look, have a drink with me; talk, explain it all - *(Glasses clink.)* Davidson? Where are you? Davidson? Davidson!

13.5 Mum's sitting room.

RUBY: Josh?

JOSH: Wossat, Ruby?

RUBY: Well, we've been seeing you on and off for weeks, and you've been telling us what it's all about, what your Dad wants, and it's brilliant, but, er –

JOSH: What?

RUBY: Well, when we gonna do something? We was going about before, and now we're sitting with you, listening…

JOSH: Well, I sort of like that.

RUBY: Oh yeh, but - you know…

JOSH: Well, just you sit tight, my girl, and you'll find out. All right?

RUBY: Right. Josh? When you're not with us…where are you?•

JOSH: I'm with my Dad. He's great company, y'know.

ALFRED: But where's that?

JOSH: Oh, in his space.

ALFRED: Where's *that?*

JOSH: Oh, he's got this smashing semi up the east end. Well, not really; but he's got the spare room all ready for you lot. Right next to mine. Um…you any closer to believing in God these days, Alfred?

ALFRED: Er…I don't know about God, Josh; but I believe in you.

JOSH: Well, that's all right, then. Thanks, Alfred, I'm very happy about that. Come on, give's a hug. Oh, Alfred. I love you.

ALFRED: Well, I – I – thanks, that's – that's mutual, Josh of course…

JOSH: Yeh, 'course it is. 'Course it is. 'Spose I'm ready now.

MUM: Oh, you *are* going on tour?

JOSH: I fancy a pint. What d'you say I tell you some really deep things down the King's Head?

13.6 The King's Head.

DAD: Well Joe, King's head. It all started in here.

JOE: Yeh, I saw the light.

SIMON: And I almost arrested you. Never did say sorry.

JOE: Well, go on then.

SIMON: Er – sorry.

JOSH: It all worked out, though, eh? You all right, Mother A.?

MOTHER ANASTASIA Thank you, yes. I'm just feeling a little obvious.

CALLUM: I don't think they get many mother superiors in here.

SIMON: Josh, I don't think we'll ever get used to this.

JOSH: Good.

SIMON: But will you always visit us like this?

JOSH: Er...yes and no. You'll have to sort of manage. Don't worry, I'm not dumping you. I'll see you again, but I'll have a Friend with me. You'll like him; he's a bit like me.

RUBY: Nobody's like you. Who's that?

JOSH: You know I talk about my Friend• sometimes, that Dad sent to me? Come down from Dad like a beautiful bird flying from heaven.

ALFRED: It's a bird?

JOSH: No, no; well, he's a bit like a dove, maybe – gentle, swooping in; but he's strong as well, like the wind. Anyway, don't rush off: he'll turn up.

ALFRED: God's new order, though? The new society. Is that not happening?

JOSH: One day there won't be anything else, Alfred. But for now, you're getting clues, demonstrations. Wanna know the biggest clue? Me.

ALFRED: You're a clue?

JOSH: Yeh. Twenty-one across, picture of God in charge, four letters.

RUBY: I got it! Josh!

JOSH: Give the lady a coconut. See, all the things I did for people, that's what it'll be like, only better, when my dad is one hundred per cent in charge.

ALFRED: And then they…

JOSH: They shot me. That bit was so clever of dad. See, all the horrible, black night in the world that's the opposite of my Dad God concentrated into death. Night fell on me and I carried the dark. Right down into deadworld. I carried it, Dad did too, in his own way. I went into the dark, so you never will.

MOTHER ANASTASIA: We can't really understand this.

JOSH: No, I'm glad you can't; but you can understand I shone in that darkness, and it couldn't make head nor tail of me.• It couldn't win; and I will shine in any darkness. Then my Dad brought me out of the dark to be the first citizen in his new order.•

CALLUM: Were you not that anyway?

JOSH: Ah well, y'see, dad never wanted death in the world, never made room for it. So I sort of fought it for him. See, when dad's order breaks in totally, there'll be nothing but life. And that day's coming into this day already – via me. I'm the biggest clue, I'm the open door, I'm the start. Things can't ever go back the way they were. The door's started opening, the light's coming through. Oh, I am enjoying meself. Oh, who's scoffed the peanuts? Was it you, mum, 'cause you have definitely got that look.

MUM: Josh, you got a wee moment?

JOSH: Oh, gotta go, folks. Over here, mum; now, what's up?

MUM: I want to tell you something.

JOSH: I know; that wasn't about the peanuts.

MUM: I've been working up to this your whole life. You know Ben, my husband, was killed.

JOSH: Yeh. Wish I'd known him.

MUM: Well, I was pregnant when we were married, but – Josh believe me, please – I'd never been with a man. You just – began.• You don't have a father, Josh. God really is your only Dad.

JOSH: God knew he could trust you.

MUM: But –

JOSH: God told me once. You're a brave woman, mum. Love you.

MUM: Josh, are you going back where you came from?

JOSH: Yeh; but don't worry, I'll still be me.

MUM: Will I still be your mum?

JOSH: Yes, you will. You'll be my mum for ever and ever.

MUM: Amen.

JOSH: Tell them all how special they are. Tell them to remember the wine.

RUBY: Come on, Mrs. D. Your gin an' tonic's getting cold.

MUM: In a minute, Ruby. Josh, do you think - ? Josh? Where - ? Oh. Oh, Josh. You came and went so quietly, so beautifully. And each time it was just you and me. Thank you, darling.•

13.7 Remembering.

DAD: Here we go, then. Nice cuppa tea.

JOE: Blimey, dad, if it was the end of the world you'd have a cup o' tea afterwards.

ALFRED: I think that's why Josh got you involved: he knew somebody'd have to make the tea.

JOE: What d'you make of that Josh's Friend thing? I don't really get that.

RUBY: Don't worry about it; it'll happen. Josh said.

JOE: I was just thinking.

ALFRED: Careful.

JOE: No, I mean, here we all are, and Josh said when we're together have a glass of wine and remember him.

ALFRED: You want a refreshment, Joe?

JOE: No, I mean do something special; something for Josh, like he said.•

MUM: I've got a bottle of port in the sideboard.

JOE: Yeh? Shall we, then? Right, off you go, Mrs. D.

MOTHER ANASTASIA: Oh, let's sit together. Dear me, this is special.

JOE: Got enough glasses?

MUM: Yes; clear the table, put them there. Here's the port and a corkscrew.

SIMON: Let's get this open. *(Corkscrew, cork.)*

MOTHER ANASTASIA: We should pray.

RUBY: I will! Dad, thanks for Josh; thanks ever so much.

JOE: You're the first, Ruby.

RUBY: First what?

JOE: You're the first person apart from Josh to call God 'Dad' straight to his face.

RUBY: Crumbs.

JOE: Now, what I'll do, everybody, is I'll pour out the wine glass at a time and give you one each. That all right?

MUM: Say something first, though.

JOE: Oh; right. Er…say something. Right: well, better stand up. Well, you all know Josh wanted us to remember him like this. So, I got this from him and I'm passing it on to you. The night he was arrested – betrayed – on his birthday, he put that new shirt on and said, 'I'll be buried in this.' You remember that. Then after the cake, his dad said to him, 'Get ready.' So he got a glass of wine and said, 'Remember me like this: say, "To Josh."' 'Remember the wine,' he said. Remember the party, remember when he died, remember the blood on his new shirt.

That was his birthday night; the night he told us to love each other. Give each other a hug or something. Right, get your wine now. Come on, Mrs. D., you first; take your glass; remember Josh. Dad, here's yours: remember Josh. Mother A.: remember Josh; remember when he died. Alfred: remember Josh; remember birthday night. Callum: remember

Josh; remember that shirt. Simon: remember Josh; remember how he saw it through. Ruby: remember Josh; remember you're the one that got him ready. Meant such a lot to him; people are always gonna say what you done• when they talk about Josh.

MUM: Here's your wine, Joe: remember Josh; remember how the dark came down on him and how he brought you into the light.

JOE: Ta, Mrs. D. Yeh, when they come for him he told Simon, 'It's not the end.' So – 'To Josh!' Remember birthday night. Till we see him again. Josh's dad, you're our Dad now; so he's our brother, we're family. *(Sound like a wind begins.)* Wossat? Somebody left a window open?•

ALFRED: Dunno.

SIMON: What's happening in here?

MUM: The lightness! I feel –

MOTHER ANASTASIA: Beautiful, fresh; so new.

DAD: It's bloomin' marvellous!

SIMON: Reality! It's reality!

ALFRED: Being, not thinking!

RUBY: He's here!

JOE: What? Who?

RUBY: Josh! Josh is here!

CALLUM: Where?

RUBY: No, no, he's just here. Oh, hello Josh!

MUM: Oh, darling, bless you!

RUBY: Look at the lights! Look at the lights!

MOTHER ANASTASIA: Oh, beautiful!

CALLUM: It is the Friend his Father sent. Swooping down like a bird: do you not feel his wings? It is like a weight upon you. Oh, the glorious –

RUBY: Hello, friend! Hello, new friend!

MOTHER ANASTASIA: So close, so close; no distance at all.

CALLUM: He came to Josh on the hill, he has come to us with him; he is the beautiful presence.

RUBY: A friend like Josh; friend, friend, friend.

ALFRED: Happy to meet you; happy to meet you.

DAD: This lark just keeps gettin' better.

13.8 Out for a walk.

DAD: Nice day for it, innit?

SIMON: I used to march up here on patrol. I'd feel those army boots hitting the street: made me feel strong.

MOTHER ANASTASIA: How do you feel today, Simon?

SIMON: I don't know. Sort of odd, I think; I used to feel I was carrying the Leader on my shoulders. I was proud of it; but he's not there now.

ALFRED: Ah, but what's taken his place?

SIMON: Nothing. There's nothing to carry.

RUBY: I think I'll have a dance. Come on, Mr. Silver. Dah-dah-dahhh...

CALLUM: Och, Ruby; it's a public street.

MUM: Good: let them see her.

MOTHER ANASTASIA: Every street should be danced in. Especially now.

RUBY: Oh, there's a gift shop: I love gift shops. Back in a minute.

JOE: Blimey, women! Bleedin' magpies! Aw, look at that, she's gone in.

MOTHER ANASTASIA: And what's wrong with a woman in a gift shop?

JOE: She'll be an hour at least, she will.

ALFRED: You're well acquainted with gift shops then, Mother A.?

MOTHER ANASTASIA: Well, they're not places a Mother Superior needs to frequent...

ALFRED: Perhaps a nice wimple with a picture of Scotty dogs?

JOE: Better than a tea-towel.

MUM: Joe! Have some respect!

JOE: Oh, here's Ruby. That was quick, girl.

RUBY: Yeh, saw something nice.

MUM: What's that round your neck, darling?

RUBY: Little thing I fancied.

MUM: Let me see, darling. Oh: a gun. A silver gun.

JOE: What d'you get that for?

RUBY: Just fancied it.

SIMON: There's more to it than that, Ruby.

CALLUM: Aye, come on.

RUBY: Well, if you gotta know, it's to remind me of Josh.

JOE: What d'you get a gun for?

RUBY: Told you: reminds me of Josh.

JOE: Why didn't you get a love-heart with his picture in it or something? What you hanging a gun round your neck for?

RUBY: 'Cos he got shot!

JOE: Come on girl, that's his mum standing there. How d'you think she feels?

MUM: No, no, it's all right. Tell me about the gun, Ruby.

RUBY: Well, he made the light shine on us.

ALFRED: But why should you - ?

MUM: Alfred. Go on, Ruby.

RUBY: Well, he had to go into the dark to do that.

MOTHER ANASTASIA: Oh. Dear child, I see; I think I see.

RUBY: He went into the dark and changed it; but he had to get shot first.•

ALFRED: A terrible injustice, though: all in the past, we don't go on about it.

JOE: Yeh, we do. Remember the wine.

ALFRED: You're going to do that again -?

RUBY: Josh took a risk. I mean, that's just so brave, letting people shoot you. That old vicar warned him, but he wouldn't run.

DAD: Yeh, he had the guts for it, he had. He stuck with us.

RUBY: So I got this little gun for round my neck. Says it all.

MOTHER ANASTASIA: Eloquently.

RUBY: You're not upset, Mrs. D., are you? You don't think it's tacky?

MUM: I don't think it's tacky at all, Ruby. I might even get one.

ALFRED: *You* wear a gun? But...Josh -

MUM: Why not? It didn't finish him; I got my boy back.

MOTHER ANASTASIA: The gun that couldn't kill Josh!

RUBY: Brilliant!

MOTHER ANASTASIA: *Gloria in excelsis Deo!*

RUBY: Eh?

MOTHER ANASTASIA: Er...hurrah for God!

13.9 The cathedral square.

RUBY: Aww, look at that old love over there, feeding the pigeons.

DAD: 'Ere, I know her - that's Annie Stallcross. Her husband had the butcher's shop down our street. She liked you, Joe, remember? Annie! Annie, over here!

ANNIE: Who's that? Oh, Mr. Silver! Hello, love!

DAD: 'Allo, Annie. Here, d'you know this feller?

JOE: Hello, Annie.

ANNIE: Is that your Joseph? Isn't he tall! Here, he's not... Joseph, didn't you - weren't you - ?

JOE: Yeh, I was, Annie. I can see now, though. Josh fixed me. Josh Davidson from Jubilee Road.

ANNIE: What, famous Josh Davidson? Was he a doctor as well, then?

JOE: No, Annie. He just touched my eyes.

ANNIE: Strewth, I wish he'd touched me.

DAD: Not so well then, Annie?

ANNIE: Me legs don't work now. There's people from the mission brings me here with me bags and I sings a song and gets a few bob in me little dish.

DAD: Where's Ernest then?

ANNIE: Passed away, years ago. Got too lonely so I married the bottle; can't remember what happened to the house.

DAD: Annie love, we'll get you a nice pie an' chips an' a cuppa, an' get you fixed up somewhere.

ANNIE: Bless yer 'eart, Mr. Silver.

DAD: Old friend of ours, everybody. Hard times: she's not so good.

RUBY: That's a real shame, that is.

DAD: Well, we'll do what we can.

RUBY: I know what Josh would do.

CALLUM: What d'you mean, Ruby?

RUBY: Well, what he did with Joe; with his eyes.

CALLUM: But Josh isn't here.

RUBY: He was there after we had the wine.

ALFRED: You're proposing something, Ruby?

RUBY: Well, Josh was trying to show us...

JOE: Oh. Oh, now hang on a minute. No...

SIMON: Ruby, I support you.

MOTHER ANASTASIA: And I'm behind you. I haven't the nerve personally –

RUBY: Well, it's scaring the knickers off me; but here goes nothing.• Annie? Hello Annie, I'm Ruby. We used to go around with Josh Davidson.

ANNIE: Did you, dear?

RUBY: Yeh. Well, Josh is sort of around; sort of. In a way - he's not sort of like standing here; but he's kind of watching us, kind of thing. With his...Friend. Least, I think he is, I dunno how it works.

ANNIE: I'm not following you at all, love.

RUBY: Er – oh, blimey. Oh look, never mind. Annie, on behalf of Josh Davidson from Jubilee Road, I'm telling you – 'cos he would, but I'm doing it – I'm telling you...get up, have a dance, run up and down, whatever you want; just...be all right. Right? You, er, you gonna do that, then?

ANNIE: Well, you look a nice girl, so I'll give it a go. I'm not one to disappoint people. Oooh! Well, I'm on me feet, that's as far as I get usually. You want me to do a dance?

RUBY: Dunno, whatever you want.

ANNIE: Er...ooh, I did a step. I did two. One and - two and – ooh, I say! I think I could run over there. I done it! I'm gonna run back again! Done that an' all! Hang on, highland fling. With a harrum and a heerum and a – oh, lummy! What d'you do to me, girl?

RUBY: Nothing! I didn't do nothing!

ALFRED: Oh my conscience, it works.

SIMON: Oh, capital; just capital.

JOE: Gawd 'elp us. Oh, Gawd 'elp us.

MOTHER ANASTASIA: *Gloria in excelsis Deo.*

ANNIE: Here, I fancy a Dashing White Sergeant! If you get my meaning! Gather round everybody, I'll give yer the best show of yer lives. One, two, three: knees up, Mother Brown, knees up, Mother Brown…

13.10 The Archbishop's Chambers.

Fr. JEREMIAS: Archbishop! Your Grace, I must inform you that associates of Joshua Davidson have gathered in the Cathedral Square.

ARCHBISHOP: Their rationale, Archdeacon?

Fr. JEREMIAS: They are telling the people that Davidson is no longer dead.

ARCHBISHOP: Desperate people. I shall deal with this myself.

Fr. JEREMIAS: Your Grace, I believe I must warn you.

ARCHBISHOP: Warn me, Archdeacon?

Fr. JEREMIAS: I believe this is God. You will not be able to stop it. You will be fighting him.•

ARCHBISHOP: Inappropriate words, are they not, from a member of this Cathedral's clergy?

Fr. JEREMIAS: I feel I may soon be called to a higher service. Good day, Your Grace.

13.11 The cathedral square 2. *(Crowd murmur.)*

JOE: I saw him, with these eyes, same feller I grew up with. They shot him, but there he was; and he said, 'I went right into the dark so you never would,' and he's here, so what about it, eh - ?

(Soldiers marching, halt. Rifles cocked.)

ARCHBISHOP: You will stop this at once!

JOE: Eh? What for?

ARCHBISHOP: Davidson was an enemy of the state; you are committing an act of civil disobedience. Now, in the name of the Church, I order you all to disperse.

JOE: What, you an' all them choirboys?

ARCHBISHOP: I warn you: I am serious. Fire over their heads, *(Rifle volley. Screams.)* Now stop this farce. Let your martyr go.

JOE: Martyr! You're admitting it, then? Set him up, did yer?

ARCHBISHOP: Do not embellish this man's sad story. The State acted to protect itself and the Church and those they serve.

MUM: God sent us Josh; you tried to take him away from the people. But God's given him back to us.

ARCHBISHOP: Give up your wishful thinking. Do not make yourselves a threat.

JOE: You making us choose? You on one side, God and Josh on the other?

ARCHBISHOP: You think this is integrity?

JOE: Yeh, I do.

ARCHBISHOP: Very well. Guns ready! *(Rifles cocked.)* I call heaven and earth to witness against you.• Joshua Davidson stands between us. Make your choice.

Notes for JOSH.

1: A nice young man.

We're interrupting our programme. Fans of the radio of yesteryear will recall Orson Welle's famous use of this device at the opening of his dramatisation of *The War of the Worlds*, when a programme of dance music was 'interrupted' to go to 'live' coverage of the Martian landing. Hopefully, *Josh* won't provoke the same degree of panic from credulous listeners, but it does show that writers can learn from their predecessors.

The People's Republic. This 'News' sequence establishes the oppressive military regime that is the equivalent of the Roman occupation of Judea. Josh grows up in this situation, a similar one to, say, that in France during the German occupation. Life goes on, but one must behave.

He's what I was spared for! The potting shed is of course a birthplace as humble as the manger that served for Jesus, but without the romanticised and sentimentalised trappings of Christian art. Mum's conviction of an angelic announcement of her son (which Edie doesn't really believe) gives her a sense of vocation and purpose even before his birth; but as we'll see, that sense of meaning goes somewhat off track.

He wouldn't say so. I would say that the movement and the understanding of life that centred on Jesus is a different sort of thing from 'religion' in the sense that many people use the word. Jesus himself certainly acted in sharp contrast to much of the official religion of his day, as well as the more popular variety, criticising both as the ethical and spiritual tradition of Israel's prophets had done before him. Part of the basis of that criticism was his understanding of the inner meaning and intention of the religious Law (Torah). Mum finds that, to represent Josh properly, she must say that 'a faith' isn't the same thing to him as God.

Wireless. Yes, I know: we have radios now, not wirelesses. However, I think of *Josh* as set against a post-war, 1945-ish background, hence the occasional dated reference. Think of the production style of *Brazil* and Burton's *1984*; but if that doesn't work for you, imagine your own setting.

She's from this wee glen. The original actress who was to play Mum was Scottish, thus giving a marked contrast to Josh's East London voice. Rather than being a problem, Mum's brogue gave some background colour and story: a Scottish girl comes south to get married, leaving a northern branch of the family that connects with Josh.

I call God my Dad. Dad? Isn't that rather childish? Or a bit irreverent? I don't think so. As you get to know Josh, you discover (I hope) that neither he nor his faith are at all childish. His relationship with God is warm, confident and intimate: he *likes* him, so I felt that 'Dad' would fit very naturally into that. When I was searching for the name that Josh would have for God, I thought of a friend of mine whose relationship with God is just as I've described. He himself is a mature, intelligent, fun person who's in love with God. How does he address God? You guessed: he calls him Dad. It comes quite naturally out of their relationship. So 'Dad' it was. As I got used to the name on Josh's lips, it came to sound perfectly natural and sat easily with the love and reverence Josh had for God. It also didn't sound 'religious' (can you imagine Jesus being *religious* about God?) and so this very natural name helped the 're-telling' along. We know that Jesus addressed God with the Aramaic name 'Abba'. This isn't really 'Daddy', as some like to think, but is more like 'Dear father.' It's still a 'family' word and carries the feelings of love and intimacy that Jesus clearly felt towards God. He can use it at his worst moment in Gethsemane (Mark 14:36), asking his dear father to take the cup of suffering from him. Paul says that the Holy Spirit enables us to share in this love-relationship, so that we find ourselves crying 'Abba! Father!' to God (Galatians 4:6); and when we do, that's the Holy Spirit agreeing with us that God has 'adopted' us into his family (Romans 8:15-16). So, all things considered, I think 'Dad' is rather good.

Callum. Josh's Scottish cousin is the John the Baptist of the piece, to begin with at least. Like John with Jesus, he is present when the Holy Spirit 'descends and remains' on Josh.

Servant. Josh is referring to the striking figure in the Book of Isaiah known as 'The Servant of the Lord.' Jesus took much of his understanding of himself and his mission from this figure. The *Ebed*

Yahweh is described in four passages known as the Servant Songs: Isaiah 42:1-9, 49:1-13, 50:4-9, and 52:13-53:12. Some suggest that Isaiah 61:1-3 is a fifth song, though the word Servant doesn't appear. God gives the Servant a vocation to be leader of the nations, but he suffers and is abused. He is to restore the nation of Israel to God, but quietly and confidently: his success will not be by political or military means. The Servant is rejected and suffers the consequences of other people's wrongdoing, but his vindication is in God's hands. There are various references back to the Songs in the New Testament. For example, Jesus says in Mark 10:45 that he has 'not come to be served but to serve' and Paul insists in Philippians 2 that Christ took 'the form of a servant' whose obedience went 'even to death.' The Jewish interpretation of the Servant is that he is a symbol of the nation Israel.

God's Spirit. The first Servant song (Isaiah 42:1-9) says that God will put his Spirit on the Servant to enable him to bring justice to the nations and succeed in his mission. The speaker of Isaiah 61:1-3 (possibly the Servant) declares that the Spirit of the Lord is upon him to enable him to bring freedom and release. Jesus quotes verses 1-2 in his 'manifesto' at Nazareth (Luke 4), but significantly stops at the speaker's statement that he will declare 'the year of the Lord's favour', thus omitting the reference to 'the day of vengeance of our God.' Jesus insisted that he performed compassionate miracles and brought freedom 'by the Spirit of God' (or 'by the finger of God', meaning the same) and that this shows that God's rule (kingdom) is arriving. The Spirit is the 'breath', the power and personal presence of God (the Hebrew *ruach* means both breath and spirit, as the Greek *pneuma* does in the New Testament). In John's Gospel, John the Baptist (John 1:31-33) is told that the person on whom the Spirit of God descends permanently (as distinct from the temporary enablings featured in the Old Testament) is the one God has sent. He witnesses this happen to Jesus when he is baptised. The same event is experienced by Jesus as an assurance of God's pleasure in him and love for him, as well as a confirmation of his calling as Messiah (the language here echoes Psalm 2:7, where God speaks to the newly appointed king). Callum is Josh's 'John the Baptist', witnessing the arrival of the new 'Friend' who will enable him to be 'Servant'.

These moors. This is the wild Scottish equivalent of the Judean desert, the 'wilderness' where the Spirit drove Jesus after his baptism. Like Jesus, Josh must now consider exactly what his vocation means. I hope I may be forgiven the presence of the sheep; but hey, it's Scotland. And Mark 1:13 tells us 'he was with the wild beasts.'

WIFIE. This lady is, I fear, one of the more wearing of Scottish saints, a lifelong practitioner of the dourest righteousness and sworn enemy of the world outside her own tiny circle. She also typifies the most oppressive forms of religious misunderstandings of God and would have been right at home in Cromwell's 'Godly Commonwealth' where those in charge knew what was right and would make you do it. There's also a swipe here at what I believe to be a worrying emphasis on 'power' (manifest in various ways) that characterises a great deal of Fundamentalist and Evangelical Christianity. 'Power' is the way forward, be in spiritual experience, unassailable knowledge, authoritarian leadership, political or nationalistic dabbling, or in peddling formulas that control reality to attract wealth or infallibly get what you want. Doctrine and the cause come before people and usually people suffer under this arrangement. Our Wifie is an incarnation of an aspect of Jesus' wilderness testing. If you are Messiah, he was asked in effect, what kind of Messiah are you? Not the kind that dazzles and forces assent, he answered. Doing things that way is 'testing' God (in an arrogant way), deliberately telling him that you know better. The Gospels tell us that Jesus consistently rejected power (in the usual sense), despite it being offered to him. If our Wifie was shown a clear comparison between her approach and Jesus', which one would she recognise?

You need a master. The apparition of the Leader offers Josh his military machine in order to see his mission fulfilled. This sheer physical force will ensure success, while Josh's 'moral crusade' will lend respectability to the regime. What could be more sensible? But Josh and the Leader are so different that such an alliance is impossible, and cannot achieve what 'Dad' really wants. Another 'Messiah' test: Jesus can be Lord of all, but only by bowing down to his enemy, an insane situation. This is the offer of power from another angle: let the 'Prince of This World' exercise his brute force on your behalf. Jesus knows he is the Suffering Servant who achieves what force cannot, and that this is the will of God. The wilderness testing left Jesus utterly sure of the kind of Messiah he was, and determined to be a true son of his Father. The strong impression is that Jesus left the wilderness determined to get on with it.

2: Starting out.

Even the Church doesn't know. Josh is now clear in his mind. His lifelong knowledge of 'Dad' and the new experience of his Friend whom Dad has sent have given him something to say that the State Church, joined to the Regime, can't say, or even understand. He has learned that God is Love and works by the Spirit of Love in the inner lives of individuals, not by absolutising state machinery, ecclesiastical structure or intellectual formulae. Notably, the New Testament insists that the prime indicators of the presence of the Spirit are the 'fruits' of mature character that embodies love. What this looks like is spelled out (somewhat shockingly) in 1Corinthians 13. But this is what God is like; this is what the Spirit is like; this is what Christ is like; and temptations to use 'power', however good it looks and however practical it seems are shown up for the shallow, destructive ways they are. Josh now knows that whatever Dad and his Friend do now, it will be along these lines. Jesus constantly found himself in conflict with the popular assumption that the hope of the Kingdom (Rule) of God was a political and military matter, the establishing of an independent Jewish state. He insisted that God's rule was manifest in the inner life of a person or community, and was shown by compassion, restoration, healing, reconciliation and right living. This Rule had arrived, but not completely, though it was very much at work in secret ways, like yeast in dough. One day the Rule of God would arrive completely, and the world would be what it was meant to be. Until then, this hope must not be politicised. Jesus warned of the consequences of insisting on this interpretation. The warnings were realised some forty years later in the Roman campaign that brutally put down the Jewish revolt of 66 AD and destroyed Jerusalem and its Temple.

3: The Lines Are Drawn.

That shilling. Yes, I know: another forties-ism. Well spotted.

Servanthood. How very ironic, considering the last episode.

Archdeacon. In the Anglican church, the Archdeacon of a diocese ranks just below the Bishop, with authority and responsibilities delegated by him. The Archdeacon is responsible, among other things, for matters that are not strictly religious.

Demob suit. Another archaism. Men demobilised from the Armed Forces after World War II received, in addition to other assistance, a decent suit to ease their return to normal life. This became known as the 'demob suit.'

Archbishop. The position of head of the Church is a rough equivalent of the High Priest of first-century Judea. Under the Roman Prefects, the religious leaders still had considerable responsibility for the actual running of the country, but were expected to do things Rome's way and make sure everyone behaved. They had a great deal of leeway (it was even possible to complain directly to the Emperor, as a Jewish delegation did to Caligula) but had to negotiate the controls that Rome held firmly in place. They also knew that Rome was prepared to make the changes that suited her. When the High Priest Annas failed to please, Rome removed him and replaced him with his son-in-law Joseph Caiaphas, who was High Priest at the time of the final confrontation with Jesus. Caiaphas himself was uninstalled some years later, but it was he who, we are told, pressed the Jewish leaders to take decisive action. To be fair to him, he was in an extremely difficult position. As a Sadducee (as most of the religious leaders were), he would have held to a policy of peaceful co-operation with Roman power, thus distancing himself from the strong anti-Roman feeling and revolutionary tone of much of the nation. They would not have seen him or the rest of the Temple hierarchy as the people to bring about their Messianic hopes. The Essene community at Qumran (who produced the Dead Sea Scrolls) saw the whole priesthood and Temple as so corrupt that they utterly rejected the whole thing to live as separatists in the desert until God should bring about a restoration. But whatever the people's hopes and ambitions were, Caiaphas knew very well what Rome's reaction would be if they spilled over in an attempt to crown a Messianic king. Jesus knew too, and constantly warned about the consequences of trying to force God's hand by violence. Whatever they knew of Jesus' thoughts on kingship, the authorities feared that his popularity might be the spark to ignite the dry tinder of revolution. John 11:48 sums up their discussions as, "If we let him go on like this, everyone will believe in him, and the Romans will come and destroy both our holy place [the Temple] and our nation." The next words show Caiaphas' realism and determination. John informs us that he told his colleagues, "You do not understand that it is better for you to have one man die for the people than to have the whole nation destroyed." It must have been clear to him that this was scarcely in line with Torah or the ethics of the Prophets, but faced with dreadful possibilities he made his grim decision. John then makes an astonishing statement. Caiaphas, he says, "did not say this on his own," meaning that, being High Priest, God enabled him to utter a prophecy about Jesus' approaching death for the people, though that death would have a significance quite different to that in Caiaphas' mind. This can be John's only meaning, as the High Priest was believed to have the gift of prophecy, and John believed that gift functioned even within such desperate decision-making. Jesus appears to have quickly learned about the decision, for he became secretive and withdrew with his disciples to a town near the desert.

The Gospels say little about Caiaphas, but our Archbishop embroils himself in activities that have no parallels in those books. His story does not reflect on the Judaism of any period, but on what a professing Christian church can become and do, while imagining itself perfectly justified. Should anyone wish to know, the Archbishop's cultured, dreamy voice in the radio recordings was based on that of Terence Stamp's character Bernadette Bassenger in *Priscilla, Queen of the Desert*. It's one of life's ironies.

Excommunicate. Joe's story is a version of that of the blind man cured by Jesus in John 9. The event is a metaphor for the 'lighting up' effect of Jesus' presence in the world. John calls him 'the real light that enlightens everybody' (1:9). Jesus' disciples see the man's blindness as an occasion for a theological discussion. Somebody must have sinned to cause this presumably deserved suffering – the standard explanation at the time – so who's responsible? Jesus sees the man's 'darkness', not as something God has inflicted, but as something that is spoiling the man's life. He therefore moves to act as God would and removes it. It's not an opportunity to discuss, but to do good to someone and thus 'do the works' of God. This emphatically does not include condemnation of people and Jesus made no connection between moral failure and illness. There's one, and only one, occasion (John 5:14) when he told someone to 'stop sinning' because there was a risk of 'something worse' (presumably a return of the recently healed condition), but we're not told what the sin was or how it contributed to the illness. It's clear that this episode is an exception and that in any case the original condition wasn't a punishment by God but something that resulted directly from the man's own behaviour. Whereas Jesus rubbed mud on the blind man's eyes, Josh dabs on some of Joe's scrumpy. I rather liked that: very appropriate.

The blind man's cure and the associated indication that Jesus is the Messiah provokes those of the religious authorities who are opposed to him. The man's insistent loyalty to Jesus leads to him being 'put out of the Synagogue'. That is, he is declared to be no longer a member of the community of the people of God, a dreadful sentence that can hardly be appreciated by anyone who is not Jewish. Perhaps the nearest thing to this is the later church practice of excommunication, which is strictly speaking a pronouncement that a person is already 'out of communion' because of some specific behaviour. When the pronouncement is made, the person can no longer function in the ministry of the church or receive the sacraments. More serious pronouncements meant that no Catholic could associate with the offender. Although the idea of all this was that excommunication was never a 'vindictive' act (designed only to punish) but a 'medicinal' one (performed in the hope that the individual would improve their life), it was a serious business for the Middle Ages, when politically-minded popes would use the threat of excommunication to bring European leaders to heel if they opposed his policies. One more thing: our Archbishop and his church do sound not unlike the Church of England, but remember this is just a device, so please don't identity the two. For the record, the C of E sees excommunication as a very extreme measure and uses it very rarely indeed. An example would be the clergyman who was excommunicated in 1909 after murdering four of his parishioners. Mind you, some Revs must be sorely tempted.

Our witness maintained. The Archbishop will not acknowledge the dark side of the situation. The Church is right because it is the Church: end of story. In following his own endless rationalisations, he has long ago sunk into denial about his own true motives and become committed to his own 'blindness'. Jesus told his religious enemies that if they truly were 'blind', genuinely not understanding the situation they would have been doing no wrong. However, they insisted that they could 'see', that they knew what was true and right. 'But now that you say, "We see",' he said, 'your sin remains.'(John 9:41) Jesus' strongest definition of evil and sin is the situation in which one deliberately calls evil good for one's own ends, a perilous place to be. This kind of denial takes many forms, not least religious ones, and can be stated convincingly in religious language

Jeremias. Fr. Jeremias is intended to mirror the Pharisee Nicodemus in John 3, a person within the circle of the religious leaders who nonetheless is sympathetic to Jesus and genuinely wishes to understand him.

4: The officer and the showgirl.

A tunnel. Yes, a tunnel. You have a better idea?

The foundations of the old terrace. You thought it was going to be the sewers, didn't you? 'They always escape through the sewers,' you said. Well, not this time. This is a highly original work of drama, you know. Sewers! Ha!

She's so thirsty. More alert readers will be wondering already if we have a reference to John 4 here. Yes, claim your coconut: you're absolutely right. The sequence with Ruby is a version of Jesus' meeting with the socially marginalised Samaritan woman at the village well. Possibly she's there alone to collect water in the middle of the day, the hottest part, when everybody else is at home for a siesta and won't be able to give her accusing stares and cold shoulders. Ruby herself is a sort of combination of this lady and Mary Magdalene, traditionally identified with the lady of negotiable affection (to use Terry Pratchett's excellent euphemism) in Luke 7:37. At any rate, having lost hope for herself, she finds herself outwith polite society, no doubt much to polite society's relief. Like Jesus, Josh uses a mysterious knowledge about Ruby, not to expose and condemn but to cut through others' rejection and the 'loser' self-image it has forced on her to bring hope and the knowledge that God disagrees with the holier-than-thou brigade.

It's a strip club. That's right, you heard correctly. To me, one of the splendid features of the Jesus of the Gospels is his complete inability to be fazed by the sins of the flesh. He appears to have a particular compassion for those who have taken that particular wrong turning. To him, the really deadly things, the things that get him very angry, are the sins of the spirit: arrogance, self-interest, self-justification, inflicting and maintaining injustice, putting religious practices before people and their needs, creating pointless burdens, withholding help, heartlessness in all its forms, especially religious ones, hypocrisy. He treats prostitutes as fellow human beings, but his teachings detest the willingness to commodify these women for gain. He loathes materialism and injustice, but still his heart warms to the young man trapped by his wealth and he seeks out Levi, the quisling extortionist of a tax man, to be a personal friend. I wonder if he enjoyed breaking the mould of what people expected a good rabbi to be. He seems to have gone out of his way to do it often enough. Jesus was too free, too himself, to be tied up in a religious stereotype. I hope Josh is too. Whatever his mother thinks.

The Governor. This gentleman is of course a re-invention of Pontius Pilate, the Roman Prefect who signed Jesus' death warrant. He's as authoritarian, tactless and brash as his original, with a few differences, as we will see. Pontius Pilatus was the fifth Prefect of Rome's province of Judea. It was regular practice to install local rulers, who would manage a province on Rome's behalf and be answerable to the Emperor and his delegates. This was the situation in Judea. However, when Herod the Great bequeathed the kingship to his son Archelaeus, the lad ruled so badly that his subjects sent a delegation to Rome asking that he be removed. Archelaeus was no doubt highly embarrassed, as he'd already gone to Rome to have his new kingship confirmed by Caesar Augustus. In the event, he was such a disaster that Rome removed him and began to rule directly through a resident Prefect (later Procurator). It's possible that Jesus' 'Parable of the Minas' in Luke 19: 12-27 (where a nobleman journeys abroad to 'receive a kingdom' and whose citizens refuse to accept his rule) reflects Archelaeus' career. The brutal reaction of the nobleman in the story certainly illustrates his way of dealing with dissidents. Contemporary sources refer to Procurator Pilate's brutality, constant executions and gross insensitivity to Jewish religious practice. No doubt the Jewish authorities derived no small pleasure from backing him into a corner over the execution of Jesus. There was in fact some instability at Rome in this period, an attempt having been made to oust Emperor Tiberius from the throne (one tradition says that Pilate was married to Tiberius' adopted niece). Anyone giving alleged revolutionaries an easy time would not be looked on kindly, and this may give added emphasis to the priests' warning, 'If you let this man go you are no friend of Caesar.' In the end, Pilate managed the province so badly he was recalled to Rome to face charges of maladministration. Some old sources say he was exiled to Gaul and committed suicide in Vienne.

The sticks. We're now well up country and far from the Capital where things began, so think of the soldiers at this base speaking with an 'Ey oop, lad' accent.

Our reputations. Mum's not quite on the same page as Josh. I think that we have hints in the Gospels that Mary didn't really grasp what Jesus was doing; but more on that anon.

Now sit down. Now Josh's capacity for real anger shows through. Mrs. Pemberton would be shocked to see her 'nice young man' now, just as many people would be shocked by the real Jesus. It's often been said that the great problem with the reconstructed 'meek and mild' Jesus who did little more than consider the lilies and tell parables about the birds all day is that it's so very hard to see why anybody would ever bother to crucify him. It's clear that Jesus could be intensely angry – at the right things. Please don't hear a polite, righteous voice as you read this scene: try to hear someone so incensed at the abuse of Ruby he doesn't care who gets rattled: in fact, he's put himself in charge and he wants to throw some offensive truths about. He's feeling the authority and drive of what Dad has called him to do.

All of you. Why do they always say that? I mean, don't blame me, I'm just serving tradition.

5: Battle joined.

Tim's getting better. These events pick up the main themes from the story of the recovery of a Roman officer's servant as Jesus simply declares it done without even seeing him (Matthew 8 and Luke 7). The Roman already has a strong confidence that Jesus can do this, joined, apparently, with a deep personal respect. Lieutenant Simon has previously had no high opinion of Josh, but has learned that he can produce the goods, perhaps thinking in the back of his mind that if he does this sort of thing he can't be that bad. At any rate, he intends to force Josh to use his 'powers' on Tim, forgetting that compassion doesn't need to be forced: thus he encounters an alternative to the mindset nurtured by his military service to the Regime. He hasn't realised it, but he's acquired faith, born of an angry desperation determined to seize what chance it can: I think Jesus would like that and would readily respond.

A smacker for you. These two sentences are Josh's version of the traditional blessing in Numbers 6:24-26, still used in blessing infants. True, 'smacker' does not appear in the Hebrew, but it's certainly in the spirit of the thing.

Well, it has; it's here. Mark tells us (1:14-15) that after his test in the desert, Jesus arrived in Galilee with good news; and the good news was simply 'God'. What's more, God's 'Kingdom' (ie. his rule) was just about to show up, so the thing to do was just believe it and live accordingly. Of course, Jesus insisted that this rule was within a person and this inevitably clashed with the idea of the Kingdom of God as a political entity God would bring about by his victorious warriors, as it had been by the Maccabean freedom fighters two hundred years before. Jesus found himself in conflict with this and with those of the religious establishment who made the Divine Law and the Rule of God a weary, burdensome thing and even manipulated it for their own ends. This led to a theme of confrontation that persisted through Jesus' public career. Josh deliberately sows the seeds of confrontation here, not for the sake of it, but because, if he's to show what 'Dad's' rule is to be like, he must announce that a new authority is active and (unavoidably) show that the current religious setup has failed the people by misrepresenting 'Dad God.' Simon, of course, knows only too well how this will sound to the ears of the Regime.

God's new order is here. Jesus insisted that his 'dynamic', powerful actions in restoring well-being (Luke 11:20, Matthew 12:28) were done by the 'finger' (power) of God or (the same thing) by the 'Spirit of God'. That could only mean, he said, that the rule of God had arrived. The sign of the Kingdom of God, for Jesus, was not a military victory but the meeting of human need and freeing people from parasitic, destructive forces. This is the idea behind what Josh says here.

Then you don't get in. To those who saw the 'Kingdom' in terms of personal or political power, the ability to dominate by one's own strength and crush opponents, Jesus said that the opposite is true. You have to let all that go and let God do it his way and define his kingdom in his own terms. Since his rule is within your life, you have to be a receptive child to be part of it, not a warrior. If you won't do that, you won't be part of the real kingdom (Mark 10:15, Luke 18:17).

He could have started a revolution. As Jesus could easily have done. A political, military Messiahship, being a 'King like David' his ancestor was his for the taking. A great theme of the Gospels is Jesus' refusal of this option. He decided in the desert that he wasn't going to be that kind of Messiah and he stuck to his decision.

6: Give me to God.

The same enemy. Or as Paul expressed it not many years after Jesus, "Our struggle is not against enemies of blood and flesh [ie, people], but against...the spiritual forces of evil." (Ephesians 6:12).

A knife in the guts. "Yea, a sword shall pierce through thy own soul also," the Angel's warning to Mary in Luke 2:35, has perhaps become rather poetic and has lost its force. Accepting her vocation to bear the Messiah must have meant dreadful pain to Mary as things unfolded.

It might be a mystery, a secret. The rule of God, said Jesus, is powerful but not necessarily obvious: God is constantly active, but you might not know. At times you have to wait till the results appear. Josh uses the same metaphors as Jesus in explaining: yeast and seed (Mark 4:30, Luke 13:21)

He'll tell you his secrets. A perk of being around Jesus is getting to understand how God's rule works (Matthew 13:11). Even if, like our friend in the cathedral, you might be a bit slow.

Passivia. I called her that because I thought that anybody with a Mother Superior like Anastasia would have to be rather passive.

That terrible voice is silent. I did wonder whether to include any representation of Jesus' practice of 'deliverance', wondering if it was a bit gross for the type of thing I was doing. I decided to go ahead since it is, after all, an integral part of the Gospels' picture of Jesus. Do forget all the 'exorcism' movies you ever saw when reading this, will you? Although Mother A. does end up on the floor, it's fairly toned down and not sensational, which Jesus seemed to prefer anyway. The entity affecting the good Mother tries to get away with it by controlling her speech and pleading for a reprieve (as in some of the Gospel accounts) before it has to go. The radio recording tried to indicate this by having one of those deep, throaty voices beloved of horror film directors speaking the lines along with Mother A. Whatever you make of these stories, they show that Jesus and his first followers believed that he was able to free people from an evil that wasn't part of any badness of their own, but associated with them from outside their personality, a spiritual parasite. I think that, whatever you may call such a thing, experience shows that people do sometimes require this kind of help, sensitively, wisely and carefully done with the authority of Christ. I think too that there are plenty of those who perceive such issues when they just aren't there and would do better to call in the psychologist. It's no accident that, not long after Jesus' time, his followers recognised the need for people who had a gift for "the discernment of spirits" (1Corinthians 12:10). But the Gospels don't recount these stories to scare us: what they're saying is that any evil must yield to Christ: there is *always* hope.

God has sent cousin Joshua. Callum has become Josh's 'John the Baptist', pointing to him as John did to Jesus.

Epistle to the Romans. Ah, you noticed. If Josh is an equivalent of Jesus, there would logically be no Epistle to the Romans at this time. However, there's nothing in the Governor's reading that is specifically Christian. The idea is simply to show people juggling political power. The Archbishop knows that the Governor, by reading this passage, will make a statement about the Church's 'loyalty', while the Governor finds that the Bible contains words with which he can cheerfully agree and use to make his own statement, even threat. Logically, a 'Josh Bible' would have no Gospels, or anything about Jesus; but hey, this is art, so let's not be too rational.

Overcome evil with good. Up to this point, the Governor's reading has been, shall we say, a bit unenthusiastic; but he really begins to build up steam from here on.

7: Life and death.

They brave rebel lads. Enter the Zealots. Or, if you prefer, the Resistance: the freedom fighters. Anyone having trouble with Andy Jamieson's grammar should realise that he's a Glasgow 'hard man' speaking in his native Patter.

That's the boy. There may or may not be a boy around when Glaswegians use this phrase. It's actually an equivalent of 'Excellent, well done!' or 'Good fellow!' or some other poncy bit of Queen's English. It has nothing to do with boys, just as the fact that a Glaswegian can address any male as 'Jimmy' doesn't mean he believes that's his name. Poetry, pure poetry.

I wish it was blazing already. If Josh sounds a bit too intense here, it's actually a version of what Jesus says about his goal in Luke 12:49, "I came to bring fire to the earth, and how I wish it were already kindled!" Andy misinterprets this as some life-denying 'unworldly' religiosity.

A white feather. The demeaning symbol handed to those non-combatants perceived as cowards during WWI.

Liquidation. Nobody managed to spring John the Baptist, Callum's original, but the outcome was the same.

Well-nigh negligible. The Archbishop has a problem with expressing his thoughts directly (not unlike certain preachers), perhaps because he feels uneasy about their content. His compulsive vagueness results in this wandering and sanitised version of John 11:50.

We welcome too. There is a certain negativity in Rev. Farquhar's tone here. He is very much the servant of the State: imagine several armed soldiers not far away.

I believe. These lines contain echoes of Jesus' words with Martha by Lazarus' tomb in John 11.

Trust me, Eilidh. Another echo of John 11. This sequence is of course a version of the raising of Lazarus.

Man, you don't mean that. We're overly familiar with the story, but removing the stone from the entrance of a burial cave was as shocking an intrusion into the realities of death as digging up a coffin.

Come from the four winds. A reference to Ezekiel 37:9, "Thus says the Lord GOD: Come from the four winds, O breath, and breathe upon these slain, that they may live." The "breath" (Hebrew, *ruach*) is the "Spirit" (also *ruach*) of God, 'The Lord and Giver Of Life.' The Spirit is seen in a similar way in the New Testament and spoken of as a Person in his own right. Remember Jesus' assertion that this Spirit, this Power of God, enabled him to perform his miracles of wholeness and life.

Forward for him. Jesus expected that, at the very end, the world would be made as God intended it to be. This final re-making, this final, complete wholeness of God's *Shalom*, would not be just a 'Golden Age' that would eventually end and come round again (as Greek thought imagined) or an ideal state that would be gradually achieved via humanity's development. It would be something done by God, in God's time: it would be the complete arrival of his 'Kingdom' and would break in from 'outside'. However, Jesus taught that this had begun already, that the powers of the End were breaking through now, that the total transformation of the End was 'coming forward' so that 'the Kingdom of God is among you.' This happens primarily through Jesus and his work; but the Kingdom isn't completely here yet: the world is the same world, despite the new inbreaking, so Jesus taught us to pray, 'Your Kingdom come.' There's a tension between 'now' and 'not yet.' Because of Christ, we live in the time when the complete meeting of human need in the day when God is all in all in the renewed earth has begun to show up in powerful works of mercy and wholeness performed in the Name of Christ by means of the Spirit. The Jewish-Christian view of history is linear: that is, it is moving towards a definite goal, and we have signs of that goal approaching. For a Jew of Jesus' day, the final End would include the Resurrection, so Josh prays that the end of the world will 'come forward' as Callum's life is renewed.

8: Close relatives.

It's Greek. The Good Mother tries to avoid embarrassing Callum further with the information that *Anastasia* in Greek means 'Resurrection.'

Lux Aeterna. 'Light eternal.' Mother A. quotes the ancient prayer for the departed, 'Let light eternal shine upon them.' She believes Callum has had a glimpse of the life of heaven.

The choir invisible. A traditional term for the unseen population of heaven, singing joyfully to God. Choir Invisible was also a Los Angeles rock band around 1981, but probably that isn't the one Mother A's thinking of.

No, he didn't. I don't believe Jesus drummed things into people, or tried to bypass their thinking processes so that they had little choice about whether to believe what he told them. That sort of thing is characteristic of authoritarian cults, is psychologically damaging and manipulative and betrays an attitude of deep disrespect for the person. Jesus wanted genuine, authentic decisions and responses, genuine belief and personal commitment, which can only come from a person honestly convinced. 'What do you think?' Jesus would say. He asked straight questions and offered straight answers that would enable a person to consider things freely for themselves and make up their minds. He even asked his disciples (at least once) if they intended to give up following him, which assumes he thought they were free to do so and he wasn't going to force them to stay. Jesus preferred reality, whether it was comfortable or not, and even thought it set you free.

Vespers. The traditional service of evening prayers.

My dad told you. Have you spotted the references to Matthew 16:13-17, where Jesus gets the disciples to tell him their personal vision of who he is? Peter gets it right, but only because God has shown him the answer.

O-a-range juice. Er…it's actually a song once sung in Glasgow that celebrated the virtues of certain luxurious foreign imports. I think. Could be wrong, mind…

Same old way. Josh echoes Jesus' lament over Jerusalem in Matthew 23:37, "Jerusalem, Jerusalem, the city that kills the prophets and stones those who are sent to it! How often have I desired to gather your children together as a hen gathers her brood under her wings, and you were not willing! See, your house is left to you, desolate." Matthew 24 contains

Jesus' expectation and warning of what would happen through pursuing the Kingdom the 'same old way' of political independence: Roman reprisals.

Don't be my enemy. Mum's possessiveness and persistence in seeing Josh's mission in her own terms has finally blossomed into a threat to his vocation. She behaves like Peter in Matthew 16 and draws down on herself Josh's paraphrase of verse 23, "Get behind me, Satan!" 'Satan' means 'enemy'.

9: A new take on it.

That's nice. Josh is very focussed here, and not in the mood for chit-chat.

Legal problem. It seems that some people tried to manipulate Jesus for their own petty ends: get the Rabbi on your side sort of thing. This gentleman, who also appears in Luke 12:13, tries it on Josh, but chooses the wrong moment.

Second fiddle to money. Or in more familiar terms, 'Ye cannot serve God and mammon.' (Matthew 6:24, Authorised Version)

Common five-eights. The average height of men requiring uniforms during WWII was five feet eight inches. Consequently 'a common five-eight' came to mean an ordinary person, the man in the street.

Admit it. Irene is one of the 'poor in spirit' whom Jesus calls 'blessed.' Matthew 5:3 can hardly mean that poor people are automatically godly or spiritually enviable. Jesus means that people who recognise their own inner, spiritual poverty (and thus know they need God's help in that department) are within God's Kingdom, in the sense that he gives them what they need; their realism means they accept his gifts. These people are to be congratulated, says Jesus. His word for 'blessed' is *makarios*, 'fortunate' or (ironically) 'well-off'. It was also a word to congratulate someone with, and was said to the groom at weddings. The Gospels show us Jesus' confrontations with many people who would rather be seen dead than admit to being spiritually poor and were convinced of their own righteousness and God's favour to them as religiously superior people. Jesus' reply to this thinking is well exemplified in Luke 18:9-14, the story told to "some who trusted in themselves that they were righteous and regarded others with contempt." A Pharisee thanks God that he is far better than the swindling, traitorous tax man with him in the Temple. The latter is disgusted with himself and asks God for mercy. "I tell you," says Jesus, "this man went down to his home justified rather than the other." So would Irene. What follows here is the Beatitudes (Matthew 5:1-13) according to Josh.

Broken your heart. I'm taking 'those who mourn' as meaning the people who were mourning for the oppressed condition of the nation in having failed God and were 'looking forward to the consolation of Israel' (Luke 2:25); and. by extension, those who are distressed by all the wrongs and sufferings of the world.

Coming to you. The merciful will receive mercy.

Wish for. People hungry for 'righteousness' will eventually get a feast.

Live in the world. You'll 'inherit the earth [or the land]' if you're one of the 'meek', ie., one of the humble people who want to give God room to work and submit to him rather than arrogantly making all the decisions. Possibly this was originally a word to the Zealots who wanted to bring God's Kingdom their way. They persisted and certainly didn't inherit the land: quite the opposite.

No muck. That is, if you're one of 'the pure in heart.'

The sort of person he is. Peacemakers will be recognised as 'children of God.' Remember that the Aramaic term 'son of' or 'child of' meant 'closely resembling' or 'characterised by'. 'Barnabas', for example, means 'son of encouragement.' The Cypriot Jew Joseph got this nickname because he was so incredibly encouraging (Acts 4:36). Jesus says that people who promote peace (*Shalom*, wholeness, wellbeing in every sense) very much resemble God.

Trying to live right. 'Persecuted for righteousness' sake.'

In good company. "In the same way they persecuted the prophets who were before you."

Pray for them. "Love your enemies and pray for those who persecute you, so that you may be children of [ie. be like, resemble] your Father in heaven." (Mat 5:44-43)

Like rotten meat without you. 'You are the salt of the earth.'

Something rubbishy. "But if salt has lost its taste…It is no longer good for anything."

Suffer with you. "Blessed are you when people revile you and persecute you and utter all kinds of evil against you falsely on my account. Rejoice and be glad, for your reward is great in heaven [ie, a great reward from God, or perhaps 'God is your great reward' – now, that is. The mention of heaven doesn't mean you have to wait till you die.]." Josh is maybe saying a few things here he didn't quite intend.

Exultate! 'Rejoice!' The word often appears in traditional Latin services.

At the name of Joshua Davidson. This scene was actually inspired by the fascinating reference in Mark 9:38-40 to somebody who had no connection with Jesus and his disciples, but who was performing exorcisms by using the authority of Jesus' name. We know nothing else about this chap, but presumably he'd seen Jesus exorcising people, or had heard that he did, and naturally thought this was a very good thing indeed. He then assumed that he could use the name of the wonder-working Rabbi to get the same results. Possibly he thought that Jesus was the Messiah, but he certainly wouldn't have had the understanding of him that the first believers arrived at a few years later. But so what? It worked! And Jesus saw the man as 'one of us' and approved. Similarly, Fr. Prendergast knows what Josh can do and suddenly wonders if he can 'do a Josh' on Fr. Jeremias' back. Had he known, Josh would have had no problems about it: perhaps we can even say he was involved; and this happened in the Archbishop's cathedral, the heart of the 'enemy camp.'

Father Blasko. If they ever film *Josh*, I would have wanted Fr. Blasko to be played by the late Bela Lugosi, creator of the elegant character of Dracula in the 1931 film. His smooth, insinuating Hungarian voice sounded in my head as I wrote Fr. Blasko's lines. He has just the right sinister respectability for a dodgy cleric. Blasko, by the way, was Lugosi's real name.

I never drink wine. Couldn't resist that one. When Dracula is offered a glass of plonk in the film, he famously and meaningfully replies, 'I neffer trink…vine.'

Much to discuss. Cue organ music. Cut to low-angle shot of Fr. Blasko staring intently at Fr. Jeremias. Cut to close-up of Fr. J. as the horrible truth dawns.

Vines. The Archbishop proves he knows at least something about the Bible by quoting Song of Solomon 2:15, "Take us the foxes, the little foxes, that spoil the vines: for our vines have tender grapes."

10: King of the world.

This late hour. This scene parallels the visit by night of the Pharisee Nicodemus to Jesus in John 3:1-21 (Jesus perhaps stops speaking at verse 12: the words after that are probably comments by the writer).

Darkness. Hey, dramatically ironic line, or what? You can write it down if you like.

No rattlesnake. This is a version of Luke 11:10-13, where Jesus links optimism about prayer with God's character: "For everyone who asks receives, and everyone who searches finds, and for everyone who knocks, the door will be opened. Is there anyone among you who, if your child asks for a fish, will give a snake instead of a fish? Or if the child asks for an egg, will give a scorpion? If you then, who are evil, know how to give good gifts to your children, how much more will the heavenly Father give the Holy Spirit to those who ask him!"

A little volatile. This was, to say the least, what worried the Chief Priests about Jesus' presence at the Passover celebrations. Many thousands of intensely excited pilgrims were crammed into a small area for the festival that was the religious high point of the year. The Romans were especially watchful. Pilate left his usual residence at Caesarea to be in Jerusalem for Passover week. If Jesus had wanted to start a Messianic revolt, it would have been the perfect time.

Another coup. 'False witnesses' made statements at Jesus' hearing before the authorities. Had tabloids been available, they may well have made use of them.

I am there. Mother A's popular quote is from a hymn by Henry Van Dyke (1852–1933), but the line itself is probably based on words from the Gnostic work known as *The Gospel of Thomas* (dated 60-140 AD), which purports to be a collection of sayings by Jesus that aren't recorded in the Gospels. Some of them are similar to sayings of Jesus in the four Biblical Gospels, but some are very strange indeed and have a different way of thinking about Jesus than that found in the New Testament, from which *Thomas* is quite separate.

And also with you. The Archbishop's 'The Lord be with you' and Josh's reply are the priest's words to the people and their reply to him in traditional liturgical worship.

His representative. The Archbishop deliberately corners Josh into declaring his self-identity and vocation, thus being true to himself, or abandoning them. The parallel is Matthew 26:63, where the High Priest, officiating at Jesus' hearing, tells him, "I put you under oath before the living God, tell us if you are the Messiah, the Son of God." Jesus' somewhat ambiguous reply is, "You have said so." Then he adds, "I tell you, From now on you will see the Son of Man seated at the right hand of Power [ie, God] and coming on the clouds of heaven." This is taken as blasphemy, a capital crime under Jewish law. Josh's reply to the Archbishop is a straightforward affirmation, but it has the desired effect of allowing the devious Prelate a good excuse to publically sever any connection in people's minds Josh may have had with the church; and particularly in the mind of the Leader and his regime. The Church is safe, he trusts; but the truth is that Josh cannot be a real part of the corrupt organisation the Archbishop leads, any more than an antibiotic can be part of an infection.

Burdens. Mat 23:4: "[The Pharisees and experts on religious law] tie up heavy burdens, hard to bear, and lay them on the shoulders of others; but they themselves are unwilling to lift a finger to move them." Jesus view of graceless, legalistic, performance-based religion. Great for certain types of ego, of course.

Before you do. Mat 21:31: "Truly I tell you, the tax collectors and the prostitutes are going into the kingdom of God ahead of you. For John [the Baptist] came to you in the way of righteousness and you did not believe him, but the tax collectors and the prostitutes believed him; and even after you saw it, you did not change your minds and believe him."

Ruined it. Mar 11:17: "He was teaching and saying, "Is it not written, 'My house shall be called a house of prayer for all the nations'? But you have made it a den of robbers.'" Having thrown the moneychangers out of the Temple, Jesus reminded the people what the Temple was for, and who it was for: that is, it was meant to facilitate God's desire to meet *everybody*. There was a huge outer courtyard where people of any race could pray, but that could hardly have been easy with the sale of sacrificial animals and the trade of the moneychangers. The latter were quite legitimate in themselves, since the Temple dues could only be paid in the approved Shekels; Jesus' objection was to crooked exchange rates raking in profit from a holy purpose in a holy place, out of the pockets of people who had little enough to start with. Such a 'house', he said, is desolate.
It's clear that Jesus had regular confrontations with religious figures over the nature of the Kingdom, the meaning of the Law, what real 'righteousness was, what God's wishes were, the place of compassion and mercy and so on. His most famous opponents were the group known as Pharisees, who mostly represented popular religion, and the Scribes, the experts in the meaning of Torah, the Law of God. Contemporary rabbis distinguished six levels of Pharisee, from good, Godly men on level one down to cold-hearted, time-serving legalists at level six. Jesus seems to have collided mostly with those of the sixth layer. Matthew 23 collects a number of Jesus' responses to the kind of religiosity these people represented and leaves us in no doubt about what he thought of it.
I've given Josh a final confrontation with the Matthew 23-type Church, building up to that instead of showing a lot of smaller incidents. Unlike Jesus, he walks away from it, but other parallels to Jesus' story still develop.

Your blindness and your rottenness. Matthew 23:16, 17, 19, 24, 26: "Woe to you, blind guides...blind fools...how blind you are!...blind guides...blind Pharisees." Matthew 23:27: "You are like whitewashed tombs, which on the outside look beautiful, but inside they are full of the bones of the dead and of all kinds of filth."

Desolate. Mat 23:38: "See, your house is left to you, desolate." Josh's parting words to the Church echo Jesus' lament over the fate of Jerusalem and its Temple. Possibly Jesus meant that the Temple as it had become was desolate because God had 'moved out', abandoned it, and so it was 'left to' unresponsive Jerusalem, God having no more use for it.

11: Into the dark.

Birthday boy. Josh's birthday party is of course a re-invention of the Last Supper, with some strands from other Gospel narratives woven in. Modern life has no real equivalent of the ancient Jewish Passover meal (which is what the Supper was, in my opinion). Passover has such powerful meaning and associations that no contemporary custom even comes close to being a suitable parallel. It's also specifically, historically and intrinsically a Jewish celebration, and the meaning of it is inseparably bound up with that Jewishness.
A birthday celebration is the kind of event that can be emotionally and relationally significant, a traditionally happy occasion that takes on a dreadful irony considering Josh has to go through it while enduring the knowledge of what's about to happen very soon. However, Just as Jesus wished to be together with those closest to him before his suffering began, so Josh wishes the same: it's the last chance to tell Mum and his friends what he knows and wants. Luke 22:15: 'He said to them, "I have eagerly desired to eat this Passover with you before I suffer."'
It's essential to read this scene remembering that Josh knows what's about to happen.

Love each other. John 13:34-35: "I give you a new commandment, that you love one another. Just as I have loved you, you also should love one another. By this everyone will know that you are my disciples, if you have love for one another."

I've done it. Josh is very focussed: his knowledge is dominating his thoughts and his emotions are whirling. He really doesn't want small talk.

Ta, mum. Josh has fallen into great sadness with the loss of Eric. The cake was a last desperate offer of friendship. It echoes Jesus' offer of a piece of bread to Judas. It was customary to do this to a valued friend or someone you wished to honour.

Not the Leader's friend. Does anybody not get this reference? Well, leave the room till you do.

Thanks, mum. Remember what he's feeling.

Lie in my coffin. This links with the incident in Mark 14:3-9 in which a woman pours fragrant ointment on Jesus' head. Mark tells us that this is only two days before Passover, thus indicating that Jesus' death is very near. Thinking ahead, Jesus sees the similarity between the pouring of the ointment and the practice of anointing the dead before burial. "She has done what she could," he says; "she has anointed my body beforehand for its burial." Ruby's gift is the shirt, which Josh sees as a preparation for his own burial. This of course is shocking, as no doubt Jesus' remark was. It has been suggested that the type of perfume mentioned in Mark was so strong and lasting that its fragrance would have been felt all through Jesus' subsequent sufferings. So too Josh will wear that shirt through everything that will soon happen to him.

Bottle of wine. Like Jesus, Josh asks his friends to remember him with an action that specifically has its origin in their last time together. Luke 22:19: "Do this in remembrance of me."

Your own Church. This scene picks up on various elements in Jesus' meeting with Pilate. See for example, John 18:28-19:12: '"Your own...chief priests have handed you over to me"... "Are you the King of the Jews?"..."I came into the world, to testify to the truth. Everyone who belongs to the truth listens to my voice." Pilate asked him, "What is truth?"..."the one who handed me over to you is guilty of a greater sin"...From then on Pilate tried to release him...' Also, John 1:3-9: 'All things came into being through him, and without him not one thing came into being. What has come into being in him was life, and the life was the light of all people. The light shines in the darkness, and the darkness did not overcome it…[John the Baptist] came as a witness to testify to the light…He himself was not the light, but he came to testify to the light. The true light, which enlightens everyone, was coming into the world.' John 8:12: "I am the light of the world. Whoever follows me will never walk in darkness but will have the light of life."

The Governor hopes he can find a way out of the delicate situation, partly for his own sake, partly for Josh's. To him, being a soldier is an honourable position and this is one reason he detests the Archbishop and those like him: he believes they have lost their honour and integrity. He has also come to be positive about Josh while not necessarily believing his message: here is a man who has kept his integrity. Perhaps he is even developing a personal liking for him. I started with the Governor as a bit of a stereotype: the conscienceless, cowardly despot who signs the death warrant to save his own skin, disinterested in Josh himself. However, when I 'met' him, he started to develop against my intentions and I found myself with a man who had a lot of good in him, but was trapped by the situation. He therefore began to be surprisingly positive, as we shall see.

Salute thee. Witty to the last, this is Andy's bitter parody of the ancient Gladiators' salute to the Emperor: 'Hail Caesar, we who are about to die salute thee.'

It's what you want. The interaction between Jesus and the two men crucified with him (Luke 23:32-43) has been moved from Golgotha to the holding cell where all three await the firing squad. Andy softens a bit towards Josh because, well, I liked him, okay? I couldn't let him keep hating Josh to the bitter end, which would have been a bit stereotypical anyway; so he became another example of the fact that life isn't back and white and neither are people. Neither is Jesus' reaction to people: he doesn't just relate to people by the rule book of cliché, tradition and expectation. Eric discovers he wants to be with Josh after all and hopes that, despite what he's done, Josh can somehow do something for him. The desperate man's thinking certainly isn't very theologically correct, but that's the last thing Jesus would worry about at a time like this. "You want to be with me? All right, you will be." I do firmly believe that you don't have to get it right about Jesus or God before they'll accept you: in fact, they accept you already and are yearning for you to do the same for them. To me, a very serious error of many Fundamentalist groups is that they easily tend to have a 'doctrine before people' approach: if you can't sign on the dotted line that you think all these details of the truth (as perceived by us) are absolutely correct, you're unacceptable to us and

God. What does this mean, except that God only likes you if you have the right intellectual opinions? To me, this approach indicates people who are seriously insecure about others and even God, so afraid that they feel a tremendous need to control others to make sure they themselves are 'safe'. They also usually hotly and sincerely deny they have this approach at all; but the message is: 'This is how we do it: submit or else.' I just can't believe that this is Jesus' way. Yes, some things are true and some things aren't, but that correctness wasn't the first thing for him. He is about relationship: people are the first thing; the only thing, really. How, for example, could a church worker define their particular Christian service? Jesus would say, I think, that it should be defined as the specific way in which God meets human need through them in particular.

Nearly time, Dad. This is Josh's 'Gethsemane' moment. Like Jesus, he admits he doesn't want to go through with what's ahead and asks God to change his plans. If this is startling, what else are we to make of Matthew 26:39: "My Father, if it is possible, let this cup pass from me"? It's clear that Jesus felt great dread and torment in Gethsemane and also later on the cross itself, when darkness descended. I believe that, in addition to the dreadful physical pain, Jesus entered an abyss of desolation, a unique suffering that tore out of him the terrible question, 'My God, why have you forsaken me?' (Matthew 27:46) We cannot hope to understand what Jesus experienced then: perhaps this moment was what he most feared in Gethsemane. I tried to give some expression to this through Josh's horror in his prison cell as he feels the Great Darkness come upon him. Still, he feels he can make it through even that because Dad is there – and then he isn't. There is an entirely new experience for Josh: a sudden emotional, relational vacuum; he is left in shock, dismay and hopelessness. These things were impossible in Dad's company, and now Dad is gone. Josh must stagger through the next events quite alone.

Dad, I felt your pain! I included this because Jesus' suffering is sometimes misunderstood as something God 'did' to him, something the Father deliberately inflicted on his Son while opting out of anything painful himself. What decent father would want to do that to his son, people ask? Sometimes this is said in order to ridicule the idea of Jesus' death achieving anything between humanity and God; but equally people ask the question out of a genuine difficulty. I believe the difficulty arises only if God's relation to Jesus' death (and to Jesus himself) is misunderstood. What I mean is this: Jesus tells God in Gethsemane that he's willing to go along with what God wants rather than his own wishes;

but do we imagine God saying, 'Son, I'd like you to let me inflict great suffering on you while I stay quite happy. Will you do that for me?' Jesus replies, 'I'd rather not, but if that's what you want, I'll let you do it.' This of course is ludicrous. I believe the account of Gethsemane lets us eavesdrop on a conversation about a decision that Jesus and his Father have already made together: for humanity's sake they will both voluntarily undergo an experience of immense suffering that will hit them where it really hurts the most - their relationship, their love for each other, the centre of who they are. Both Jesus and his Father become vulnerable; both of them go into the dark. It follows that the Spirit does too, though the New Testament doesn't spell this out. John 14 – 17 speaks of the love between Father and Son, and the relationship of the Spirit to both. We also have a clue in Hebrews 9:14, where we're told in 'sacrifice' language that when Jesus entered the dark in dying he gave himself to God 'through the eternal Spirit.' This suggests that somehow the Spirit enabled the agonising act of self-giving to truly take place and to *work*, to reach the Father who is in his own agony as, with the Spirit's pained involvement, that mutually agreed strategy of willing suffering with its visible expression at Golgotha becomes effective for our sakes. We see all this only from the human side. We catch the words at Gethsemane, read words like "[God] did not withhold his own Son, but gave him up for all of us" (Rom 8:32), witness Jesus' cruel execution and fail to see the whole picture. But the truth is that, if God is who we know he is, Father, Son and Spirit felt each other's agony as each of them suffered for us.

One of the most terrible theological blunders ever was one that goes against God's very nature, namely the medieval doctrine of God's Impassibility. Theologians meant by this that God was *incapable* of suffering. They were trying to protect the idea of God's greatness and majesty, but they got it terribly wrong. The fact is that God chooses to be vulnerable, to be able to be hurt. If you think about it, how else could it be? God is Love, and if you love someone that gives you the potential to be hurt. They may not love you back, for example, or something may happen to them, or they may turn to the bad, all things that would be very painful to you. All suffering people, even if all their questions aren't answered, can know that God is there, identifying with them, feeling all their pain, that Jesus is suffering with them because he's been there and still is. I want a God like that.

Getting it wrong! The awful circumstances reveal that to an extent, Mum has been supporting Josh on her own terms. Now that it looks as if she'll lose him if he sticks to his vision, she urges him to forget the whole thing and is ready to tell the authorities he's 'not well'. What Mary did during Jesus' imprisonment and interrogations we don't know. Perhaps she herself, like the disciples, was in danger: if a crowd had been ready to call for Jesus' death, what might they do to his mother? She may have hidden, at least on the Thursday night, in the home of John Mark (to whom she was related) or other friends who would give protection and support. Maybe she joined the crowd outside Pilate's headquarters on Friday morning to wait for news - less likely, perhaps, because so risky. At any rate, she was loyal to the end and did the only thing she could for her son, by simply being there for him as he died.

But how much had Mary grasped what Jesus was doing? Once, at home in Nazareth, Jesus' presence created such a disruption that 'when his family heard it, they went out to restrain him, for people were saying, "He has gone out of his mind."' (Mark 3:21) Later, Mark records that, on another visit home, Jesus remarked, "Prophets are not without honour, except in their hometown, and among their own kin, and in their own house." (Mark 6:4) In fact, the degree of negativity he experienced towards himself at Nazareth astonished him. But what was the effect on Mary when she didn't see the powerful cast down from their thrones, as she had sung years before (Luke 1:46-55)? Quite the opposite in fact. Had God really "helped his servant Israel, in remembrance of his mercy"? Whatever Messianic hopes Mary may have had regarding Jesus didn't seem to be coming to fruition during his career; and all hopes were dashed when 'the powerful' eventually killed him. So, in a way, Mary too went into the dark for our sakes as 'the powerful' forced her to make her own sacrifice.

If you followed him. In her distress, Mum grabs at the theological comfort blanket that says the sign that you're in line with God is material success, absence of trouble, perfect health or what have you. If Josh will just give up his calling all will be well and she can have him back. Jesus made it clear that trouble is a part of life in this world and that following him might lead to even more, though he added, "take courage; I have conquered the world." (John 16:33) The cruel side of the unchristian 'comfort theology', in contrast to Jesus' realism, is the effect on people who awkwardly don't get rich, healthy or trouble-free. They are left to conclude (and are often told directly) that it's their own fault, since they obviously have insufficient faith, are disloyal, haven't 'given' enough money or have somehow sinned. Apart from the cruelty of this (in her distress, Mum slips into it a bit), and the get-out clause it provides for those whose 'ministry' hasn't worked, it's in direct contradiction to Jesus' refusal to see sickness or misfortune as the inevitable indication that someone has sinned or failed (John 9:2-3).

I don't know. John the Baptist, whom Callum represents, found himself in prison. Despite his own successful activity and despite being the one to point out Jesus as Messiah, he wondered during this dark time if he'd got it right after all and sent a message to Jesus asking if he really was who he'd said he was. No doubt Jesus understood, because he didn't criticise John and simply pointed to what he himself was accomplishing as an indicator, adding, "Blessed is anyone who takes no offense at me." (Luke 7:22-3). Despite John's doubts, Jesus went on to tell people that his cousin was the greatest person in history till that time. (Luke 7:28)

Your mum now. John 19:27: 'Then he said to [John], "Here is your mother."'

I forgive you. Luke 23:34: 'Then Jesus said, "Father, forgive them; for they do not know what they are doing."' Jesus probably means the Roman squaddies detailed to carry out the execution. He knows it's all in a day's work for them and that they have no idea who he is. Likewise, Josh offers his forgiveness in advance to the firing squad.

When I decide. Jesus carried a strong awareness that the ending of his life, his 'time', was not in the hands of anybody but himself and would happen only when he was ready. "For this reason the Father loves me, because I lay down my life in order to take it up again. No one takes it from me, but I lay it down of my own accord." (John 10:17-18) John may suggest that Jesus chose the moment when he gave up his spirit to God. '[Jesus] said, "It is finished." Then he bowed his head and gave up his spirit.' (John 19:30)

Here I come, Dad. Whatever he felt earlier, it's clear that Jesus died aware of his Father's presence and welcome. If 'Here I come' seems to trivialise this, may I say I think not? I think it very natural language for someone who's just had the delight of a loved one's company returned to him when he thought it was gone; and the door is opening that will enable them to be reunited. Josh's pain is ending as he is released into joy, and the confidence, eagerness and triumph he feels is, I hope, a good reflection of the completion and peace that Jesus felt as he died with the Jewish night prayer on his lips, the last prayer before sleep. "Father, into your hands I commend my spirit."(Luke 23:46)

12: Never look back.

In death. Fr. Jeremias uses the traditional words of the Funeral Service from the Book of Common Prayer.

That's me. Note for non-Scots: Mum betrays her Caledonian origins with the phrase 'That's me,' meaning 'I'm ready,' or 'I'm off.'

Round the King's Head. A down-to-earth version of "Why do you look for the living among the dead?" (Luke 24:5) After all, the Angel seems to say, why not check the pub? People who aren't dead tend to behave as if they were, well, alive.

Spam. If Spam sandwiches seem a bit mundane at a time like this, we should remember that Jesus proved he was the same, solid person his friends had known before his death by asking for something to eat, then wolfing down a bit of fried fish. Not really a hyper-spiritual, ethereal sort of thing to do.

Once I've got through this. Hebrews 12:2 describes Jesus as 'the pioneer and perfecter of our faith, who for the sake of the joy that was set before him endured the cross.'

Bullet holes. Mum becomes the 'doubting' Thomas of the piece, unable to believe what the others say. Like Thomas, she can't surmount the physical realities of it all. John 20:25: 'The other disciples told [Thomas], "We have seen the Lord." But he said to them, "Unless I see the mark of the nails in his hands, and put my finger in the mark of the nails and my hand in his side, I will not believe."'

We are all together. Actually, when I was typing this line my mind ran ahead and I found myself singing the opening of *I Am The Walrus*;

hence this last phrase. I do think that Josh would be in such a happy, light-hearted mood at the time (wouldn't you be?), that he might well do that. And they *are* all together: Josh, Mum and Dad.

13: Remember the wine.

Back to how it was. Josh's resurrection doesn't just mean he'll now carry on where he left off as if his death was only a brief interruption to his career. This echoes Jesus words to Mary Magdalene as she joyfully hugs him: "Do not hold on to me, because I have not yet ascended to the Father. But go to my brothers and say to them, 'I am ascending to my Father.'" (John 20:17) We can hardly imagine Jesus objects to the hug, but he seems to be telling Mary that he'll be going back (ascending) to God, so she and his friends mustn't get used to relating to him the way they did before. Josh just moving back into his old bedroom would be a bit of an anti-climax, don't you think?

The scripture saith. 1Thessalonians 5:21, if you must know. However, I would be failing in my responsibility if I didn't point out that Paul is not referring specifically to apricot scones. One should not use this verse in developing a Christian understanding of home baking.

Couldn't be anyone else. The sight of the entry wounds of the bullets confirms the faith that has secretly and mysteriously grown up already. Luke 10:21 tells us that Jesus was delightedly grateful that his Father was the kind of God who could be understood without human cleverness, who in fact would bypass the smarty-pants of this world to be known by kids and other unsophisticated people. I think Mrs. Pemberton is one of the latter. Not overly bright, a crashing bore at times; but she *knows*. Luke says, 'Jesus rejoiced in the Holy Spirit and said, "I thank you, Father, Lord of heaven and earth, because you have hidden these things from the wise and the intelligent and have revealed them to infants; yes, Father, for such was your gracious will."'

Hello, Governor. I think it's very significant that this scene is the kind of thing you *don't* get in the four Biblical Gospels, the ones Christians decided to trust. After all, what better material to include than a clincher where Jesus appears after the resurrection to Pilate, the High Priest or whoever and says, 'See: it's all true.' Or a scene where he does a walkabout in Jerusalem to confront the people who yelled for his execution, or meet the soldiers who carried it out. That would really have got the new movement off the ground. But no: what we get are meetings with the friends who will later be the ones to tell everybody else about it, including that gathering of about 500 people that Paul refers to years later, when most of the 500 are still around to confirm or deny it. Maybe there were others too, but we don't know. There were of course loads of 'Gospels' and other writings doing the rounds, but the Famous Four are the only ones the Jesus-movement eventually committed themselves to. The other stuff contained all kinds of stories, like Jesus making clay birds fly when he was a little boy. But an interesting one is something known as *The Gospel According to the Hebrews*, (not to be confused with the New Testament Letter to the Hebrews), which was very well thought of. Some people think Luke might have got some information from it. Anyway, this work tells us that James, Jesus' brother, vowed not to eat bread until he saw Jesus alive again after his death. Subsequently, we're told, Jesus did meet him and said, "My brother, eat your bread, for the Son of man is risen from among them that sleep." The Biblical Gospels tell us that Jesus' brothers didn't believe in him during his public activity (John 7:5), but Paul says clearly that he met Jesus after the resurrection (1Corinthians 15:7). We also know that he became the leader of the Christian community at Jerusalem. Obviously something changed his mind, so could *The Gospel According to the Hebrews* be correct? Of course, even such a meeting wouldn't be the same kind of encounter as, say, a meeting with Pilate as a 'proof' to an outright enemy. The exception to that, of course, is Saul of Tarsus' encounter with Jesus outside Damascus while still violently opposed to his followers. Later, as Paul, he tells us that he was the last person to see Jesus after his resurrection, which is part of his qualification to function as an Apostle (1Corinthians 15:8).

So why does Josh invite himself to the Governor's office? Well, partly because I'd grown to like the Governor and didn't want to just leave him steeped in regret, partly because I thought it would be a fascinating scene to write (I also wanted to highlight Christ's respect for honest unbelievers) and partly because, well, Josh (or Jesus) would just do that sort of thing. If Jesus took the initiative in meeting Paul, how many other non-sympathisers has he unexpectedly introduced himself to? Kallistos (Timothy) Ware, the Orthodox Archbishop of Britain, was furiously reading Mark's Gospel as an atheist in order to refute the priest who was to address his student society. As he read, he said, he became aware that Jesus was in the room with him. 'The doctrine of the resurrection has never been a problem to me,' he said later. 'I have experienced it.'

Than you have. We might consider Matthew 8:10 here: 'When Jesus heard [the Centurion], he was amazed and said to those who followed him, "Truly I tell you, in no one in Israel have I found such faith."'

Where are you? Good question. Personally, I believe that when Jesus spent time with his friends after his resurrection these spells were 'visits' *from* 'heaven' and that the last one (which ended with what we call the Ascension) seemed so much like a final departure to show that things were now well and truly into the new situation as regards Jesus' relation to this world. Actually, it wasn't exactly the last visit: there was the encounter with Saul outside Damascus, for example; and many people since then have been quite sure of Jesus' literal company, seen or unseen. But it appears that extended spells in Jesus' company 'like it used to be' ended with the 'Ascension'. When I say that Jesus appeared to his friends 'from' heaven, I don't mean a rapid transit back and forth from some location beyond Alpha Centauri. I understand heaven as meaning God's 'space', to borrow an excellent phrase from NT Wright. This isn't 'up there' somewhere, but can be described more in terms of the idea of a 'parallel universe' that intersects with our world at every point. Jesus' 'visits', then, are more like opening a door and stepping through from the place that's only a hairsbreadth away anyway. Heaven and earth are cheek by jowl, overlapping even, and the Christian hope of the final, complete arrival of God's Kingdom, means that we look towards the day when God's 'space' breaks though and heaven and earth will be joined, fused together and everything is renewed. As Jesus taught, this has begun: the Kingdom is showing up already, and one day there will be nothing else. 'See, the home of God is among mortals. He will dwell with them; they will be his peoples, and God himself will be with them; he will wipe every tear from their eyes. Death will be no more; mourning and crying and pain will be no more, for the first things have passed away..."See, I am making all things new."' (Revelation 21:3-5)

My Friend. Jesus promised the arrival of the Holy Spirit in a way never before known. In John's Gospel, he calls him the Advocate, ie., someone called over to help you. The name based on John's Greek word is Paraclete, which means the same. Some translations just have 'Helper' (Josh calls him Friend). The word was used to refer to a lawyer pleading for you in court or a priest praying for you, but the idea is just somebody who's there for you, who actively helps you. Jesus later told his friends to wait in Jerusalem for 'the promise of the Father.' By this, he meant that the ancient Jewish hope that God would pour out his Spirit would find fulfilment in God's giving of the Holy Spirit. 'I will pour out my spirit on all flesh; your sons and your daughters shall prophesy, your old men shall dream dreams, and your young men shall see visions.' (Joel 2:28) Jesus had made it clear that it was by the Spirit of God that he performed his miracles and now he says that this same Spirit will be 'in' his followers, a permanent and utterly close relationship, as opposed to temporary 'touches' for specific purposes as in times past. Acts 2 records how, forty days later, the disciples were joyfully aware that the Spirit was here at last and Peter uses the Joel text to explain to the crowd what has happened. Paul understood the Holy Spirit as 'the Spirit of Christ', someone very like Jesus and very close to him, but not the same person. He 'lives' within the community of Christians and in each Christian individually, the indicator of that being the development of mature, loving character like that of Christ. The Spirit enables us to know Christ's presence, he speaks on Christ's behalf, he enables us to understand the facts about Christ and works powerfully and amazingly, as Jesus did. His activity is still the way in which God's kingdom shows up. John 14:16-18 "And I will ask the Father, and he will give you another Advocate, to be with you forever. This is the Spirit of truth, whom the world cannot receive, because it neither sees him nor knows him. You know him, because he abides with you, and he will be in you. I will not leave you orphaned; I am coming to you."

Head nor tail of me. John 5,:1,9 refers to Jesus as a light: 'The light shines in the darkness, and the darkness did not overcome it [or, didn't understand it]...The true light, which enlightens everyone, was coming into the world.'

First citizen. Paul refers to Jesus as 'the beginning, the firstborn from the dead.' (Colossians 1:18)

Began. You thought I'd missed out the Virgin Birth, didn't you? Aha.

Thank you, darling. That was actually the Ascension, yes. Why so quiet? Why no blaze of light and shining clouds? Well, as the cover says, this is a re-telling and a Biblical Epic treatment would really have shattered the mood in the King's Head. I also enjoyed tying up the loose ends in Josh's relationship with his Mum and the last few minutes of his physical presence, a gift to her alone, gave me a great chance to do that.

Mary was presumably present at Jesus' ascension (strange if she wasn't) and I imagine he had a special goodbye for her. The fact that Ruby, Joe and the rest miss Josh's farewell isn't such a big deal, I think. After all, there were lots of people who weren't there at Jesus' farewell who would have wanted to be.

Like he said. And so we have the first 'Remembering', as Josh wanted. We don't know the occasion of the first Communion Service, Lord's Supper, Eucharist, Mass (or whatever your preferred understanding may be) but it was soon established as the special 'meal' that was the reminder of Jesus' death, something that will 'proclaim' or 'makes known' that death and its special significance for the remainder of history. Paul says he received this 'from the Lord', meaning that the details of the practice had been handed down, starting from Jesus, from believer to believer until they reached him. He himself now hands on the memory of how Jesus took bread and one of the cups of wine that featured in the Passover meal and told his disciples to think of tearing the bread as a symbol of the injuries he would soon receive and of pouring the wine as a picture of how he was about to shed his blood. The cup of wine, Jesus said, signified the sealing of what he called the new covenant (or agreement) 'in my blood' (ie., by his death). This refers back to Jeremiah 31:31, where God (rather shockingly) says that although he made an agreement with Israel when they left Egypt that they were his people (something that was of the utmost importance to the Jews), he will one day establish another agreement of a different kind. Under this agreement God's will, his Law, won't be written on stone tablets but written on the inside, on his people's hearts, so that they each have a personal knowledge of him with all failure and wrongdoing forgotten by God. Jesus says that this agreement will come into effect by means of his death, and wants to be remembered with the bread and wine that are pointers to that death 'which is for you.' It follows, says Paul, that this is no mere ritual, but something to be taken very seriously. His example comes from the practice of the Christians at Corinth of meeting for a communal meal that included the bread and wine that was the reminder of Jesus' death. However, gluttony and selfishness meant that people who (apparently) hadn't the means to bring food were humiliated and left hungry while others indulged to the point of drunkenness. This is not the Lord's Supper, says Paul. It actually shows contempt for the family of believers and Paul believes this behaviour may actually rebound with physical ill-effects. (1Corinthians 11:19-26) There's no modern ceremony that could be a echo of the Passover meal. Josh instead takes something from a different celebration: a glass of wine at a birthday party. He passes that on to his friends as something to remember his death by, something to stand for the blood that would soon stain the shirt Ruby had given him. In pouring the wine and doing what Josh asked, Joe recalls the various features of 'Birthday Night'. It's not hard to imagine his impromptu reminiscences becoming so familiar with repeated use that they turn into the words that will always be said when people celebrate 'Josh's Party.'

What you done. As Ruby unintentionally got Josh 'ready' for his death with the gift of the new shirt, so the woman at Bethany who poured oil on Jesus' head was said by him to have 'prepared' his body for burial. Full of gratitude, he then said, "Truly I tell you, wherever the good news is proclaimed in the whole world, what she has done will be told in remembrance of her." (Mark 14:9)

Somebody left a window open? We're now out of the Gospels and into Acts chapter two with the arrival of our friend The Holy Spirit. The phenomena mentioned in Acts (the sound like a rushing wind and the appearance of something resembling flames 'resting' on each person) are the prelude to an experience of joyful release and delight in God. Peter then explains to the people outside (in very Jewish terms) what it all means (Acts 2:14-39). The explanation includes the significance of Jesus, who, Peter says, has caused all they're seeing and hearing. Speaking of a rabbi who, less than a couple of months previously, was walking around the very streets where the audience are standing, he says, "Being therefore exalted at the right hand of God, and having received from the Father the promise of the Holy Spirit, [Jesus] has poured out this that you both see and hear." (Acts 2:33) The disciples' delighted awareness of God and Christ is important. Marvellous as demonstrations of God's power are (and I don't want to downplay them or create a false division), the surest signs of the Holy Spirit's presence are quality of life, experience and character and a love for Christ and people. Paul says that the kingdom of God (ie., God's rule showing up) isn't making sure you stick to nit-picking rules, but it's something bigger and better, namely 'righteousness, peace and joy in (inspired by) the Holy Spirit.' If you serve Christ that way, says Paul, you'll please both God and people. (Romans 14:17-18)

He had to get shot first. I was once chatting to a lady who, although she had certain 'spiritual' beliefs, wasn't keen on the Christian thing at all. The Cross was mentioned and she said, 'But do you think that if Jesus had been shot, his followers would have worn little revolvers round their necks?' I told her, much to her surprise, that yes, I thought they would. After all, the thing about the Cross is that, despite being one of the most appalling ways of killing someone ever devised, it became the means by which God, in Christ, personally took on death and evil and won. A means of destruction became simultaneously the means of conquest. The Cross is where Jesus died, but that makes it the prelude to the resurrection: go through the door of death and you find you've stepped into life. The two bits of wood nailed together to crush somebody become a symbol of the fact that Jesus, when willingly crushed as much as a person can be, showed that utter death wasn't big enough to keep him back from life. And we get to share his achievement. The awful gibbet is a celebration of Jesus' courage, loyalty, dedication, mercy; and also a huge irony: a promise of hope, a sign of love, a spring of joy, the measure of the heart of God, the declaration that death is the disabled enemy that will be destroyed. And that's why Ruby bought a little silver gun.

Here goes nothing. Annie's cure is a version of the healing of the disabled man by the Temple Gate (Acts 3:1-10). You usually get the impression that Peter was so bursting with faith that he hadn't the slightest doubt the man would walk. Well, maybe he was: after all, he'd been on the job with Jesus, watching him do this very thing. But maybe he wasn't: this was his first opportunity to 'have a go' out on his own, so to speak. We're not actually told how confident he was. I've imagined Ruby as being not very confident at all (and hey, Ruby just had to be the first one to do this, 'cause I love her), but moved by compassion for Annie, her knowledge of what Josh would do and the assurance that Josh's 'Friend' is there, she goes for it. So she has faith; and so do the others, who support her although they're not quite at the stage of having a go themselves. After all, 'faith' isn't some kind of 'stuff' you can amass and keep under the bed until you have a lot of it; it's confidence in, reliance on, God. It's moving over to let God do what he wants. Jesus said you only need a speck of this attitude for God to get a mountain shifted (Matthew 17:20. He was perhaps looking at Mount Tabor in Galilee when he said it).

Fighting him. Fr. Jeremias repeats, in his own way, Rabbi Gamaliel's warning to the Jewish authorities about the new followers of Jesus. After recalling other Messiah-movements that had failed tragically, he says, "if [this movement] is of God, you will not be able to overthrow them - in that case you may even be found fighting against God!" (Acts 5:39)

Interestingly, it was the greatly respected Gamaliel who was mentor to the young rabbi Saul of Tarsus, better known to history as Paul the Apostle.

Witness against you. The Archbishop ironically uses the words of Moses to the Israelites on the eve of their entry into the Promised Land: "I call heaven and earth to witness against you today that I have set before you life and death, blessings and curses. Choose life so that you and your descendants may live." (Deuteronomy 30:19)

www.ingramcontent.com/pod-product-compliance
Lightning Source LLC
Chambersburg PA
CBHW070722160426
43192CB00009B/1284